# Student's Guide to Writing College Papers

Chicago Guides
to *Writing*, Editing,
and Publishing

# Student's Guide to Writing College Papers

## FIFTH EDITION

### Kate L. Turabian

REVISED BY GREGORY G. COLOMB,
JOSEPH M. WILLIAMS, JOSEPH BIZUP,
WILLIAM T. FITZGERALD, AND THE
UNIVERSITY OF CHICAGO PRESS
EDITORIAL STAFF

University of Chicago Press    *Chicago and London*

Portions of this book have been adapted from *The Craft of Research*, 4th edition, by Wayne C. Booth, Gregory G. Colomb, Joseph M. Williams, Joseph Bizup, and William T. FitzGerald, © 1995, 2003, 2008, 2016 by The University of Chicago.

The University of Chicago Press, Chicago 60637
The University of Chicago Press, Ltd., London
© 2010, 2019 by The University of Chicago

Published 2019
Printed in the United States of America

28  27  26  25  24  23  22  21  20  19      1  2  3  4  5

ISBN-13: 978-0-226-49456-2 (cloth)
ISBN-13: 978-0-226-43026-3 (paper)
ISBN-13: 978-0-226-43043-0 (e-book)
DOI: https://doi.org/10.7208/chicago/9780226430430.001.0001

Library of Congress Cataloging-in-Publication Data

Names: Turabian, Kate L., author. | Colomb, Gregory G., editor. | Williams, Joseph M., editor. | Bizup, Joseph, 1966– editor. | FitzGerald, William T., editor.
Title: Student's guide to writing college papers / Kate L. Turabian ; revised by Gregory G. Colomb, Joseph M. Williams, Joseph Bizup, William T. Fitzgerald, and the University of Chicago Press editorial staff.
Other titles: Chicago guides to writing, editing, and publishing.
Description: Fifth edition. | Chicago ; London : University of Chicago Press, 2019. | Series: Chicago guides to writing, editing, and publishing
Identifiers: LCCN 2018060157 | ISBN 9780226494562 (cloth : alk. paper) | ISBN 9780226430263 (pbk. : alk. paper) | ISBN 9780226430430 (e-book)
Subjects: LCSH: Dissertations, Academic—Handbooks, manuals, etc. | Academic writing—Handbooks, manuals, etc. | Report writing—Handbooks, manuals, etc.
Classification: LCC LB2369 .T82 2019 | DDC 808.06/6378—dc23
LC record available at https://lccn.loc.gov/2018060157

♾ This paper meets the requirements of ANSI/NISO Z39.48-1992 (Permanence of Paper).

# Contents

# Preface for Teachers

We are pleased to share this book with fellow teachers who believe in the importance of writing, research, and critical thinking, and, equally, in our students' ability to do these things.

In college, and in courses leading up to college, students write many papers in which they gather information and present the contributions of experts. These are valuable skills to acquire, but we think students can and should do more. We believe that they should learn to think and write like researchers themselves, and that they should discover firsthand how rewarding research can be.

This book, therefore, does more than teach students to report on and document information; it shows them how research is, fundamentally, a process of inquiry. Through research, we find answers to questions worth asking. While this book focuses on academic research, it stresses that research is everywhere in our places of work and in our daily lives, and it insists that the fundamental gestures of research-based argument—offering good reasons and evidence that might move someone to think or act differently, and demonstrating a willingness to be so moved in turn—are vital to civic life. We hope that this book leads students to set out on an ever more productive path as critical thinkers and problem solvers.

Why do so few students do research well? Perhaps it is because they too often experience research as a mechanical process cut off from their ordinary intuitions about how to use information to solve problems or convince others of some point. In contrast, this book encourages students to understand academic research and argument as special applications and extensions of the kinds of research and argument they engage in every day.

The *Student's Guide to Writing College Papers* follows in the footsteps of the University of Chicago Press's guides for advanced students and practicing researchers, *The Craft of Research* (4th edition, 2016) and *A Manual for Writers of Research Papers, Theses, and Dissertations* (9th edition, 2018). Like the previous edition, it reframes the ideas and practical wisdom of these other guides for novice researchers. Most of the topics are the same, as are all of the principles and a good bit of the advice. But students who are just learning what it means to write a college paper will find in this book explanations of academic research practices, as well as examples, models, and templates, that are designed to make this guidance concrete and accessible *for them*.

In updating the book, we sought to stay true to the vision of the authors responsible for the fourth edition: Gregory G. Colomb and Joseph M. Williams, and also Wayne C. Booth, their coauthor on earlier editions of *The Craft of Research* and *A Manual for Writers*. Although these authors are no longer with us, this revision is very much an ongoing collaboration. An essential point of the book is that arguments are conversations, and throughout our work, we sought to subject their ideas to the kind of skeptical yet generous scrutiny the book tells researchers to expect from their own readers. Conversely, when considering a particular revision, we always asked ourselves, *Could we have persuaded Booth, Colomb, and Williams to accept this change?* Only when we felt that the answer would most likely have been *yes* did we make the change. We hope that the result of this process has been to sharpen and refine the approach to research and writing that made the previous edition such a success.

We have also recast the book to enhance its use in the contemporary classroom. This edition is informed by the many insights that came from a unique two-year program the Press sponsored called the Turabian Teacher Collaborative, which placed the fourth edition into the hands of more than two dozen high school teachers and their students for two school years (see the acknowledgments section for details). In particular, we have revised the examples that run throughout the book, and we have broadened the book's notion of what the products of a research project might be. While the book still focuses on teaching students to write good college-level research papers, it also acknowledges more explicitly than did the previous edition that every research project need not culminate in a formal paper.

Now for a word or two about some of our specific decisions. One of the most vexing issues students face in writing papers for college is the use of the first person. In many curricula, its use is discouraged if not forbidden. Our view is that the first person has a place in student academic writing, as it does in professional research. Throughout the book, we use the first person ourselves (as here!), and we feature its use in multiple examples. We acknowledge the good pedagogical reasons that lead some teachers to prohibit or forestall its use, but we also endeavor to show students how the first person can be used appropriately in academic writing. For a detailed treatment of the first person in academic writing, see pp. 154–55.

We also use some terms for the elements of an argument that differ from those with which students may be familiar from high school. In particular, we do not use *thesis* or *thesis statement*; instead, we use *claim* to identify the main point of an argument. Likewise, we do not use *counterclaim* but refer instead to forms of *acknowledgment* and *response* to questions and beliefs of others. Our terms are not at odds with these others, but we have chosen them to reinforce the book's position that academic argument requires not mere dispute but real intellectual conversation in search of understanding. Thus, for example, we encourage students to carefully consider and address rather than merely counter the alternative views they discover in their reading and research. Doing this is hard intellectual work, but we believe today's beginning college students are up to the task. Again, our terminology is not inconsistent with other common terminologies for teaching research and argument, but it is specifically chosen to emphasize the book's position that responsible argument must be a genuine conversation.

This book has three parts:

Part 1, "Your Research Project," is a guide to producing the paper, from starting an assignment to responding to a teacher's comments. This part is designed so that students can engage it in three ways: to gain an overview of the research process and its rationales, to learn about the specific stages of that process, and to perform the specific actions that go into those stages. We present this material as a coherent sequence but emphasize throughout the productive messiness of the process.

Part 2, "Citing Sources," offers guidance on issues of style and format in bibliographic citations. It presents models for three common citation styles—Chicago, MLA, and APA—and reflects the latest updates to these styles. This part begins with a chapter on the general theory and practice of citation, including use of citation software, but is generally intended for reference, to be consulted as the need arises. We have limited its coverage to those sources beginning researchers are most likely to rely on.

Part 3, "Style," offers guidance on issues of style ranging from hyphenation and punctuation to the forms of numbers. It follows *The Chicago Manual of Style* (17th edition, 2017). This part is also intended only for reference, to be consulted as the need arises, and we have limited the coverage to those matters we judge to be most useful to students.

The first of three appendixes covers the format for class papers, with some sample annotated pages. A second offers a glossary of terms used in the book. A third is a guide to reference works that students can use to get started.

For more information about the book, go to Turabian.org.

*Joseph Bizup*
*William T. FitzGerald*
*The University of Chicago Press Editorial Staff*

# Acknowledgments

This book is in the lineage of three classic texts published by the University of Chicago Press: *The Craft of Research*; *A Manual for Writers of Research Papers, Theses, and Dissertations*; and *The Chicago Manual of Style*.

The first of these books began as the work of a triumvirate: Wayne C. Booth, Gregory G. Colomb, and Joseph M. Williams. Following the deaths of these remarkable authors, Joseph Bizup and William T. FitzGerald have assumed the mantle of revising *The Craft of Research* and the chapters derived from it both in this work and in *A Manual for Writers*. The influence of Booth, Colomb, and Williams continues to animate all of these books.

Both this book and *A Manual for Writers* were originally prepared by Kate L. Turabian, the longtime dissertation secretary at the University of Chicago. "Turabian style" for citations, hyphenation, punctuation, and the like is now synonymous with "Chicago style," as outlined in the more comprehensive *Chicago Manual of Style*. Note, however, that this book also covers two other widely used citation styles, MLA and APA, in addition to Chicago's own notes-bibliography style. Revisions to parts 2 and 3 and appendix A were carried out by Russell David Harper, who has also updated the comparable material in *A Manual for Writers* and served as chief reviser for recent editions of *The Chicago Manual of Style*.

Of the two Turabian books, *A Manual for Writers* is intended for advanced undergraduates, graduate students, and researchers, while the *Student's Guide to Writing College Papers* is designed for all those learning what it means to research and write a college paper. The idea that this book might be useful even at the high school level first arose when the Press commissioned Booth, Colomb, and Williams to help rethink it for the fourth edition, its first revision in more than thirty years (Booth, who died before the revision started in earnest, is not formally credited on the book). Joe Flanagan of York High School and his colleagues were particularly helpful to the authors in this effort. Others who aided with the fourth edition include Christine Anne Aguila, Jo Ann Buck, Bruce Degi, Laura Desena, Robin P. Nealy (and her students at Wharton County Junior College), Kathleen Dudden Rowlands, and Joseph Zeppetello.

In 2013, Press staff members Ellen Gibson and Mary E. Laur approached Bonnie Stone Sunstein and Amy K. E. Shoultz of the University of Iowa's College of Education for help in assembling a team of high school teachers to test the fourth edition with their students and offer feedback for creating the fifth. Under advisors Sunstein and Shoultz, twenty-six teachers and nearly a thousand students from urban, suburban, and rural schools across four states participated in the Turabian Teacher Collaborative during the 2013–14 school year. Sixteen of these teachers continued to teach from the book the following year. Members of the Turabian Teacher Advisory Board, and their affiliations at the time of their participation in the program, were as follows (two-year members marked with an *):

*Deb Aldrich, Kennedy High School, Cedar Rapids, Iowa

Kara Asmussen, Kennedy High School, Cedar Rapids, Iowa

*Deidra Baker, Keota High School, Keota, Iowa

Shelly Chandler, Marshalltown High School, Marshalltown, Iowa

*Angela Conrad, Keota High School, Keota, Iowa

*Michael Di Iacova III, Edwin G. Foreman High School, Chicago, Illinois

*Beth Fettweis, Iowa City High School, Iowa City, Iowa

Nate Frese, Iowa City West High School, Iowa City, Iowa

Christina Frum, University of Chicago Woodlawn Charter School, Chicago, Illinois

*Nathan Fulcher, Santa Monica High School, Santa Monica, California

*Michael Goldberg, Marshalltown High School, Marshalltown, Iowa

Annette Hennessy, Naperville Central High School, Naperville, Illinois

*Arthur Hunsicker, Revere High School, Revere, Massachusetts

*Mackenzie O'Connor, Clear Creek Amana High School, Cedar Rapids, Iowa

*Tisha Reichle, Santa Monica High School, Santa Monica, California

*Marybeth Reilly, Naperville Central High School, Naperville, Illinois

Steve Riley, Columbus High School, Columbus Junction, Iowa

Joanne Sapadin, Naperville Central High School, Naperville, Illinois

*Amy Shoultz, Iowa City West High School, Iowa City, Iowa

Margaret Shullaw, Iowa City West High School, Iowa City, Iowa

Laura Starke, Naperville Central High School, Naperville, Illinois

*Bonnie Sunstein, University of Iowa, Iowa City, Iowa

Wendy Watson, Columbus High School, Columbus Junction, Iowa

*Brad Weidenaar, Marshalltown High School, Marshalltown, Iowa

*Nicole Weiss, Naperville Central High School, Naperville, Illinois

*Susan Yates, Edwin G. Foreman High School, Chicago, Illinois

Several members of this group also led a workshop following the 2014 National Council of Teachers of English convention based on their experiences teaching the principles in this book. Workshop participants included teachers from a variety of states, including Texas, Florida, California, Ohio, Michigan, Virginia, and Maryland, as well as an American teaching at an international school in the United Kingdom.

Insights from the two-year Turabian Teacher Collaborative and the NCTE workshop are reflected throughout this fifth edition, from revised examples of research topics and clarified terminology to new illustrations and more practical advice on source citations. Sunstein and Shoultz have also prepared resources for teaching the book to high school students, which are available at Turabian.org.

At the Press, this edition was overseen first by David Morrow and later by Mary E. Laur, with assistance from Rachel Kelly Unger and Susan Zakin and support from editorial directors Christie Henry and Alan G. Thomas. Ruth Goring copyedited the book, while Amber Morena proofread it and Meg Wallace provided the index. Marketing manager Ellen Gibson, with assistance from Tristan Bates and Susannah Engstrom and support from marketing director Carol Kasper, was instrumental in leading the Turabian Teacher Collaborative. After Gibson's departure from the Press, Jennifer Ringblom, Lauren Salas, Carol Fisher Saller, and Russell Harper led the efforts to bring the book to students and teachers.

Finally, Bizup and FitzGerald would like to thank their families for their support and also the many scholars, teachers, and librarians who have graciously shared their ideas, practices, and perspectives, thus making this a better book.

# Introduction
# Writing, Argument, and Research

If you are reading this book, chances are you are a college student, or soon will be. Our goal in writing it is to help you do three things that are crucial to most college-level work: to write, to argue, and to research. You probably do these things every day already. But they have special meanings in college, meanings you must understand to get the most out of your college education. This book shows you how to bring these activities together so that you can write a successful college paper.

## What Is a College Paper?

So just what *is* a *college paper*? That question is not as simple as it seems, and in fact, it has several good answers. From one perspective, a college paper is simply a piece of writing you produce in college. Understood in this sense, it might be almost anything: a report, a critical essay, a response paper, a project proposal, a white paper, a personal narrative, a story. Some of this writing will be printed out on paper. A small bit of it may be handwritten. But increasingly, much of it will be submitted electronically or even published on the web, for your class or for the world. This understanding is valuable, for it requires students and teachers—at both the high school and college levels—to acknowledge the incredible breadth of writing that twenty-first-century college students do. But this understanding, for our purposes, is too broad. For if we take a college paper to mean *any* kind of writing, we could offer you only the most general advice about how to write one.

Some students and even some teachers have a much narrower understanding: they think a college paper is a particular kind of assignment—a paper with five paragraphs, each with a topic sentence and an example—that they imagine students doing in an old-fashioned first-year English or composition class. This understanding is less valuable, but it is not entirely wrong: there is a long tradition of teaching college students to do just this sort of writing. But that tradition is fading, and to pretend that it is sufficient for today's students would be to do them a grave disservice.

We take up the middle ground between these two views. For the purposes of this book, we understand a college paper to be any piece of writing done in college (or in a college-preparatory curriculum in high school) that uses the products of research to make an argument addressing a question its readers care about. This notion of a college paper includes much of the writing that students do in college, but not all of it. That limitation, though, is valuable. We can't tell you how to do *every* kind of writing you could possibly be asked to do in college. But we can show you how to do research that addresses real questions, how to make arguments that not only assert your point but also consider the views of others, and how to communicate these arguments in writing that your readers will recognize not only as clear and coherent but also as contributing to their own knowledge.

We said that college-level work requires writing, argument, and research, and we will have much to say about each of these throughout the book. But to get started, we'll just introduce some basic principles.

## How to Think about Writing

As a college student, or almost one, you have already been writing for years: if you are like most students, writing more than any other activity, except perhaps reading, has defined your education. It will continue to be at the center of your education in college, and it will be even more important in your career and the rest of your adult life.

In fact, the further you advance in almost every profession, the more writing you will do and the more important your ability to write will become. Newly hired engineers, for example, work on technical problems. Advanced engineers may do that too, but they will also draft proposals for prospective clients; write emails, progress updates, and performance reviews for coworkers, bosses, and subordinates; and produce reports on their projects for colleagues, shareholders, and perhaps even the general public. Similar observations could be made about law enforcement officers, health care providers, teachers, or people working in almost any profession. And don't forget about all the writing you will need to do in your daily life, whether posting about your vacation on social media or explaining your car accident to an insurance company.

Here are some things to keep in mind when you think about writing as a college student:

- *Write to discover ideas.* Writing is a complex process involving many different activities: everything from jotting down your first notes to proofreading your final draft is part of your writing process. We say *your* process because nobody's way of writing is exactly like anyone else's, and a big part of being a student is figuring out what works for you: Do you write best in short bursts or in longer sessions? Do you make detailed outlines or loose plans? Do you craft your sentences slowly and deliberately or dump words onto the page or screen to refine later? But whatever the specifics of their processes, all accomplished writers know that writing and thinking are intimately connected. They understand that writing is not just a matter of capturing in words ideas that have already crystallized in their minds and that their ideas will inevitably grow and change *as* they write. Student writers, who are often working to tight deadlines and who can be uncomfortable with the uncertainty of not knowing their final thoughts before they start, can be tempted to deny this basic truth. That's a mistake that leads not to efficiency but to frustration. If you accept that your thoughts will evolve as you write, you'll write better and smarter papers.

- *Write for readers other than your teacher.* All writers need readers to tell them how well they are doing: you may think your paper is brilliant, but only your readers can tell you if it actually is. As a student, you write as a novice for a reader—your teacher—who knows more about your subject than you do and who reads your writing less out of interest than because it's her job. But outside of school, the situation is exactly the reverse: you will almost always write as an expert for readers who know *less* about your subject than you do and who read your writing because it helps them in some way. If you write only as a student, you will never learn to serve these readers. So you have to try now to write for readers—real or imagined—other than your teacher, even when you are doing assignments for your class. Many teachers understand this and will help you by defining a reader for you to write for. The advice in this book will also help you.

- *Write consistently and widely.* Everyone knows that the way to get and stay in shape is to exercise regularly by doing not just one activity but a whole range of them. Writing works the same way. The more you write, and the more ways in which you write, the better your writing will get. Don't just do the assignments you are given: keep a journal, write a blog, contribute to a school publication, craft a short story. In fact, the most productive writers commit themselves to writing *something* every day. So should you.

The final thing we have to say may not make you happy, but it is true. Students often hope they will eventually get to a point where writing becomes easy. Probably not. For a lucky few, writing is a pleasure, as natural as taking a walk on a sunny spring day. For most of us, though, writing will always remain a challenge. We get better through instruction, reading, and practice, but the writing tasks we face get harder too. The good news is that if you stick with it, you'll learn to manage this difficulty, as we all have. We can't guarantee that you'll enjoy writing, but we can guarantee that if you follow and practice our advice, you can learn to do it well.

## How to Think about Argument

When we hear the word *argument* we typically imagine some sort of heated discussion between parties at odds. In disputes of this kind, the parties tend to talk past one another, shout over one another, or otherwise try to knock down their opponents' arguments.

We think of argument in a different way: not as something people *have* but as something people *make*. Most importantly, we think of arguments as something people make *together*. In this sense, arguments are at the core of university life. In this book (and in our wider experience) we understand argument as intellectual conversation, at times intense conversation, but conversation nonetheless. In writing arguments, we join ongoing conversations and we invite our readers to converse with us.

It's true that writing can seem a *one-sided* conversation in which we do all the talking and our readers all the listening. But as you will discover, the great thing about writing, especially writing as a product of research, is that the arguments we make are always an opportunity to connect with others, to imagine our readers' beliefs and interests, to anticipate their questions and concerns. When you think of your readers as allies, not as adversaries, you enter into an intellectual community with a proper spirit of humility.

## How to Think about Research

In this opening discussion of writing, argument, and research, we saved research for last because it is the one that students are least likely to appreciate and most likely to misunderstand. When you think of a researcher, what do you imagine? If you're like most people, you probably picture someone in a lab coat peering into a microscope or a solitary figure taking notes in a library. Those pictures aren't wrong. But you might also have pictured NBC's Hoda Kotb, Amazon's Jeff Bezos, or the New England Patriots' Tom Brady: anyone who prepares extensively to do his or her job. Like just about every successful person, they are experts not only in doing research but in using the research of others. In fact, that's part of what makes them successful. More than ever, knowing how to find, evaluate, and use information is essential for success in any profession. If you know a lawyer, a doctor, a business executive, a marketer, an event planner, a construction manager, or any other professional, then you know someone whose job depends on research. These days the key to most jobs is not just how much you know but how good you are at finding out what you don't.

But do you also think of yourself as a researcher? The fact is you do research almost every day. You are a researcher whenever you dig up the information you need to accomplish a goal—from selecting the most popular chemistry teacher, to finding an affordable apartment that allows pets, to figuring out which new phone to buy. Typically these searches are too quick to feel like a research "project," but you are doing what good researchers always do: collecting information to solve a problem or answer a question.

Do you think of your teachers as researchers? You should. We college teachers teach, but most of us also do research. That research begins in our areas of expertise, with what we know, but what gets us excited are the things we *don't* know but wish that we did: *What's the connection between morality and the biology of the brain? Will knowing grammar rules make you a better writer? Can we reduce climate change by removing the greenhouse gases already in the atmosphere? Did the Neanderthals die out naturally, or did our human ancestors kill them off?* We teachers spend much of our working lives with research questions like those, either asking and answering our own or studying the questions and answers of our colleagues.

Why should the research experience of teachers matter to you? For one thing, it's good to know that we practice what we teach. More importantly, our commitment to a life of research colors the kind of learning that we value most—and that we expect from you. New college students are often surprised to discover that just knowing the facts is not enough for most teachers. It's not enough in our own work: more than knowing things, what energizes us is our habit of seeking out new questions, the cast of mind that drives all research. And it's not enough in yours: more than checking that you know the facts, we want to see what you can *do* with the facts, what new questions, combinations, possibilities, or puzzles you discover—or invent. We value and reward good answers, but we reward good questions more. That's a perspective we invite you to embrace as well.

---

**YOUR FIRST RESEARCH ASSIGNMENT**

**Researching Research in the Workplace**

Here's a useful way to start thinking about research: Professionals do research because they need the answer to a question in order to accomplish some goal. Let's suppose that you have a goal—to motivate yourself to care enough about your research assignments that you will do good work on them. And to achieve that goal, you need the answer to a question: is *research really that important in the workplace?*

So your first mini-assignment is to research the answer. Find five people you know with jobs that you might like to have—not your perfect job but work that you can imagine doing. Ask them about research on their job. Don't just stop with those activities they call research. Ask about any tasks that require them to find out something they didn't know in order to accomplish some goal. Also ask how much those skills matter in their evaluations of their colleagues. Share your results with your classmates.

## Why You Should Learn to Do Research Now

What this book teaches you about research is relevant to your future profession and your adult life generally. But our focus is on academic research, the kind of research your teachers do and the kind of research you will do as a college student. Research is at the heart of every college curriculum, and it will show up in your classes in both obvious and hidden forms. Colleges have been this way for centuries, but it's not just tradition that explains why we expect you to learn research.

The first reason is practical: it concerns your economic future more than your current education. You may not yet be a practicing professional who depends on research, but the chances are good that you will be. The research you do now will prepare you for the day when your job depends on your ability to find answers for yourself or to evaluate and use the answers of others. It will also prepare you to *get* that job in the first place: although potential employers care about what you know, the workplace changes so quickly these days that they care more about how prepared you are to find out what you don't yet know.

The second reason has to do with your education, now and for a lifetime of learning. When you understand research, you are better able to avoid the trap of passive learning, where your only choices are to absorb, or not, what some textbook or teacher says. Doing research, you'll discover how the knowledge we all rely on is only as good as the research that supports it. You'll also discover that what you learn from the research of others depends on what questions you ask—and don't ask. And doing your own research will let you experience the messy reality behind what is so smoothly and confidently presented by experts on the job or in the media. As you learn to do research, you'll learn to distinguish biased and unsupported assertions from reliable research reported clearly, accurately, and with appropriate qualification.

Our third reason you might think idealistic. We teachers ask you to do research because it is the most intellectually exciting part of any education. We hope you too will experience the sheer pleasure of solving a research puzzle and the pride and self-confidence that come from discovering something that no one else knows.

We must be candid, though: doing research carefully and reporting it clearly can be hard work, consisting of many tasks that will often compete for your attention at the same time. And no matter how carefully you plan, research follows a crooked path, taking unexpected turns, sometimes up blind alleys, even looping back on itself. As complex as that process is, we will work through it step by step so that you can see how its parts work together. When you can manage its parts, you can manage the often intimidating whole and look forward to your next research project with greater confidence.

### Our Promise to You

This book reflects its authors' decades of dedication to understanding how writers write, how readers read, and how researchers do their work. What you find here is grounded not in our mere opinions but in our own efforts to answer these questions through our own research. It also reflects our collective experience as teachers of writing and research at more than a dozen universities. We know what it means to be a college student, and you can rest assured that we will give you the most practical advice we know how to give. We know what it is to have to get a paper out the door, and we'll respect your need to get your papers done. But we'll also show you how to get them done right.

Finally, we have written this book in the hope that it will inspire some of you to think of yourselves not just as students learning what others have already discovered or as preprofessionals training for your careers. We hope that some of you will experience for yourselves the joys of writing and research: the thrill of discovery and the feeling of accomplishment that comes from making and sharing new knowledge.

# PART I  *Your Research Project*

We know how anxious you may be feeling if you are facing your first big research project. *What should I write about? How do I find information on it? What do I do with that information when I find it?* But you can handle any project if you break it down into its parts, then work on them one at a time. In the first part of this book, we show you how to do that.

You may think that some matters we explain are beyond your immediate needs. We know that a five-page paper differs from a PhD dissertation. But both require the same skills and habits of thought that experienced researchers began learning when they were where you are now. In that sense, this book is about your future, about starting to think in a new way—like a researcher.

We have organized this book as though you could devise and do a research project by progressing steadily through a sequence of steps, from selecting its topic, to finding data, to writing it up. But no researcher, however experienced, ever marches straight through those steps. They move forward a few steps, go back to earlier ones, even head off in an entirely new direction. So while our sequence of chapters looks like a steady path, when you read them you'll be reminded regularly that you can't expect to follow it without a few detours, perhaps even some new starts. We'll even tell you how to check your progress to see if you might need to go back a step or two.

You can manage that kind of looping, even messy process if you know that behind it is a series of tasks whose order makes sense, and that with a plan based on them you can work your way toward a successful paper.

There are four stages in starting and completing a research project.

- In chapters 2–3, we focus on how to find a topic and then in it a research question whose answer is worth your time and your readers' attention.
- In chapters 4–6, we show you how to find information from sources and how to use them to back up an answer.
- In chapters 7–11, we show you how to plan and draft your paper so that you make your best argument.
- In chapters 12–15, we show you how to revise that draft so that your readers will see that you based your answer on sound reasoning and reliable evidence.

Several themes run through those chapters:

- You can't jump into a project or even a part of it blindly. You must plan, then keep in mind the whole process as you take each step.
- A researcher does more than find data on a topic and report it. Your job is to gather *specific* data to answer the *specific* question that *you* are asking.
- From the first day of your project to its last, you must keep in mind that your paper is a conversation with your readers. You have to bring them into that conversation by asking on their behalf the questions that they would ask if they were there in front of you. And then you have to answer them.
- You should try to write every day, not just to take notes on what you read but to clarify what you think of it. You may not use much of this early writing in your final draft, but you will be prepared for that scary moment when you have to begin writing it.

We have described a research project as if it must culminate in a research paper because that is the most common product of research. But a paper is not the only possibility. In fact, just doing the research itself can be a valuable learning experience. But you won't get the full benefit of that experience unless you also communicate your conclusions to others in some way: in a presentation, a website, a research poster, or even an informal discussion or question-and-answer session with your class.

We challenge you in this book to think about your research and writing as professional academic researchers do. That can be a tall order for a student just starting out. But don't feel overwhelmed: we have designed this book so that when you get confused or lost, you can hunker down with our mini-guides and checklists just to get the job done. Rely on these aids when you need to: you can always go back later to consider the larger issues about the nature of research, argument, and writing we raise. Eventually—probably not today, and maybe not next month or next year, but someday soon enough—you will find that your success on a job or in life will depend on your understanding of that mindset of a researcher.

**How to Use Part 1**

In part 1, we lay out all the goals, plans, strategies, steps, models, formulas, and everything else we know that will help you to understand, first of all, the mindset you need to do research well, then the processes and forms you must master to manage a research project, and finally the specific things you must do to get your paper done. We hope that you will engage our book in all three ways. Here's how we suggest you do that:

1.  Read all of part 1 to get an overview. Read the introduction and chapter 1 carefully, then the rest as quickly as you can. Slow down when we explain what research is like, how researchers think, what the stages are, and why you need them. Speed up when we cover small details that you won't remember anyway.

2.  Before you start a new stage in writing your paper, reread the chapters that cover it—for instance, read chapters 2 and 3 before you pick a research question, chapters 7 and 8 before you outline a draft. Use this reading to create a mental plan for how you will get through that stage.

3.  As you work on your paper, look in the relevant chapters for checklists, models, and other guides that will help you go step by step.

If your deadline looms and you cannot squeeze out the time for this big-to-little-picture approach, you can work the other way around: start from the checklists, models, and guides. If you understand what to do looking at them alone, do it. If not, read the surrounding text until you do. We hope you won't be so pressed for time that you have to take this shortcut, but we designed this book so that you can. If you do, go back and read the sections you skipped after you turn in your paper. You'll be glad you did.

# 1    Imagining Your Project

All successful researchers do at least three things: they raise questions readers want answered, search out answers to those questions, and argue for those answers in their papers, presentations, or reports. In this chapter, we show you how to get started by finding or inventing a research question that will be interesting enough for readers to care about and challenging enough that you have to research its answer. Then we show you how to plan your project by mapping out the parts of the argument you will need to support that answer.

## 1.1   How Researchers Think about Their Projects

All researchers set out to discover things they don't already know: facts about the world that we'll call *data*. But they undertake their projects for different reasons. Some just want to satisfy their curiosity: baseball fans memorize statistics about their favorite players and teams; foodies investigate the ingredients that go into a fine meal; space buffs read everything they can about NASA's space program. These sorts of people do research just for the fun of it. They don't have to care whether others are interested. They can research in whatever way they want without bothering to write up what they find.

Most researchers, however, pursue their projects not just for themselves but also for others, their readers or audience. They do their research to share it—because their colleagues or clients need it, because they think their question and its answer are important to other researchers, or just because they want others to know something interesting. But when researchers share their results, they have to offer more than just whatever data they happen to dig up on their topic. They seek out certain *kinds* of data—those they can use to show that they have found a sound, reliable answer to a research question, such as *Why did the Apollo moon landing become a symbol of America's identity?* In other words, they look for data that they can use to build an argument—that is, data they can use as *evidence* to support a *claim* that answers a *question.*

The best researchers do more than just try to convince others that their answer is right. They also show why that answer is worth knowing by showing why their question was worth asking in the first place. For example, in a business setting, researchers usually show why their research helps someone decide what to do:

> If we can understand why our customers are moving to the competition, we can know what we have to change to keep them.

But in an academic setting, researchers usually show how the answer to their research question helps others understand some bigger, more important issue in a new way:

> Historians have long debated about how nations construct their individual identities. If we can figure out how the Apollo moon landing contributed to America's national identity in the 1960s, we can better understand how symbolic events shape national identity in general.

If you cannot imagine yourself appealing to an audience of historians, you can still imagine one closer to home: your class. Locate that larger issue in the context of what you are studying:

> A major issue in this class has been how interest in space exploration has waned since the end of the Apollo mission. If we can figure out why getting to the moon was so important in the 1960s, we can better understand how such events shape national identity.

You can find out whether your question is worthwhile by describing your project in a sentence like this one:

> 1. Topic: I am working on stories about the Apollo mission to the moon,
>> 2. Question: because I want to find out why it was deemed so important in the 1960s,
>>> 3. Significance: so that I can help my classmates understand the role of symbolic events in shaping national identity.

In its second and third parts, this sentence takes you beyond a mere topic to state a question *and* its importance to readers.

When you state why your research question is important to your readers, you turn it into a *research problem*. A research problem is simply a question whose answer is needed by specific readers—your audience—because without it they will suffer a cost. That cost is what transforms a question that is merely interesting to you into one that you can expect others to care about.

**TQS: How to Identify a Worthwhile Research Question**

You can help yourself think about your project by describing it in a three-step sentence that states your Topic + Question + Significance (or TQS):

TOPIC: I am working on the topic of _____,

QUESTION: because I want to find out _____,

SIGNIFICANCE: so that I can help others understand _____.

Don't worry if you cannot at first state your question's significance. As you do your research and develop your answer, you'll find ways to explain why your question is worth asking.

Note: Like all of the formulas you will find in this book, the TQS formula is intended only to guide your thinking. Use it to test and refine your question, but don't plan to use it in in your paper in exactly this form. In your introduction you will use the information from each part of this TQS sentence but not the sentence itself (see chapter 13).

That three-step TQS sentence is worth a closer look because your project's success will depend on your ability to discover or invent a good research question.

### 1.1.1 Topic: "I am working on the topic of . . ."

Researchers often begin with just a topic, something that sparks their curiosity, such as *the Apollo mission*. But if you stop there, you've got problems. Even a focused topic is a poor guide to your work, because a topic alone gives you no principled way to decide what data to look for or, once you have them, which data to use in your paper and which to discard. When that happens, students often run into trouble, producing a *data dump*. They dump everything into a paper that reads like a grab bag of barely connected facts. Most readers quickly become bored, asking, *Why are you telling me this?* They might read on if they are already interested in the topic, but even those readers will want to know: *What do these facts add up to?*

### 1.1.2 Question: ". . . because I want to find out how or why . . ."

More experienced researchers begin not just with a topic but with a research question, such as *Why was the Apollo mission to the moon important to America's national identity?* You may have to do some preliminary reading about your topic to come up with a question, but in every research project, formulating that question is a crucial early step. Experienced researchers know that readers will think their data add up to something only when they serve as evidence to support an answer. Only with a question can a researcher know what data to look for and, once obtained, what to keep—and not just data that support a particular answer but also data that test or discredit it. As we'll see later, with sufficient evidence to support an answer, a researcher can respond to data that seem to contradict it. In writing a paper, the researcher tests that answer and invites others to test it too.

1.1.3   **Significance / So What: ". . . so that I can help others understand how or why . . ."**

Experienced researchers also know that readers won't be interested in just any research question. Readers want to know not just your answer but also why that answer is worth knowing. So expect your readers to respond to your question with one of their own: *So what?* Think of it this way: What will be lost if you don't answer your question? Maybe nothing: you just want to know. That's good enough to start but not to finish, because eventually your readers will want an answer beyond *Just curious.*

All questions, in short, are not equally good. For example, you could ask the question *Who was taller, Neil Armstrong or Buzz Aldrin?* But you would have trouble answering *So what?* to the satisfaction of any but the most fanatical NASAphiles. Readers ask *So what?* about all research questions, not just the off-the-wall ones. If you ask the question *Why was the Apollo moon landing a symbol of America's national identity?*, you should also expect readers to ask in turn: *So what? Why should I care about that?* But this time you can justify your question by pointing out the significance of its answer: *If we can answer that question about the Apollo mission, we might better understand the bigger issue of how such events in general shape national identity.* Readers care about a question only when its answer makes them say *That's worth knowing!*

Of course, professional researchers have a big advantage: they already know what questions their readers care about. Students, especially beginners, usually have less to go on. So don't worry if at first you cannot find some great significance to your research question. Keep hunting for a good *So what?*, knowing that all won't be lost if you don't manage to find one. As long as you find a question that is relevant to your class, you can always explain its significance in terms of the class (for more on this, see 13.1.3):

. . . so that I can help my classmates understand how such regional myths have shaped America's sense of a unified national identity, which has been an important issue in our study of American diversity.

1.2   **Conversing with Your Readers**

Experienced researchers understand that genuine research must matter not only to the researcher but also to others. That is why our formula—*I am working on the topic of X because I want to find out Y so that I can help others understand Z*—

is so powerful: because it emphasizes that informing others is the real end of research.

Whenever you read a text, you silently converse with its authors. The same goes for *your* readers when you are the author. But imagining and then entering into such conversations can be difficult for beginning researchers—and especially for students, who sometimes misunderstand the kind of relationship with readers they should strive to create. Your task as a student researcher is not simply to rehearse whatever facts you've managed to turn up, in order to prove to your teacher that you've learned enough to get a good grade. Doing that might be—at best—a useful student exercise, but it is the opposite of genuine research. You may, it is true, receive some assignments that ask you simply to regurgitate information. But the best assignments will do more: they will invite you to experience genuine research by imagining and contributing to a community of readers who care about your question. In such research you become a kind of teacher yourself who says to your reader (even if she is your teacher), *Here is something that will help you remedy a situation that troubles you* or, more typically, *Here is something that will help you better understand something you care about.* When you present your research in this way, you write for others who are open to learning from you and even to changing their minds—if you can make the case.

We now understand the goal of genuine research, at least in its pure form: it is not to have the last word, as some students mistakenly believe, but to keep the conversation going. The best questions are those whose answers raise several more.

There is yet another reason to think of yourself as conversing with your readers: it will prod you to produce a better, richer, more thoughtful argument. Imagine your readers as interested and inquisitive colleagues, as a community of fellow researchers and even partners who want an answer as much as you do. Imagine that conversation taking place not in a classroom but around a table. Your question grabs the attention of your peers because they recognize that they'll be worse off if they don't get an answer. You share not just your answer but all the information you can find that is relevant to deciding whether your answer is a good one. In sharing that information, you try to anticipate their questions. You are candid enough to acknowledge any information that challenges or complicates your answer, and you address objections they might have. Even so, they have many more questions, alternative explanations, and other issues— each of which you consider and address as fairly as you can.

If you can imagine your readers in this way, your paper will be better. If you think of your project in these terms, you'll make more good decisions and waste less time as you write your paper. But just as importantly, you'll be preparing yourself for the day when your readers are indeed colleagues who need from you the best answers you and they can find.

1.3    **How Researchers Think about Their Answers/Arguments**

For researchers who see themselves as participating in such extended conversations, arguments are not just edifices of data but responses to questions readers can be expected to ask. Students are often surprised to realize that what they had thought was the main job of research—looking up information on a topic—is only a small part of a successful research project. Before you can even begin, you may have to do some preliminary reading to help you figure out a good research question. That question will then guide your work: you won't just look up information on your topic in the library or online; you will search for information—in the library but perhaps also in the field or the lab—to help you answer your question and then to test the strength of that answer. And once you think you've found an answer that satisfies you, you'll still have to justify it to your readers. Readers won't accept that answer just because you believe it: you have to give them reasons to believe it themselves. And they won't just take your word that your reasons are good ones: you have to support each reason with reliable evidence. In short, readers expect you to offer a complete and convincing argument that uses the data you have found to explain and support your answer.

1.3.1    **Think of Your Readers as Allies, Not Opponents**

By *argument*, we do not mean anything like the heated exchanges you see on cable news shows, where anything goes because all anyone cares about is winning. Unfortunately, many students imagine all arguments are like that, partly because the loud and angry ones are so memorable but also because the language we use to describe argument makes it sound like combat:

> I will *defend my position* from the *attack of my opposition*; then I will *marshal* my most powerful evidence to *counterattack*. I'll *probe for weak spots* in the other position, so that I can *undermine* it and *knock down* its key claims. We will *fire away* at each other until one or the other of us *gives up* and *surrenders*, leaving only the *victor* and the *vanquished*.

Experienced researchers know that they cannot treat readers like enemies to be vanquished. To succeed, researchers must *enlist readers as allies* who agree, at least provisionally, to follow along in the hope of learning something new. As we've said, a good research paper is like a silent conversation with your readers, and it's much easier to converse with an ally than with an enemy.

You can make allies of your readers—encourage them to be receptive rather than defensive—by treating their values, ideas, and perspectives with respect. That does *not* mean telling them only what you think they will agree with or want to hear—after all, your ultimate goal is to expand or change their minds. But you do have to attend closely to what you know (or imagine) your readers already believe, so that you can move them from where they are to where you would lead them.

> **CAUTION**
>
> **Don't Pander to Teachers**
> Students sometimes think they will be rewarded for writing papers that tell teachers what they want to hear by repeating what the teacher has already said. But that can be a grave mistake, in college and even in high school: it bores your teachers, who think it is not enough that you just rehash what's said in class and in the readings. Your teachers want to see not only that you know the class material but also that you can use that knowledge to think for yourself. If your papers, especially your research papers, merely summarize what you've read or repeat back your teacher's ideas, you will get that dreaded comment: *This does not go far enough.*

When your teacher says that you must *make* an argument to support your answer, don't think of *having* an argument, in which everyone stakes out a position and no one changes his or her mind. Instead imagine an intense yet amiable conversation with people who want to find a good answer to your question as much as or even more than you do. They don't want unsubstantiated opinions; they want claims you can support with reasons, and they want the evidence that makes you think your reasons are true. As in a conversation, they will also expect you to consider their points of view and to address any questions or concerns they might have. And they'll expect you to be forthcoming about any gaps in your argument or limitations in your evidence. In short, they want you to work *with* them to achieve the best available answer, not for all time but for now.

## 1.3.2    Think of Your Argument as Answers to Readers' Questions

You can think of the parts of your argument as answers to different sorts of questions readers might ask. If you can imagine these questions, you can write your argument.

### 1.3.2.1    *The Core of an Argument: Claim + Reasons + Evidence*

Your answers to the first three questions readers ask constitute the core of your argument.

1. **Claim: *What do you want me to believe?*** Once you raise your research question, readers naturally want to know the answer. We call this answer your *claim* because it is a statement that you are *claiming* to be true. Papers can have many claims running through them. A paper's main claim is also called its *thesis*.

Although some people still believe that early education should focus only on reading, writing, and math, elementary schools should actually make teaching languages other than English a priority.*claim*

2. **Reasons:** *Why should I believe that?* Unless your answer is obvious (in which case the question was not worth asking), readers will not accept it at face value. They'll want to know why they should accept your claim as true.

Although . . . , elementary schools should actually make teaching languages other than English a priority*claim* because we acquire languages best and most easily when we are young,*reason 1* because those who begin second languages as adults rarely attain fluency,*reason 2* and because language instruction fosters an awareness of cultures and societies beyond one's own.*reason 3*

3. **Evidence:** *How do you know that?* Even when your reasons seem plausible, responsible readers won't accept them just on your say-so. They expect you to base each reason on data you've discovered through your research. These data are your evidence.

Although . . . , elementary schools should actually make teaching languages other than English a priority*claim* because . . . *reasons* Studies of childhood language acquisition show that . . . *evidence for reason 1*

The terms *reason* and *evidence* are often used interchangeably, but they aren't synonyms. We will say more about this distinction in chapter 6. But for now, it is enough for you to understand that reasons are *statements* that support claims, and evidence is *data* on which those reasons rest.

1.3.2.2    *Honoring the Conversation: Acknowledgment and Response*
A claim supported by reasons that are based on evidence is the core of every argument. But if your argument consists *only* of these three elements, thoughtful readers may feel unsatisfied. When you make an argument for a community of readers, you make it not in a vacuum but in the context of all the arguments about your topic that have been made before. Careful readers therefore want to know not only that you can support your claim but also that you have thoughtfully considered the views of others—especially when their views differ from your own. Of course you can't address *every* claim that has come before your own, but you can honor the conversation by anticipating and responding to questions your claim might raise for your readers.

4. **Acknowledgment and Response:** *But what about this other view?* You cannot expect your readers to think exactly as you do. They will know things you don't, they will believe things you don't, and they may even distrust the kind of argument you want to make. If you adopt a genuinely cooperative stance, then you are obliged to acknowledge and respond to at least some of the questions that arise because of those differences.

Although some people still believe that early education should focus only on reading, writing, and math, elementary schools should actually make teaching

languages other than English a priority, because . . . *claim + reasons + evidence* To be
sure, widely introducing language instruction in elementary schools would be
expensive, and it would require giving less time to some other subjects. *acknowledgment* But the long-term benefits both to individual students and to society at
large far outweigh these costs. *response*

There are several types of acknowledgment and response, including *rebuttal* or *counterclaim*, in which you note and then challenge a competing view; *reflection*, in which you describe the evolution of your views or weigh your claim's
strengths and limitations; and *concession*, in which you accept another position's
merits before asserting the merits of your own. But all of these forms have a common purpose: to show your readers that you recognize the limitations of your own
ideas and that you have thoughtfully considered the views of others before ad-
vancing your own. These are things you must do. If you want readers to take your
arguments seriously and possibly to change their minds in response to them, then
you have to show that you are open to having your own mind changed as well.

1.3.2.3    *Explaining Your Logic: Warrants*
In some cases, researchers make arguments in which they have to explain not
only their reasons and evidence but also the principles that guided their reasoning. Suppose, for example, you were visiting your friend Paul in Cajun country.
It is a warm July evening, so he invites you to go for a walk on the levee, and then
he adds, "You might want to put on long sleeves." This makes no sense to you, so
you ask, "Why?" "Because the sun's going down," he replies. Now you are truly
baffled. You understand Paul's claim, and you can see the sun going down. But
you just cannot understand why that means you should wear long sleeves on a
warm July night. His reason is true, and his evidence is good. But his argument
so far fails.

That's when we need a *warrant*, or a principle that connects reasons and
evidence to a claim. So you ask again, "Why does the sun going down mean
that I need long sleeves?" As it happens, Paul has a good answer. "Ah," he says.
"You don't know about swamp country. You always need to protect yourself from
mosquitoes, and when the sun goes down, they come out in droves. If you don't
cover up, they will eat you alive."

Now it all makes sense. As an expert in swamp-country living, Paul was able
to reason in a way you couldn't. First, he knows a factual correlation you don't:
*When the sun goes down, mosquitoes come out*. That lets him apply a general principle of reasoning—a warrant—to reach his conclusion: *And when mosquitoes
come out, you want to protect yourself*. That warrant lets Paul connect his reason
to his claim: *So put on long sleeves*. (You still might wonder why anyone would
want to go walking among those mosquitoes in the first place.)

5. **Warrant:** ***How does that follow?*** A warrant is a principle stating that

when some condition (a reason, evidence) is true, we can draw some conclusion (claim). For example, you would have to supply a warrant if some readers asked, *But why does it matter that people learn languages best when they are young?* To which you would have to reply with a general principle:

From a developmental perspective, we should teach children things when they are most capable of learning them. <sub>warrant</sub>

Researchers usually leave their warrants unstated, because they expect their readers to know them already. But you may need to state your warrants if your readers are unfamiliar with your subject, or if your subject is controversial, or if your research methods are unconventional, or if you are writing for readers whose way of seeing the world is very different from yours. Such situations arise only occasionally when you write a paper for a class, so we will not dwell on this fifth question. But you should know that readers might ask it.

### 1.3.3   Use the Parts of Argument to Guide Your Research

A research question helps guide your research project because it tells you generally what information to look for: whatever is relevant to answering your question. But in the parts of argument you have an even better guide. As you plan and conduct your research, remember that you will need to answer at least four questions that every cooperative argument must address.

---

**Plan Your Research around the Questions of Argument**

Every argument must answer the three questions that define the core of a research argument, and cooperative ones must also answer a fourth.

c ⌐ 1. What's the answer to your research question?   **Claim**

o

r 2. Why should I believe that?   **Reasons**

e ⌐ 3. How do you know that reason is true?   **Evidence**

4. But have you considered this view? [or this   **Acknowledgment** evidence, complication, objection, etc.]   **& Response**

Create a plan to search for and read sources so that you have good answers to each of these questions:

1. **Claim.** If you begin without a plausible claim that answers your research question, start by reading general treatments of your topic in order to get ideas for possible answers.

2. **Reasons.** Once you have a claim that can serve as an hypothesis, make a list of the reasons why you think that claim is true. If you think of too few

---

plausible reasons, do some more general reading. If you still can't find any, look for another claim.

3.  **Evidence.** Once you have a list of reasons, search for specific data that might serve as evidence to support each one. Depending on the kind of reason, that evidence might be statistics, quotations, observations, or any other facts. If you cannot find evidence for a reason, then you have to replace that reason. If you find evidence that goes against a reason, keep the evidence. You may need to acknowledge it in your paper.

4.  **Acknowledgment & Response.** As you read for claims, reasons, and evidence, keep a record of anything that might complicate or contradict your argument. You will need to acknowledge and respond to it through rebuttal, counterclaim, reflection, or concession—if you think it might also occur to your readers.

We discuss these steps more fully in chapters 6 and 7.

## 1.4    How You Can Best Think about Your Project

You have learned a great deal new about writing research papers, and it's only the end of the first chapter. We'll cover this ground again in later chapters, where we'll go step by step through the process of planning, researching, drafting, and revising your paper. Don't expect to walk though those steps exactly as we lay them out—research is too messy, with lots of looping back and jumping forward. But if you stay flexible and take it one step at a time, you'll get through the process confidently enough.

For now, we would like you to focus not on the steps but on creating an overall mental picture of research that you will keep in mind as you work. Unfortunately, three common pictures are false ones that distort the nature of true research.

In the first, you think of your project as just a matter of meeting the demands of an assignment. All that matters is finding enough information to fill up the required number of pages.

Q: *How's your project going?*

A: Good. I've found enough information for four pages already. I only need two more pages of material.

This picture is false because just doing the assignment is *never* the point of an assignment. Under pressure, students sometimes choose projects they think will be easy rather than projects that genuinely interest them. But when you make this choice you shortchange not only your teacher but also yourself. You will do better work, you will learn more, and you will *enjoy* your project more if you pick one you care about.

In the second, you think of your project as no more than gathering data. All that matters is the hunt. Your argument is an afterthought:

Q: *How's your project going?*

A: Good. I have a ton of sources (even including a bunch of print sources from the library), and I've dug up lots of information. I just have to organize my notes, and then I can write it all up.

This picture is false because data don't speak for themselves: your data become meaningful when you use them to make an argument addressing a question your readers care about.

The third picture is the reverse of the second. Before you even begin your research, you settle on a claim, and you think of your project as just backing it up:

Q: *How's your project going?*

A: Good. I wrote a three-point outline, and I found enough stuff to back up the first two points. I just need to research the third point and I'm done.

This view is false because the point of research is not to confirm what you already believe but to discover something new. When you begin a research project, you should have some idea of what your claims might be. But you should also expect those claims to change as you learn more.

If you think of your project in these ways, you'll miss out on what research is really about.

As we have said, the end product of a research project is usually a paper, but that product can take other forms as well, anything from a research poster to an informal class discussion. No matter the end product, the process is the same: (1) you find a research question important to you *and* to your readers; (2) you decide what information you need to find based on the question you ask; (3) you use the information you find to select and then test the best answer to your research question; and (4) you finally present that answer and its support in a way that anticipates readers' questions.

As you begin to plan for your project, let these principles be your guide:

- Find a project that interests you. *You will do better work and you will enjoy your work more when you research something that matters to you.*
- Start by asking questions and gathering data that help you answer them. *Your task is to ask and answer a research question that interests you and your readers.*
- Begin with a claim in mind, but be willing to adjust it as you learn more. *Research is not about backing up what you already believe; it is about discovering something new.*

- Most importantly, don't think of research as a solitary endeavor. *Keep your readers with you from start to finish.*

If right from the start you focus on the conversation you are creating with your readers—on *asking and answering questions*—then you'll find it easier to do the things that will produce a successful paper.

---

WORKING IN GROUPS

**Find Surrogate Readers**

You can help yourself think of your paper as a conversation with readers if you talk about your work to your family, friends, and classmates. Later we will suggest that you form a writing group for testing your storyboard and draft. But it may not be too early to form an informal group even before you find a question. Recruit three or four classmates who will join you for coffee or lunch just to talk over your earliest ideas. At this point you don't need suggestions, just a sympathetic ear. You will also learn just from listening: the more you experience what your readers will, the easier it will be to imagine them.

# 2   Defining a Research Question

A research project begins well before you search the internet or head for the library and continues long after you have collected all the data you think you need. Every project involves countless specific tasks, and so it is easy to get overwhelmed. But in all research projects, you have just five general aims:

- Ask a question worth answering.
- Arrive at an answer that you can support with good reasons.
- Find reliable evidence to back up your reasons.
- Draft an argument that makes a good case for your answer.
- Revise that draft until readers will think you met the first four goals.

You might even post this list over your desk.

    Research projects would be much easier if we could march straight through these steps. But you will discover (if you have not already) that the research process is not so straightforward. Each task overlaps with others, and frequently you must go back to an earlier one. The truth is, research is messy and unpredictable. But that's also what makes it exciting and ultimately rewarding. You can manage these tasks with a plan, as long as you are prepared to depart from it. But the first step in any research project is to find a good research question.

> CAUTION
>
> **Start with a Question, Not Your Favorite Answer**
> Students sometimes think that a shortcut to a research paper is to argue for something they already believe so strongly that nothing could change their mind. Big mistake. Not only will you lose the benefits of the research experience, but you'll come to your paper with the wrong frame of mind: to say whatever is necessary to support your position rather than to find out what will help you discover the truth. Even when they are confident that they know what the answer will be, true researchers follow where the facts lead them rather than force the facts to go their way. Plan to answer a question, not defend an opinion.

## 2.1  Questions and Topics

Most students start a research project without a good question, often without even a topic. That puts them a couple of steps behind most professionals, who start with their research question in mind.

Often researchers start with a question that others in their field already think is worth answering: *Did Neanderthals use pigments, bones, or feathers to decorate their bodies?* Anthropologists asking this question would know why their colleagues think it is significant. *So what? Well, if we knew whether Neanderthals decorated their bodies, that would help us answer a bigger question: Were Neanderthals able to think abstractly using symbols, or is that capacity unique to modern humans? And if we knew that, then we might also understand . . .* (*So what?* again. See 1.1.3.)

Then there are those questions that just pop into a researcher's mind with no hint of where they'll lead, sometimes about matters so seemingly trivial that only the researcher thinks they're worth answering: *Why does a coffee spill dry up in the form of a ring?* Such a question might lead nowhere, but you can't know that until you see its answer. In fact, the scientist puzzled by coffee rings made discoveries about the behavior of fluids that others in his field thought important—and that paint manufacturers used to improve their products. You can't know where a question might lead until you try to answer it.

> QUICK TIP
>
> A researcher's most valuable asset is the ability to be puzzled by seemingly obvious things, like the shape of coffee rings or that the hair on your head keeps growing while body hair doesn't. If you cultivate the ability to see what's odd

in the commonplace, you'll never lack for research projects as either a student or a professional. Questioning the obvious is also the first step in critical thinking, which is a skill much prized in the workplace. But if you don't start practicing it now, you won't do it well then.

If your assignment allows it, you too can start with a question that's been eating at you, whether it's related to a practical issue or a personal interest. One source of questions might be a problem that you or a family member has faced. If your neighborhood is near a chemical plant, research the health risks. If you know someone afflicted with a disease, research any new or experimental treatments. A second source might be a cause to which you are devoted. If you volunteer for Habitat for Humanity, research how well those houses suit their owners ten years after they are completed. A third source might be something you love to do. If you love fashion and hope to be a designer, research the economic challenges for a start-up design company.

If you begin with only a topic, you should still consult your interests. Is there some mental itch you'd like to scratch? *I've played the piano for years, but I have no idea how it was invented.* You might not know exactly what will puzzle you about the origins of your instrument, but your project gives you a chance to find out, to scratch that itch. Even if you must begin with a topic so unfamiliar that you can't imagine what could be puzzling about it, look hard for something that sparks your interest. The more *you* care to have an answer to your research question, the easier it will be to show why your readers should care too, and the longer you can work on finding it before you weary of the search.

### How to Use the Rest of This Chapter

If you are reading this chapter before you start your project, to learn how research questions work, read on from here to the end. But if you are using it to develop a question for a project, go to the section designed for your stage in the process:

1. If you already have a promising research question, skip to 2.6 to learn how to test it.
2. If you are working from a text, skip to 2.5 to learn how to find a research question in your response to it.
3. If you have a general topic, skip to 2.4 to learn how to find a question in it.
4. If you are starting from scratch, move on to the next section.

2.2    **How to Choose a Topic**

A standard piece of advice when starting a research project is to narrow your topic. That's not wrong, but it is misleading. What makes your paper work is a focused research question, not a narrow topic. So as you work through this section, keep in mind that at every stage you are looking for a good, focused research question. As soon as one comes to mind, skip to 2.6 to test it. Until you find a question, keep narrowing your topic: a specific topic is a better source of questions than a general one. But remember, it's not the topic but the question that matters most.

---

QUICK TIP

**The Value of Surprise and Disagreement**

Keep in mind as you look for a research question that what is surprising or wrong catches our attention most easily. Look for ideas, claims, facts, or anything that makes you think, *Wow, I didn't know that!* or *How can that be true?* Not only will those matters hold your attention longer, but they will make it easier to get the attention of your readers.

---

2.2.1    **How to Find a Topic Based on Your Personal Interests**

If you can pick any topic, start with something that intrigues, amuses, surprises, irritates, or otherwise interests you.

- What special interests do you have—chess, manga, basketball, knitting, electronic music? The less common, the better. Investigate something about it that you don't know.
- Where would you like to travel? Find out all you can about your destination. What particular aspect surprises you or makes you want to learn more?
- Can you find a social media page focused on issues that interest you? Pay attention to what others, especially those whose points of view differ from yours, are saying about these issues.
- Visit a museum or a "virtual museum" on the internet that appeals to you. What catches your eye that you would like to know more about?
- Does your library have rich resources in some field? Ask your teacher or a librarian.
- What intrigues you in your reading? What connections do you see among different things you are reading?

You might find a topic in your disagreements with others:

- Is there an issue you have debated with others, then found that you couldn't back up your views with good reasons and evidence?

- Is there a common belief that you suspect is simplistic or just wrong? Do research to make a case against it.
- Tune in to talk radio or interview programs on TV until you hear a claim you disagree with. Can you make a case to refute it?

You might also find a topic if you think about your future:

- What courses might you take later? Find a textbook and skim its study questions.
- If you have a dream job, what kind of research project might help you get it? Employers often ask for samples of an applicant's work.

Keep in mind that you may be living with your topic for a long time, so be sure it interests you enough to get you through the inevitable rocky stretches.

2.2.2    ## How to Work with an Assigned Topic

In most classes you won't be able to write about just any personal interest; you'll be expected to find a research question related to the subject matter of your class. Even if you are passionate about military history, you may be hard-pressed to write about it in a class on Buddhism. But you should still look for a topic that might engage you, not just because doing that will help you do better in the class but also to practice finding *new* interests in subjects and material that hadn't interested you before. If you try to stick only to projects related to your preexisting personal interests, you risk missing out on one of the most exciting aspects of learning.

If your assignment specifies a general topic—for example, *Buddhism and war*—skip to section 2.2.3 to narrow it. But if you are free to choose any topic related to the theme of your class, look for one that interests you in the following places:

- Do any of your personal interests overlap with the class theme?
- Review your course readings and notes. What has surprised or irritated you?
- Look over any course readings that your teacher skipped.
- Skim other books and articles by the authors of your assigned readings, looking for matters related to your class. Did an author write an earlier work that is inconsistent with the assigned text? Did she apply some of the same ideas in a wholly different context?
- Skim a textbook for a more advanced class on the same or a related subject.
- Look through the archive for an online discussion list that covers the subject of your class. What topics have been discussed?

QUICK TIP

**Interpreting Assignments**

When experienced researchers talk about their projects, they often describe them as topics: *I'm studying online poker.* But such statements are really a shorthand for that whole Topic-Question-Significance formula we showed you in chapter 1: *I'm studying online poker because I want to find out how amateur players bet so that I can help others understand how people make decisions in the absence of complete information.*

Teachers use a similar shorthand when giving assignments, and you have to learn to read between the lines to complete them successfully. Assignments often include phrases like these:

| | | |
|---|---|---|
| *explore X* | *discuss X* | *analyze X* |
| *explain X* | *critique X* | *investigate X* |

But these phrases, like that researcher's description of her project as *studying online poker*, describe only the first step. As a student you have to infer the rest. An assignment to *discuss X* really means something more like this:

*Find an issue in X that raises a question about a specific aspect of X, whose answer will help us understand some larger theme, feature, or quality of X.*

In using such shorthand, your teachers are not trying to fool you. They just assume that you already understand what they mean. Now you do.

## 2.2.3    Make Your Topic Manageable

If you pick a topic whose name sounds like an encyclopedia entry—*railroads, birds, musical instruments, sports*—you'll find so many sources that you could spend years reading them. You have to carve out of your topic a manageable piece. You can start by limiting it: What is it about, say, sports that made you choose them? Think about your topic in the context of something you know or care about and that is also likely to matter to others. Then add words to your topic that both limit and enrich it:

sports
    politics and sports
        political protests and sports events
            politics and the Olympic Games
                political *protests* at the Olympic Games
                    political *protests* by *athletes* at the *1968* Olympic Games

You might not be able to focus your topic sufficiently until after you've read something about it. (Did you know that athletes from several countries engaged in protests at the 1968 games?) That takes time, so start early. Begin with a general online encyclopedia like the *Encyclopaedia Britannica* or even Wikipedia (but see the Caution below). Since you are just looking to prime your thinking, you can search the internet for ideas without too much concern for the reliability of what you find (although your sources' reliability will be crucial later if you want to draw on them for evidence). Your goal for the moment is simply to put your topic into a context that makes it meaningful for both you and others.

> **CAUTION**
>
> **How to Use Wikipedia**
>
> When you need information quickly, Wikipedia can be a godsend. It covers almost every topic you can think of, and studies show that it is generally reliable. But it is usually incomplete, and it does have errors, sometimes outrageous ones. As a result, many teachers ban its use as a source. If you have easy access to an established encyclopedia such as *Britannica*, use it. Otherwise, feel free to use Wikipedia for ideas or citations to pursue. But unless Wikipedia is a focus of your research (and unless your teacher says it is okay), do not use it for information you must cite. When you access a Wikipedia article, check out its "Discussion" tab, which will help you decide how much confidence to place in that article.

## 2.3   Two Kinds of Research Questions

You'll be better able to find a question in your topic if you know the different types of questions researchers ask. That's because not every kind of question will work in every situation or class.

Research questions come in two varieties. One kind of question concerns what we should do to address some tangible problem. We call such questions *practical*. Practical questions are common in the professions, business, and government. The other kind of question concerns what we should think. We call such questions *conceptual*. Conceptual questions are also common in the professions, business, and government, when their answers help us understand what causes a practical problem, but they are most common in the academic world. You need to be able to distinguish these two kinds of research questions because your teachers will expect you to write about one kind or the other (in high school or college, usually conceptual ones) and because you have to answer these two types of questions differently.

### 2.3.1   Practical Questions: What Should We Do?

The answer to a practical question tells us what to do to change or fix some troublesome situation. You can recognize a practical question by looking at the third step in the TQS formula: that step states both the practical problem and something we should do to change it.

> **T:** I am working on the topic of X, (*What's interesting about that?*)
> **Q:** because I want to find out Y, (*So what if you do?*)
> **S:** so that I can help others **decide what to do** to fix Z.

The significance of a practical question is that answering it empowers us to take action to improve some situation in the world.

Suppose, for example, someone asked about your research as an intern in the Dean of Students office:

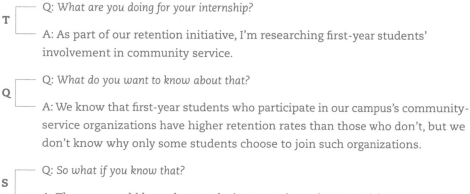

T
> Q: *What are you doing for your internship?*
>
> A: As part of our retention initiative, I'm researching first-year students' involvement in community service.

Q
> Q: *What do you want to know about that?*
>
> A: We know that first-year students who participate in our campus's community-service organizations have higher retention rates than those who don't, but we don't know why only some students choose to join such organizations.

S
> Q: *So what if you know that?*
>
> A: Then we would know how to design our orientation materials to persuade more students to sign up, which should increase retention.

What makes this *practical* research is that you are interested in the question chiefly because you want to use the answer to decide what to do about a troublesome practical problem, in this case, lower-than-desired retention rates. (In this example, you can imagine receiving a further response: *How do you know that students' involvement in community service actually affects retention? Maybe those students likely to remain in college are also likely to participate in community service?* That's a good question, and for your research to hold up, you would need a reason to believe that participation in community service does not merely *correlate* with higher student retention but actually *contributes* to it: *Well, nothing in our admissions data allows us to predict which students will join a community-service organization, so . . .*)

2.3.2     **Conceptual Questions: What Should We Think?**
Academic researchers usually ask a different kind of question. Its answer doesn't tell us what to do to change the world but only how to *understand* it better: *How does* The Simpsons *reinforce traditional conservative values? When does a cult become a religion?*

You can recognize a conceptual question because its significance in the third step concerns not what we do but what we understand:

> **T:** I am working on the topic of X, (*What's interesting about that?*)
> **Q:** because I want to find out Y, (*So what if you do?*)
> **S:** so that I can help others **understand** how/why/whether Z.

The significance of a conceptual question is that answering it puts us in a position to answer some other broader or more important question.

Suppose, for example, that you had to ask your teacher's approval for the topic of your research paper:

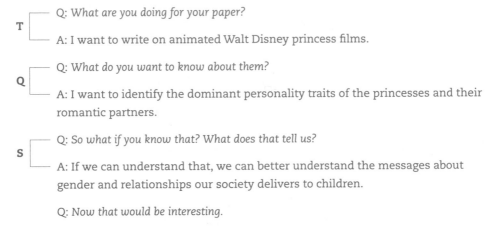

T
- Q: *What are you doing for your paper?*
- A: I want to write on animated Walt Disney princess films.

Q
- Q: *What do you want to know about them?*
- A: I want to identify the dominant personality traits of the princesses and their romantic partners.

S
- Q: *So what if you know that? What does that tell us?*
- A: If we can understand that, we can better understand the messages about gender and relationships our society delivers to children.

Q: *Now that would be interesting.*

### 2.3.3 The Challenge of Answering *So What?* for Conceptual Questions

Students can be impatient with conceptual questions because they seem irrelevant to "real world" issues. Many can't even imagine answers to *So what?* questions like these:

- *So what if we don't know why Shakespeare had Lady Macbeth die offstage?*
- *So what if we don't understand the psychology of the zebra fish?*
- *So what if we don't know how language originated?*

Trust us: there are research communities that can answer each of those *So what?* questions, even if you can't. In contrast, no one asks *So what?* of a researcher trying to understand how to cure Alzheimer's, because the practical significance of that research is obvious.

But here's a trap: you know now, following our TQS formula, that you should identify the significance of your research question. But stating the significance of a conceptual question can be harder than stating the significance of a practical one, especially when you're a student. That's because you are probably not yet a member of a specific research community, like professional historians or marine biologists, so you might not see how your research question bears on larger ones.

But even if you can't quite state the significance of your conceptual question, you should resist the temptation to assert a practical significance instead:

> **T:** I am studying the rise of the shōguns in twelfth-century Japan
> **Q:** because I want to understand why Japan gravitated toward military rule
> **S:** so that we can resist dictatorship today.

Most readers would find the link between that conceptual question and its asserted practical significance a stretch.

You can look forward to a day when you can answer conceptual questions relevant to the practical problems that beset us. Before we can solve important practical problems, we almost always have to do conceptual research to understand them better. And sometimes the answer to a conceptual question helps us address a practical problem in ways we did not initially expect. For example, research modeling the flocking of birds is being used to optimize the efficiency of hybrid vehicles.

So try to be patient if at the start of your project you cannot think of any good answers to *So what?*—even the most experienced researchers sometimes have to find their results before they can say why they are worth knowing. Remember that you'll need *some* answer by the end, and keep your eye out for larger issues as you do your reading. (We'll show you what to look for in chapter 4.) The more often you imagine others asking *So what?* and the more often you practice answering it, even if only to your own satisfaction, the more confident you can be that you can succeed at every researcher's toughest task—convincing others that your work is worth their time.

## 2.4    Question Your Topic

Now that you know the types of research questions you can ask, you are ready to find one in your topic. A topic is only as good as the questions it raises. So make a list of all the questions that you can imagine asking about your topic, then choose the most interesting among them.

### 2.4.1    Ask Your Own Questions

Here are some questions you can ask for yourself about almost any topic. The categories are loose and overlap, so don't worry about keeping them straight. Suppose you have settled on the topic of the Olympic Games.

1.  Start by asking how your topic fits into larger contexts: a larger history, a larger system, or a larger category that includes things like it.

- **How does your topic fit into a larger history?**

  What motivated the creation of the modern Olympics? How are the modern Olympics related to the ancient games in Greece? What national or international sports competitions preceded the Olympics? How are the Olympics connected to the civil rights movement?

- **How does your topic work as a part of a larger system?**

  How do different countries use the Olympics to encourage patriotism? Do cities benefit economically from hosting the Olympics? How profitable are the Olympics for advertisers? How are the Olympics related to professional sports? To education? To politics? To warfare? To the arts? To the media?

- **How does your topic compare to and contrast with other things like it?**

  How are the Olympic Games like or unlike other international sporting competitions? College sports? Professional sports championships? Nineteenth- and twentieth-century world fairs? Political conventions? Outdoor music festivals?

2. Next, ask questions about the parts of your topic.

   - **What are the histories of parts of your topic?**

     When and why did the biathlon become an Olympic sport? Why do NHL players play on national hockey teams? When did women first compete in the Olympic Games? Why were the second Olympics held in Paris?

   - **How do the parts of your topic work together as a system?**

     How are the Olympics organized and governed? How does a sport qualify for inclusion in the Olympics? Why did the International Olympic Committee relax its prohibition against the participation of professional athletes? What role do national Olympic committees play in organizing the games?

   - **How many different categories of your topic are there?**

     How many sports are represented in the Olympics? How often have nations boycotted the Olympics? What other sporting events are modeled on the Olympics?

3. Next, set your imagination loose with speculative questions.

   - **What's *not* true about your topic?**

Why aren't Olympic athletes paid a salary? Why can't Olympic athletes use performance-enhancing drugs? Why aren't the games held every year? Why aren't darts and chess Olympic sports?

- Ask *What if?* questions:

What if corporations could field Olympic teams? What if the Olympics did not award medals? What if Olympic athletes could train for only six months prior to competition? What if countries sanctioned by the United Nations were not allowed to compete? What if the Olympics were broadcast freely over the internet?

4. Finally, turn positive questions into a negative ones:

How have the Olympics not succeeded in fostering international understanding and cooperation? Why have some cities chosen not to host the games? What factors are not important to the International Olympic Committee when it chooses host cities? In what ways is competition not important to the Olympics?

### 2.4.2    Borrow Questions

Researchers often study questions first raised by others. Unless your teacher specifically says you must devise your own question, you too are free to find your question wherever you can. If you are concerned about plagiarism, you can cite the source of your question, but you do not have to.

Some questions you can find online:

- Find a social media page or online discussion forum on your topic, then "lurk," just reading for the kinds of questions those on the page raise. You can also visit the websites of professional organizations concerned with your topic. Look for questions that also interest you.
- Look for study guides related to your topic. You can find them both in textbooks and online. Many questions will be unsuitable because they ask for a rehash, but some will be thought provoking.
- Find online syllabi for classes on topics like yours. Some of them will list proposed questions for papers.

You can also find questions in your classroom. Listen in class discussions for issues that are left unresolved, for points on which a classmate seems confused, for statements that you cannot accept. All of these can be turned into potential research questions.

2.5       How to Find a Topic and Question in a Source

Teachers often ask students to find their topics and questions in course readings or other sources. When you read, pay attention to what surprises, puzzles, or provokes you. Here are several ways to find topics and questions in a source.

2.5.1     Build on Disagreement

Nothing motivates us to argue more than disagreement, and our quarrels with a source often generate some of our best ideas. But your readers won't like disagreement for its own sake, and you don't want them to think you are merely disagreeable. But they will if you set out only to show that a source is wrong, wrong, wrong. So look for *creative* disagreements, the kind that lead you to think hard not just about what your source says but also about what you think in response. You'll know you've found one when you show not just that a source is wrong but that something else is right.

---

**USEFUL FORMULA**

**Smith claims _____, but I will show _____.**
When you find a creative disagreement, you state your research question in terms of the difference between what a source says (in the first blank) and what you will show (in the second):

   Smith claims that _____ is true, but I will show that _____ is really the case.

(In all of these examples, our generic name for the source will be *Smith*.)

---

In stating this formula we have used the first person ("I") to emphasize the conversational nature of research arguments: in your claim or thesis statement, you are responding to Smith, and others (you can hope) will be motivated by your ideas to respond to you in turn. But we also know that teachers differ on whether the first person should be used in formal writing. Our view is that the first person *can* be appropriate in formal writing, but we also understand why some teachers may ask you to avoid it (see 15.2.2).

If you are not supposed to use the first person in your class, this formula, and our others, will still work for you. You will just have to rephrase your sentence when you put it into your paper:

Smith claims that _____ is true, but _____ is really the case.

Here are a few of the many ways you can create a research question based on your disagreements with a source, grouped by the type of disagreement:

**Kind**

- Smith claims that _____ belongs in category A, but I will show that it really belongs in category B.

Smith claims that fringe religious groups are "cults" because of their strange beliefs, but I will show that those beliefs are no different in kind from those of standard religions.

- Smith claims that _____ is normal/good/significant/useful/moral/etc., but I will show that it is really [*something else*].

Smith claims that organized religion does more harm than good, but I will show that it is the misuse of religion that does the harm, not religion itself.

**(You can reverse all of the forms in this list: Smith claims that a religion is not a cult, but I will show that its beliefs are too strange to count as religious.)**

**Part-Whole**

- Smith claims that [*whole*] always has [*part*] as one of its defining features/ components/qualities, but I will show that [*part*] is not essential.

Smith claims that competition is the essence of sport, but I will show that, even by her standards, competition is only incidental to the way most people actually play sports.

**Change**

- Smith claims that _____ is changing in a certain way, but I will show that it is really the same as it was.

Smith claims that social media will kill off mainstream media, but I will show that mainstream media will find ways to survive because people still want what only they can offer.

- Smith claims that _____ is changing in a certain way, but I will show that it is really changing in a different way.

Smith claims that targeted online marketing will let consumers get the products they want and need, but I will show that such techniques really let companies manipulate their customers more than ever.

- Smith claims that _____ is a stage/process in the development of _____, but I will show that it is not.

Smith claims that people suffering from drug or alcohol addiction must hit rock bottom before they can commit to change, but I will show that new early intervention programs can save people before they bottom out.

**Cause and Effect**

- Smith claims that _____ causes _____, but I will show that it really causes _____.

Smith claims that persistent poverty causes crime, but I will show that it really causes despair, which sometimes leads to crime and sometimes does not.

- Smith claims that _____ is caused by _____, but I will show that it is really caused by _____.

Smith claims that the collapse of the banking system was caused by greed and a lack of government oversight, but I will show that the real cause was that financial instruments became so complicated that no one could evaluate their risks.

- Smith claims that _____ is sufficient to cause _____, but I will show that _____ is also necessary.

Smith claims that big-time athletics programs can debase the educational mission of a college, but I will show that athletics programs alone are not enough: there also have to be alumni and other stakeholders who are more passionate about success on the field than in the classroom.

## 2.5.2   Build on Agreement

It can be affirming to find a source whose problem you care about and whose argument you find convincing. But you can't create a paper out of that agreement alone: *Same here!* is not a very interesting claim. You may, however, be able to build on that agreement by extending or elaborating on that source's claim. Here are some ways to do that:

**Provide Better Support**

- Smith gives limited/old/partial/weak evidence for _____, but I will show _____ using better evidence.

Smith gives only anecdotal evidence that exposure to violent cartoons does not encourage violence in children, but I will show that Smith's conclusion is affirmed by recent studies of child brain development.

**Confirm Unsupported Claims**

- Smith speculates _____ might be true, but I will show that it is in fact true.

Smith recommends visualization to improve sports performance, but I will use new findings from sports psychology to show why that is good advice.

**Apply a Claim More Widely**

- Smith argues _____ is true in one context, but I will show that it is true in another / a more general context.

Smith argues that medical students learn physiological processes better when they are explained with many metaphors rather than with just one, but I will show that the same is true for novices in technical professions generally.

---

**USEFUL FORMULA**

**Smith claims _____ about this, and I will show _____ about that.**
When you build on agreement, you apply the problem and answer of a source to a different object of study. You state your research question in terms of how you can show that what Smith has shown to be true about one thing is also true (or not) about another:

Smith claims that _____ is true in the case of _____, and I will show that it is/is not true in the case of _____.

---

### 2.5.3    Use a Source as a Model

Whether you agree or disagree with a source's claims, you may still be impressed by the *way* it answers its question or makes its argument. In that case, you might use that source's method of analysis or way of making its argument to answer a different question of your own.

### 2.5.3.1    *Apply a Source's Method of Analysis to a New Subject*

Researchers routinely borrow methods from each other. In many fields they even repeat other researchers' projects to confirm their findings. You can do the same. Suppose you want to find out whether violent video games affect adolescents' capacity for empathy. You are excited about your question, but you don't know how to begin answering it. Then you come across a source that shows you a way: the author used a survey to show that men who are fans of action flicks tended to drive faster than men who aren't. Interestingly, the author reports no similar correlation among women. Perhaps, you think, you could create a survey of your own to explore the emotional effects of video games. And you also have another question: if action flicks seem to influence male and female drivers differently, might violent video games also affect adolescent boys and adolescent girls differently?

### 2.5.3.2    *Pattern Your Own Argument on an Argument from a Source*

A typical case is when you read an essay that analyzes a creative work in a way that you find convincing, so you apply it to a different work. Suppose you are taking a class on Asian American literature. You enjoy an assigned article by Dan

Yoshita on Maxine Hong Kingston's 1976 memoir *The Woman Warrior*, so you use it as both inspiration and a model for your own analysis of Chang-rae Lee's 1995 novel *Native Speaker*:

> Yoshita argues that although Kingston styles her book a memoir, she knowingly adopts a fictional register to prevent her mainly non-Chinese readership from treating her as an objective cultural informant. In his novel *Native Speaker*, Chang-rae Lee draws on the low-literary conventions of the spy novel for a similar purpose . . .

This approach involves lots of borrowing, but as long as you fully acknowledge the source, you are in no danger of plagiarism. Your paper may be less original than if you had thought up the problem yourself, but that is rarely a problem for beginners. In fact, professionals create research questions in this way all the time.

## 2.5.4   Look for Surprises

When you work from agreement or disagreement, you build on the *argument* of your source text. But you can't do that if you are working from a text that does not make an argument or if what interests you is not its argument but how it is put together. In that case, rather than ask whether you agree with the text, look for what seems puzzling, confusing, out of place, or otherwise a surprise.

When you look for surprises, try the three-step approach we call E-S-P:

> **E:** When I first read this text, I **expected** to find _____.
> **S:** So I was **surprised** when instead I found _____.
> **P:** I have a **problem** because my old understanding of this text/author/argument makes sense only with [*what you expected*], not with [*what you found*].

This kind of problem gives you four ways to create an argument.

- Figure out how you have to change your understanding of the text:

  > At first it made sense to understand the text [*the way you did*], but I will show why we should really understand it in a different way.

- Figure out how and why you were wrong to expect what you did:

  > At first it made sense to expect the text to do [*what you expected*], but I will show why that is based on a mistaken understanding of the text.

- Figure out how and why what you found actually fits in:

  > When the text did not do [*what you expected*], I first thought that I was wrong to expect it. But I will show that [*what you expected*] would have fit perfectly.

• Show that the text would have been better, or at least more consistent, if the author had done what you expected rather than what you found:

> It seemed surprising that the text did not do [*what you expected*], and I will show that it would have been better if it had.

Among the advantages of this approach is that it gives you an easy way to create a context that shows why your question is significant: you can use what you expected to set up a contrast that defines your question. You are still responding to a source, only this time that "source" is your former self and belief. Here is a compressed version (to learn how to expand it, see 13.1):

> In view of the position Kaufmann takes on amnesty, education, and other issues concerning undocumented immigrants, it would be natural to expect that he would favor, or at least not oppose, English-only legislation. But in fact, his fifth chapter not only criticizes English-only movements but makes a strong case for a multilingual society. In this paper, I will show . . .

---

**WORKING IN GROUPS**

**Bounce Ideas off Friends**
You can use your classmates for all of the above strategies for finding questions in sources. Ask your friends (or your writing group, if you have one) for their ideas about your topic. They may have ideas that are interesting but in your view wrong, that are in your view right but not properly developed, or that just plain surprise you. If so, plug their ideas into the appropriate formula and you have a candidate for a worthy research question.

---

## 2.6    Evaluate Your Questions

Finally, evaluate your questions and scrap those unlikely to yield interesting answers. Most important, you don't have a good question if no one would disagree with your answer. To test this, imagine yourself arguing for the opposite of your actual view; if the argument sounds absurd rather than merely wrong, abandon your question.

Here are some other signs of a question you can't use.

1. You can answer the question too easily.
   • You can just look it up: *What city hosted the first Winter Olympic Games?*
   • You can just quote a source: *What does Fisher say about the role of professional athletes in the Olympic Games?*
2. No one could plausibly *disprove* the answer, because it seems self-evident. *Were the modern Olympic Games inspired by the games of the ancient Greeks?* The answer is obvious: *Yes.*

You cannot make a good argument if you cannot identify the best evidence for it.

3. You can't find factual evidence to support the answer
    - The relevant facts do not exist, or the question is purely speculative: *Would Japan have participated in the first modern Olympic Games if invited?*
    - It's a matter of personal taste or opinion: *Is skiing or snowboarding the more exciting sport?*

4. You would find so many sources that you cannot look at most of them: *What is the role of sport in society?* (This usually results from a question that's too broad).

QUICK TIP

Don't reject a question because you think someone must already have asked it. Most interesting questions have more than one good answer. Don't reject a question because you think your teacher already knows the answer. You should target your paper not at an expert like your teacher but at someone whose knowledge is more like yours.

The crucial point is to find a question that *you* really want to answer. Too many students, even advanced ones, think that education means memorizing the right answers to questions someone else has asked and answered. It is not. Among your most important goals for your education should be to learn to ask your own questions and find your own answers.

# 3    Working toward an Answer

At the end of chapter 1 we cautioned you against three false views of how researchers work: that they just want to fill up pages, that what matters most is the process of gathering data, and that they do it to back up claims to which they are already committed. We urged you instead to view research as a process of discovery that allows you to *arrive* at good claims and to *craft* good arguments to support them. In this chapter we take up that idea again, by showing you how *starting* with a claim to which you are *not* fully committed—what we call a *working answer* or *hypothesis*—can help you plan and execute your research project.

## 3.1    Propose Some Possible Answers

Before you get far into your project, try one more preliminary step. It's one that many beginners resist but that experienced researchers rely on, so start practicing it now. As soon as you have a question, imagine some plausible answers, no matter how sketchy or speculative. At this stage, don't worry whether they're right. That comes later.

For example, suppose you ask, *How do females of some species of sea turtle get back to the same beaches where they were hatched to lay their eggs?* You might speculate:

- Maybe they rely on their memories?
- Maybe they are guided by astronomical information?
- Maybe they follow ocean currents?
- Maybe they can sense the earth's magnetic field?

That question about sea turtles is a conceptual question, but you can approach practical questions the same way (see 2.3 for these two types of questions). Suppose you are writing a proposal to restructure the way classes are scheduled at your school. You ask, *What would happen if high schools and colleges started classes at 10:00 a.m. rather than at 8:00 a.m.?* You might speculate:

- Maybe students' academic performance would improve if they could sleep later into the morning?
- Maybe students' physical and mental health would also improve?
- Maybe students would participate in fewer sports and extracurricular activities?
- Maybe a later start time would increase what schools pay for electricity, heat, and air conditioning?

You can start gathering data with only your research question to guide you, if you stay on the alert for the answers those data suggest. But your research will go better if it is guided by possible answers. You will then see more readily which data might support (or contradict) a possible answer, helping you focus your research even more.

---

QUICK TIP

**Write, Don't Just Think**

Even early in your project, write out your answers as fully as you can. It is easy to think that you have a clear idea when you don't. Putting a foggy idea into words is the best way to clarify it—or to discover that you can't.

---

### 3.1.1   Decide on a Hypothesis

If one answer seems most promising, consider it your working answer or *hypothesis*. Even the most tentative hypothesis helps you to think ahead, especially about the *kind* of evidence that you'll need to support it. For example, will you need numbers? Quotations? Observations? Images? Historical facts? If you can imagine the kind of evidence you'll need before you start looking for it, you'll recognize the data you need when you see them.

Some new researchers are afraid to consider *any* hypothesis early in their project because they fear it might bias their thinking. There is indeed a risk that your hypothesis might blind you to better ideas or keep you from giving it up when the evidence says you should. In research as in romance, it is dangerous to fall too hard for your first love: the more you like it, the less easily you'll see its flaws. Even so, it's better to start with a flawed hypothesis than with none at all.

If you can't imagine any plausible hypotheses, consider changing your question. That might cost time in the short run, but it may save you from a failed project. Under no circumstances put off thinking about an answer until you begin drafting your paper or, worse, until you've almost finished it. Drafting and revising can be acts of discovery, but you should be writing throughout your project, not just in its final stages (see 5.4 and also the introduction).

3.1.2    **If You Can't Find an Answer, Argue for Your Question**

We have focused on answering questions so much that you might think your project fails if you can't answer yours. In fact, experienced researchers regularly argue that a question that isn't being asked should be, even though they can't yet answer it. Similarly, you can write a good paper explaining why your question is important and what it would take to find a good answer.

3.2    **Build a Storyboard to Plan and Guide Your Work**

For a two- or three-page paper, you might not need much of a plan—a sketch of an outline might do. But for a longer project, you'll need more. The first plan that comes to mind is usually a formal outline, with its *I*'s and *II*'s and *A*'s and *B*'s and so on. An outline is better than no plan, but the problem with an outline is that it can force you to lock down your paper before you've done your best thinking. So if your teacher requires an outline, be ready to change it at the first sign that you can do better.

Many researchers, especially those outside the academic world, plan long papers on what is called a *storyboard*. A storyboard is like an outline broken into pieces and spread over several pages, with lots of space for adding data and ideas as you go. Storyboards are more flexible than outlines. You can leave storyboard pages unfinished until you are ready to fill them, and you can move pages around as you figure out your argument and the organization of your paper. You can spread pages across a wall, group related pages, and put minor sections below major ones so that you can see at a glance the design of your whole project and your progress through it. Picturing your project in this way can help you identify places where your argument needs to be developed more fully, and it can let you try out different ways of organizing your paper so that you can choose the best one.

Figure 3.1 shows part of a storyboard for a research project on teaching languages in elementary schools (see 1.3.2). In her first page, the researcher has stated her question and current hypothesis along with some alternatives, including one she has entirely rejected (see 3.2.1). She has arranged her reasons into two groups, one focused on when languages are best learned and the other on their benefits. She has added an acknowledgment and response (see 6.4), but her page for cultural awareness is almost blank, because she has not yet discovered the right evidence to support that reason (she plans to do more research on this point). And of course, this storyboard is a snapshot of her thinking at the present moment; it can, and should, change as her research progresses and her ideas develop.

3.2.1    **State Your Question and Hypothesis**

To start a storyboard, write at the top of its first page your question and hypothesis as exactly as you can. At the bottom, add alternative answers so that

**Question:** Should elementary schools teach languages other than English?

**Hypothesis:** Elementary schools should make teaching languages other than English a priority.

**Alternative Hypothesis 1:** ~~Elementary schools should focus on teaching reading, writing, and mathematics (the "three R's"), not languages.~~

**Alternative Hypothesis 2:** Elementary schools should teach languages other than English only if doing so does not interfere with other more important priorities.

**Reason:** Children's learning ability

Children learn languages more easily when they are young.

> (Group with point about adult language learners' level of proficiency: relevant to <u>when</u> languages are best taught.)

**Evidence:**

Johnson 2013: Comparative study of child language learners of different ages. Good quantitative data.

McDaniel 2015: Cognitive psychology research. Argues that young children are "neurologically receptive" to languages.

Teacher interviews: Our group interviewed four teachers who have taught Spanish at different levels. Teachers report younger language learners picking it up more quickly.

> (How do our interviews compare with Johnson's findings? Do teachers' perspectives align with Johnson's perspective?)

**Reason:** Adult language learners' proficiency

Adult language learners struggle to become fluent.

> (Group with "children's learning ability": also addresses <u>when</u> languages are best taught.)

**Evidence:**

Johnson 2013: Comparative study of child language learners of different ages. Good quantitative data.

Franklin 2009: Study of multilingual households in New York City. Reports that many first-gen adult immigrants continue to speak their first language primarily.

**Figure 3.1. Part of a storyboard for a research project**

you can see more clearly the limits and strengths of your favored one. Add new answers as you think of them, and cross off those you prove wrong. But save them all, because you might be able to use a rejected one in your introduction (see *I used to think . . . , but . . .* in 7.3.2).

**Reason:** Mental training

Learning a second language trains the mind and makes better, more flexible thinkers.

(Group with "cultural awareness" as a <u>benefit</u> of language learning. Could this point be one of our main reasons? Which is more important, cultivating cultural awareness or mental training?)

**Evidence:**

Yamato 2001: Reports that students in schools with language programs do better on tests of quantitative reasoning.

(How generalizable is this study? Does the specific language studied affect the result?)

**Reason:** Cultural awareness

Learning a second language teaches students about other cultures.

(Group with "mental training" as a <u>benefit</u> of language learning.)

**Evidence:** ???

**Acknowledgment:** Conflict with other priorities

Teaching languages might distract schools from teaching the "three R's": reading, writing, arithmetic.

**Responses:**

Fixed-pie fallacy?

Use Yamato 2001? If students who learn languages perform better on quantitative reasoning tests than those who don't, doesn't that mean that language learning is helping with at least one of the "R's"?

Chase 2002 makes a similar point.

**Acknowledgment:** Resources

Some schools lack the staff or the funding to teach languages.

**Responses:**

A lack of resources does not mean that teaching languages is not valuable or should not be a priority.

Teaching languages in some schools is still better than not teaching languages at all.

Are there alternative sources of funding available? State or federal grants? Private foundations?

### 3.2.2    State Your Reasons

Imagine explaining your project to a friend. You say, *I want to show that elementary schools should devote more time to teaching foreign languages,* and your friend asks, *Why do you think so?* Your reasons are the sentences that back up your answer: *Well, first, people learn languages much more easily when they are young. Sec-*

*ond, those who learn languages as children generally attain greater fluency than those who learn them as adults. Third, foreign language instruction increases awareness of other cultures and societies. Fourth, . . .* and so on. List each reason that might support your hypothesis at the top of a page, one reason per page.

If you have only one or two reasons, you'll probably need more. Make your best guess about possible reasons, and put them at the tops of separate pages: *Reason 4: Something about the effect of learning a language on cognitive development??* Each reason, of course, needs support, so for each reason, ask: *Why do I think that? What evidence will I need to prove it?* That will help you focus your search for data to use as evidence.

If you're new to your topic or early in your project, *all* of your reasons may be only educated guesses that you will have to change as you learn more. In fact, if you don't change any of your reasons, you might not be self-critical enough. But a list of reasons is the best framework to guide your research and focus your thinking. No matter how speculative, a list of reasons is certainly better than no reasons at all.

---

QUICK TIP

**Try Out Several Orders**

When you plan a first draft, you will have to decide what is the best order for its parts, so you might as well try to find a good one now. Lay out your storyboard pages on a table or tape them to a wall. Then step back and look at their order. Can you see a logic in that order? Try out different ones—chronology, cause and effect, relative importance, complexity, length, and so on. (For more principles of order, see 7.2.) Don't be afraid to play around with this storyboard: it's not your final plan, just a way to guide your thinking, plan your research, and organize what you find.

---

3.2.3    **Sketch In the Kind of Evidence You Should Look For**

Every field likes to see its own kinds of evidence. Economists, chemists, and political scientists look for numbers. Literary scholars and historians want quotations. Field biologists like to see observations, pictures, and diagrams. So for each reason, sketch the *kind* of evidence that you think you'll need to support it. If you can't imagine the kind of evidence you'll need, leave that part of the page blank.

Although you may be used to finding all of your evidence in the form of quotations from secondary sources, focus here on primary evidence from primary sources (see 4.1.1). Don't just read *about* the Gettysburg Address or Martin Luther's Ninety-Five Theses; get a copy. And don't neglect quantitative data. In today's world, researchers of every sort—even literary critics—use numbers, and if you are not comfortable using quantitative data, you will find yourself limited in the kinds of research you can do and the kinds of arguments you can make. Today you have easy access to more quantitative data than ever before, as well as to online tools for visualizing data and producing charts and graphs. It's just not sufficient to assert that Americans seem less willing to move than ever before when, with just a few clicks, you can find out from the US Census Bureau that in 2016 the percentage of Americans who relocated was the lowest ever (11.2%).

---

WORKING IN GROUPS

**Tell and Retell Your Elevator Story**

As soon as you have a working answer and a few reasons, create an *elevator story*. Imagine that you step into an elevator and find your teacher, who asks, "So how's the paper going? What do you expect to say about your topic?" You have only a couple of floors to sum up where you are. Early on, you can use this plan:

I am working on the problem of [*state your question*].

I think I can show that [*state your working answer*] because [*state your reasons*].

My best evidence is [*summarize your evidence*].

If you have a writing group, have everyone tell their elevator story at the start of every meeting. If not, tell yours to anyone who will listen—even your dog will do. As you learn more and your argument develops, refine your elevator story and tell it again. The more often you encapsulate your argument in an elevator story, the sooner your paper will come together.

# 4 Doing Your Research

Research—systematically seeking out data that will help you answer a question—can take many forms, depending on the question you ask and how you try to answer it. Some researchers do experiments in laboratories; some observe the natural world or human behavior; some administer surveys or conduct interviews. As a student, you might do any of these kinds of research, and still others. In this chapter, however, we focus on source-based research, for two reasons. First, it is a kind of research that every student is asked to do. And second, because it is often the *first* kind of research that students are asked to do, it serves for many as a model for other sorts of research they may do in college and beyond.

In this chapter we focus on locating, evaluating, and recording sources. In the next we focus on using them in your argument. But don't think that those are separate steps—first you find all your sources, and then you read them and take notes. Rather, once you find one good source, it will lead you to others. As you fill your storyboard with notes, you'll think of new questions that will send you looking for new sources. So while we discuss finding and using sources as two steps, you'll more often do them together.

As you develop your project, plan to do your reading in three phases. First, read just to learn enough to know what to look for. This phase won't be very systematic; it may well depend on what online search engines turn up. Second, read to get an overview of your topic and question. This reading will be mostly in reference works like encyclopedias. Third, search out the specific sources that you will use in developing your argument. For this phase, you'll need a careful plan.

## 4.1    Three Kinds of Sources and Their Uses

Beginning researchers often think of research as just finding information to put into their papers. So they fire up a search engine and get started. That, of course, is a wrong picture of research. In fact, one of the most common complaints about new researchers is that they offer up as evidence the first (and only) bit of relevant data they find. They assume that all evidence is the same and that one bit of evidence is enough. But all researchers—including students—are expected to consider not just *relevant* evidence but the *best available* evidence. Therefore, as you plan your research project, you have to think not just about finding *enough* sources but also about how you will *use* those sources to answer your research question and then to explain and justify your answer in your argument.

To do that, you need to know the different kinds of sources and how researchers use them. Sources are conventionally grouped into three categories: *primary*, *secondary*, and *tertiary*. Their boundaries are fuzzy, but knowing these categories can help you plan and conduct your research.

### 4.1.1    Consult Primary Sources for Evidence

Primary sources are "original" materials that provide you with the "raw data" you will use as evidence to develop and test your hypothesis and ultimately to support the reasons in your argument. In history, primary sources are artifacts or documents that come directly from the period or event you are studying: letters, diaries, objects, maps, even clothing. In literature or philosophy, your main primary source is usually the text you are analyzing, and your data are the words on the page. In arts criticism, your primary source would be the work of art you are interpreting. In social sciences such as sociology or political science, census or survey data would count as primary sources, as could data obtained through observation or experiment. In the natural sciences, reports of original research are sometimes characterized as primary sources (although scientists themselves rarely use that term).

### 4.1.2    Read Secondary Sources to Learn from Other Researchers

Secondary sources are books, articles, papers, or reports that are based on primary sources and intended for scholarly or professional audiences. Articles in scholarly journals analyzing news coverage of the Apollo 11 moon landing, representations of gender in *Grand Theft Auto*, or how children learn languages would be secondary sources for researchers working on those topics. The best secondary sources are books from reputable university presses and articles or papers that have been *peer reviewed*, meaning that they were vetted by experts in the field before they were published. Secondary sources also include specialized encyclopedias and dictionaries that offer essays written by scholars in a field. Secondary sources were once available mainly through college and university libraries, but now they are also available through online catalogs and databases including CQ Researcher, EBSCOhost, Gale Power Search, Academic One File, and many others. In addition, school libraries often have books that bundle collections of secondary sources on a topic for students.

Researchers use secondary sources for four purposes:

1. *To substitute for unavailable primary sources.* Professional researchers are generally expected to rely on primary sources for their data and evidence. As a student, you too should get your data and evidence from primary sources when you can. But if you can't, your teacher will probably allow you to report the data from a secondary source. Be sure to ask.

---

CAUTION

**Always Cite the Source You Consult**

Some students think that when they use data reported in a secondary source they should cite the original, primary source. But they are only half right. If you cite just the primary source, you imply that you consulted that source yourself. If you cite just the secondary source, you imply that it is the ultimate source of your data. Both mislead readers. Instead you should cite *both* sources. For example, if you use a secondary source written by Anderson for primary data in an article by Wong, your citation would look like this (using APA style; see part 2):

(Wong, 1966, p. 45; quoted in Anderson, 2005, p. 19)

---

2. *To learn what others have written about your topic.* Secondary sources are the best way to learn what other researchers have said about your topic. You can also learn from secondary sources the kinds of questions experts in the field think are important, not only from their research questions but from any additional questions they mention at the end of articles. You may be able to model your question on theirs or even to use a question they mention but do not address.

3. *To find other points of view.* Beginning researchers sometimes believe they will weaken their case if they mention ideas that contradict their own. The truth is actually the opposite: when you acknowledge opposing views, you show readers not only that you have considered those views but also that you can respond to them (see 6.4). Your paper will be complete only when you imagine and respond

to your readers' predictable questions and disagreements. You can find those in secondary sources. What alternatives to your ideas do they offer? What evidence do they cite that you must acknowledge?

More important, you can use the arguments of others to test and improve your own. You cannot understand what you think until you know why a rational person might think differently. So as you search for sources, look not only for those that support your views but also for those that challenge them.

4. *To find models for your own research and writing.* You can use secondary sources to find out not just *what* others have written about your topic but also *how* they have written about it. If most of your sources use headings, charts, and lots of bullet points, then you might consider doing the same; if your sources never use them, you probably shouldn't. Notice things like the language (technical or ordinary?), paragraphs (long or short?), and how they use other sources (quotation or paraphrase?). Pay special attention to the kinds of evidence most of them use and the kinds of evidence they rarely or never use.

You can also use secondary sources as models for your own argument. You cannot reuse a source's *specific* claims and reasons, but you can use the same *kind* of reasoning in your own argument, perhaps even following the same organization. So if you come across a source that's not on your exact topic but treats one like it, skim it to see what you can learn about how to argue your case. (You don't have to cite that source if you use only its logic, but you may cite it to give your own more authority.)

> QUICK TIP
>
> You may find secondary sources hard to read because they are intended for advanced researchers. They assume a lot of background knowledge, and many aren't clearly written in the first place. If you're working on a topic new to you, don't start with secondary sources. Begin with an overview in a specialized encyclopedia or reliable tertiary source; then use what you learn there to tackle the secondary sources.

## 4.1.3   Read Tertiary Sources for Introductory Overviews

Tertiary sources are books and articles that synthesize secondary sources for general readers. They include textbooks, encyclopedias (including Wikipedia), and dictionaries, as well as articles in publications for broad audiences, like *Time* and the *Atlantic*. In the early stages of research, you can use tertiary sources to get a broad overview of your topic. But if you are making a scholarly argument, you should rely on secondary sources because these make up the conversation in which you are seeking to participate. If you cite tertiary sources in a scholarly argument, you will mark yourself as a novice or outsider, and many readers won't take you—or your argument—seriously.

QUICK TIP

Professional academic researchers are expected to consider *all* the evidence that might be relevant to their claim—not just one letter in which Einstein describes his creative process but every letter in which he mentions it. Business researchers are expected to consider all the evidence that might change their claim significantly—interviews not just with one customer but with several of the most important ones. Students can't be held to these standards, however, because they rarely have the time, resources, or expertise to assemble such complete bodies of evidence. So find out your teacher's ground rules before you start: How many sources are you expected to consult? When must you use primary sources? When can you substitute secondary sources? Will a tertiary source be acceptable if its author is a respected scholar? Then you can plan your search to find the kind and amount of evidence you will need to convince amiable but skeptical readers of your claim.

## 4.2 Search for Sources Systematically

Knowing where to begin your search for sources can be overwhelming at first. It is tempting simply to enter terms into a search engine like Google and see what comes up. We do this too, but we also know that there are more systematic and productive ways for discovering useful, credible sources. Many school libraries offer curated collections of sources intended specifically for students. In college, though, you can't rely on such collections but must build up your own. Make the library the focus of your search strategy, using not just its physical collections but also the online resources it offers.

### 4.2.1 Ask a Librarian

Students often imagine libraries as collections of materials, as places to study, or as portals to various online resources. But don't forget about the *people*: be sure to consult the reference librarians and (in larger libraries) subject area specialists who are there to help you. They can show you how to use the catalog to locate materials held by your library or by other libraries (and obtainable through interlibrary loan); they can teach you about the library's other online resources and databases; they can help you refine your search strategy and guide you to the right tools for your project. They may also have created research guides for specific topics and courses, identifying relevant reference works and online databases.

And don't be shy. Librarians love to assist researchers of all levels and at all stages of the research process. They can help you formulate your research question and plan, develop search terms, and inventory your results to ensure you haven't overlooked something of value. The only embarrassing question is the one you failed to ask. If you already have your research question, share it: *I'm looking for data on X because I want to find out . . .* If you have a working hypothesis and reasons, share them too: *I'm looking for data to show Y [your reason] because I want to claim Z [your hypothesis]*. Rehearse your questions to avoid wasting your time and theirs.

### 4.2.2    Consult Reference Works

Look up your topic in a specialized encyclopedia or dictionary such as the *Encyclopedia of Philosophy* or the *Concise Oxford Dictionary of Literary Terms*, where you may find an overview of your topic. You will also usually find a list of standard primary and secondary sources.

### 4.2.3    Search Your Library Catalog

Search your online catalog using keywords from your question or hypothesis—*space exploration, female astronauts, Sally Ride*. If you find too many titles, limit your search to those published in the last ten years. If you find too few, search a catalog service like WorldCat (if your library supports it) or go to the Library of Congress catalog at http://www.loc.gov. It has links to large university catalogs. Start early if you expect to get books from interlibrary loan.

**Articles**. If most sources on your topic are articles, locate a recent one in your library's online databases. Its database entry will include a list of keywords. Use them to find more articles on your topic. In most cases you can just click on them. Some databases provide abstracts of journal articles. Use these keywords to search the library catalog as well.

**Books**. Once you find one book relevant to your topic, look it up in your library's online catalog to find its Library of Congress subject headings (at the bottom of the entry). Click on the subject headings to find other books on the same topics. Many of those sources will have more subject headings that can lead you to still more sources. It can turn into an endless trail.

### 4.2.4    Explore Online Resources

Libraries also have online resources that are not freely available on the internet: subscriptions to general and specialized indexes, databases, and collections on a vast array of topics. After books, these are arguably a library's most valuable assets, since they give researchers access to materials of high scholarly quality they could not obtain otherwise. Major research libraries offer the most comprehensive access, but most college libraries, and even many high school and public libraries, offer online tools and resources that greatly extend their actual collections. The best way to find the right online tools and resources for your project is to talk with a reference librarian (4.2.1).

Many academic databases either provide abstracts or direct you to articles that include abstracts. Looking at these can help you decide if an article itself is worth reading carefully. Some databases allow you to access full-text articles or books. But beware: if your library does not subscribe to a particular journal included in a database, you might be asked to pay a fee to access a full-text article. Before doing so, *always* speak with a librarian about other means of access.

## 4.2.5 Follow Bibliographical Trails

Every secondary source you find will include a bibliography. If a source looks useful, scan its bibliography for promising titles. Once you locate them, scan their bibliographies. One good source can set you on a trail to all the sources you'll need.

## 4.2.6 Browse the Shelves

Today's libraries provide a wealth of online resources, but don't forget about their physical collections. If you are allowed, go into your library's stacks—where the books and journals are kept. If you don't, you may miss crucial sources that you can only find there. More important, you'll miss the benefits of serendipity—a chance encounter with a source that you find only in person. Find the shelf with books on your topic, then scan the titles on that shelf and the ones above, below, and on either side, especially for books with new bindings published by university presses. Then turn around and skim titles behind you; you never know. When you spot a promising title, skim its table of contents, then its index for keywords related to your question or its answer. Then skim its bibliography for titles that look relevant to your project. You can do all that faster with books on a shelf than you can online.

You can check tables of contents for many journals online, but browsing in the journals area of a library can also be productive. Find the journals that have promising articles. Skim tables of contents for the prior ten years. Most volumes include a yearly summary table of contents. Then take a quick look at the journals shelved nearby. Skim their most recent tables of contents. You will be surprised at how often you find a relevant article that you would have missed had you done your work entirely online.

If a book or article looks promising, skim its preface or introduction. If it still looks promising, set it aside for a closer look. Even if it doesn't seem immediately relevant, record its Library of Congress call number and bibliographic data (see 4.4), and in a few words summarize what the book seems to be about. A week or two later, you might realize that it's more useful than you thought.

## 4.3 Evaluate Sources for Relevance and Reliability

You will probably find more sources than you can use, so you must evaluate their usefulness by skimming quickly for two criteria: relevance and reliability.

QUICK TIP

If you are new to a field, you can get a rough idea of a journal's quality by its look. If it's on glossy paper with lots of illustrations, or even advertisements, it might be more journalistic than scholarly.

### 4.3.1    Evaluate Sources for Relevance

Once you decide a source might be relevant, examine it more closely. If your source is a journal article, do this:

- Read the abstract, if it has one.
- Skim the introduction and conclusion; if they are not marked off by headings, skim the first six or seven paragraphs and the last four or five.
- Skim for section headings, and read the first and last paragraphs of those sections.
- Check the bibliography for titles relevant to your topic.

If your source is a book, do this:

- Skim its index for your keywords, then skim the pages on which those words occur.
- Skim the first and last paragraphs in chapters that use a lot of your keywords.
- Skim its introduction, especially its last page, where writers often outline their text.
- Skim its last chapter, especially the first and last several pages.
- Skim prologues, introductions, summary chapters, and so on.
- If the source is a collection of articles, skim the editor's introduction.
- Check the bibliography for titles relevant to your topic.

Be sure that you're looking at a book's most recent edition. Researchers change their views over time, refining them, even rejecting earlier ones.

If your source is online, still follow these steps, but you can also search the whole text for your keywords. If your source is not an article or book, adapt these steps as needed to judge its relevance.

### 4.3.2    Evaluate Sources for Reliability

You can't judge a source until you read it, but there are signs of reliability.

#### 4.3.2.1    *Library-Quality Sources*

We value libraries not just for the ready access they provide to a wealth of primary, secondary, and tertiary sources, but also because we know we can trust them. The first question you should ask about a source is whether it is *library quality*. Libraries are so important to researchers not just because they provide access to books and other sources but also because those materials are chosen by trained librarians who are specialists in judging their value and quality. For a source to be library quality, you do not have to find it in an actual library. But it does have to meet an academic library's standards. To determine whether a source is of library quality, look for these signs:

- It is part of a library's collection of physical books, articles, recordings, and other materials.
- It is provided as part of a library's online resources, including article databases, electronic books, electronic archives, and so on.
- It is provided by an online scholarly journal associated with a university or academic publisher.
- It is provided online by a reputable scholarly organization, such as the Rhetoric Society of America (research and other sources on rhetoric), the ARTFL Project (works by French authors), or the Pew Forum on Religion & Public Life (religion and social issues).

4.3.2.2    *Evaluate the Reliability of Internet Sources*

When you search online, you will encounter hundreds of sites whose material does not appear to be of library quality. Evaluate each one carefully. The number of reliable online sources grows every day, but they are still islands in a swamp of misinformation. Before you use data from the internet, look for these signs of reliability:

1. The site is sponsored by a reputable organization. Some sites supported by individuals are reliable; most are not.
2. It is related to a reliable publisher or professional journal.
3. It is not an advocacy site. It is not sponsored by an organization with a political or commercial agenda, and it avoids one-sided advocacy on a contested social issue.
4. It does not make wild claims, attack other researchers, use abusive language.
5. It does not include errors of spelling, punctuation, or grammar.
6. It says who is responsible for maintaining the site and when it was updated. Trust a site only if careful readers would trust those who maintain it. If you don't know who maintains it, or if it has no date, be cautious.
7. It is not too glossy. When a site has more decorative graphics than words, its designers may care more about drawing you in than about presenting reliable information.

Finally, remember that biased or partisan sites often mimic the features of more reliable ones. For example, they may contain academic- or official-looking seals or logos and be published by groups with professional-sounding names. Don't be fooled by such false signals: compare the site you are evaluating to others on the same topic. Don't just follow links in the site itself, because sites advocating similar views often link to each other. Instead, do a new search on some of the site's key terms. What other sites come up on its topic? Likewise, if you don't know about the group responsible for a site, find out. Again, turn to your library for help.

4.3.2.3    *Evaluate the Reliability of Library-Quality Sources*
In most cases, student researchers are not expected to screen their sources as carefully as a professional must; library quality is usually enough. But when you have to be more demanding, look for these additional signs of reliability:

1. **The author is a reputable scholar.** Most publications cite an author's academic credentials; you can find more with a search engine.
2. **The source is current.** How quickly a source goes out of date varies by subject, so check with someone who knows the field. For articles in the social sciences, more than ten years pushes the limit. For books, figure fifteen or so. Publications in the humanities have a longer shelf life.
3. **The source is published by a reputable press.** You can trust most university presses, especially at well-known schools. You can trust some commercial presses in some fields, such as Norton in literature, Ablex in sciences, and West in the law. Be skeptical of a commercial book that makes sensational claims, even if its author has a PhD.
4. **The article was peer reviewed.** Most scholarly journals, both print and online, publish an article only after it has been peer reviewed by experts. Few popular magazines do that. If an article hasn't been peer reviewed, use it cautiously.

Those signs don't guarantee that a source is reliable, but they should give you some confidence in it. If you can't find reliable sources, admit the limits of the ones you have.

4.4    **Record Citation Information Fully and Accurately**
Once you decide a source is worth reading, record all of its bibliographic information so that you can locate the source again later and, as important, so that you can cite that source if you use it in your paper.

We have to be candid: recording citations is the least exciting part of doing research, but it is nevertheless important. Citations help readers understand your work by seeing whose work you have relied upon. They also help readers find your sources to check your work or to use in their own research. Finally, your citations help readers decide whether you are a careful researcher whose work they can trust. Nothing will label you as an untrustworthy researcher faster than citations that are incomplete, inaccurate, or inappropriate. You may have software or an online tool that automatically formats citations for you, but these aids cannot substitute for your own care.

So we urge you to be doggedly systematic in creating your citations, whether or not you use software or an online tool to help. If you get the information down right the first time, you won't have to go back to do it again.

### 4.4.1 Determine Your Citation Style

Most fields require a specific citation style. The three most common ones are described in detail in part 2:

- Chicago style (also known as Turabian style), from the University of Chicago Press. This style is widely used in the humanities and qualitative social sciences.
- MLA style, from the Modern Language Association. This style is widely used in literary studies.
- APA style, from the American Psychological Association. This style is widely used in the quantitative social sciences.

If you are uncertain which style to use, consult your teacher. Before compiling your list of sources, read the general introduction to citations in chapter 19.

### 4.4.2 Record Bibliographic Data

You don't need to memorize the details of citation formats, but you do need to know what information to save. Copy this checklist or use it to create a template for recording the data as you go.

For books, record

- ☐ author(s)
- ☐ title (including subtitle)
- ☐ edition or volume number (if any)
- ☐ title of multivolume work or series (if any)
- ☐ city and publisher
- ☐ year published
- ☐ title and pages for chapter (if relevant)
- ☐ URL (for books read online)

For articles, record

- ☐ author(s)
- ☐ title (including subtitle)
- ☐ title of journal, magazine, website, etc.

☐  volume and issue number (if any)
☐  date published
☐  pages for article (if any)
☐  URL (for articles read online)

For some online sources, the information you need is less predictable. Record as much of the above as applies, along with anything else that might help readers locate the source. You will also need at least these:

· date posted or last modified
· date of access (for undated sources)
· sponsoring organization

You might also record the Library of Congress call number. You won't include it in bibliographic citations, but you'll need it if you have to find the source again.

## 4.5  Using People in Research

One of the paradoxes of twenty-first-century research is that even as new technologies allow us to access an unprecedented wealth of materials with ease, research has also become more personal. So as you undertake your project, don't forget about the human element.

Most obviously, people can be sources of primary data collected through observation, surveys, or interviews. Be creative when using people for primary research: don't ignore people in local business, government, or civic organizations. For example, if you were researching school desegregation in your town, you might go beyond the documents to ask the local school district whether anyone there has memories to share. We can't explain the complexities of interviewing (there are many guides to that process), but remember that the more *exactly* you plan what you want to ask, the more efficiently you will get what you need. You don't necessarily need to ask an interviewee a fixed list of questions, but prepare in advance so that you don't question your source aimlessly. You can always reread a book for what you missed, but you can't keep going back to people because you didn't prepare well enough to get what you needed the first time. And always remember that when conducting primary research that involves people, you must adhere to rigorous ethical standards (see the Quick Tip at the end of this chapter).

People can also lead you to good secondary sources or serve as such sources themselves. We have already encouraged you to discuss your research with one kind of expert—your reference librarian—but you can also benefit from talking directly with experts on your topic. Ask them about the important open questions in the field. Ask them what they think of your project or provisional thesis. Ask them to suggest secondary sources for you to read. This kind of personal guidance can be invaluable to a beginning researcher, and many experts will be happy to talk with you (or at least engage in a little email correspondence).

All of us have made these kinds of queries with great success in our own research, and all of us have responded to them in turn by helping those who have contacted us. One of us once invited an eminent scholar to talk about his research process to a group of first-year college students. He began his talk by saying, "I don't really have a research process; I just ask my smart friends what I should read." This scholar was being at least a bit tongue in cheek, but we could all do worse than to rely on such smart friends, at least to get us started.

---

QUICK TIP

In recent years, colleges and universities have become increasingly aware that using people in research may inadvertently harm them—not just physically but by embarrassing them, violating their privacy, and so on. So every college or university now has a committee that reviews all research directly or indirectly involving people, whether done by students or by professional researchers. These committees go by different names—Human Subjects Committee, Institutional Review Board, Ethics Research Board, and so on—but they all aim to ensure that researchers follow the maxim that should govern research as it does medicine: *Do no harm. If you plan to do any sort of research involving people—interviews, surveys, experiments, even observations—talk first with your teacher about your plans and any approvals you might need.* If you don't, you could harm those who help you, and you may even damage your institution.

# 5   Engaging Sources

In this chapter we show you how to get the most out of your sources, especially your secondary sources. The ways that researchers find or create their data, and the kinds of data readers expect as evidence, vary wildly from field to field. But every field has its body of secondary sources, sometimes called its *literature*, that document the field's conversation. And researchers in all fields engage these sources in similar ways. In this chapter we show you how to read sources as experienced researchers do: not just for data but more importantly for questions, problems, and arguments that spur your own thinking.

    Once you find a source worth a close look, don't read it passively or mechanically, recording only what it says. If you simply pass along what you find, untouched by your own ideas, your paper will be just a summary. You must record the words and data you take from a source accurately, but you have to go further to engage its ideas: *Why does the author use those words? How is this section connected to the next? Are these ideas consistent with earlier ones?* So talk back to your source as if its author were sitting with you, eager to hear what you have to say—and imagine your readers engaging you in the same way.

5.1    ## Read Critically

The ability to read critically is perhaps the most important skill you can develop as a researcher. If you can't read critically, you will struggle not only to make sense of your sources but also to ask good questions of them—and of yourself. Some beginning researchers think reading critically means just picking a source apart. But that's only part of it. We've said that researchers understand *argument* in a special way, not as mere verbal conflict but as a kind of conversation that lets all parties improve their understanding (see 6.1 and the introduction). Similarly, researchers understand being *critical* to mean not just finding fault but deliberately assessing an idea's value. To do this well, you have to read both generously and skeptically.

It is hard to read in both of these ways at the same time, so if you can, read a promising source twice. First, try to make sense of it on its own terms. Focus on understanding and even believing it, not only as information but also as an argument. Don't look for disagreements right away. (Disagree too soon and you'll misunderstand or exaggerate a weakness if your source presents an argument that challenges yours.) Then reread it as if you were amiably but pointedly questioning a friend: imagine the writer's answers, then question them. When you read a passage, think not only about what it says but about how you would respond. Record those responses in your notes or—if you own the source or a copy of it—in the margins of the source itself.

In other words, read not passively as a mere transcriber copying information into your notes, but actively and creatively. Here are some ways to do that.

5.1.1    ## Read Generously to Understand

Reading generously can be difficult because we are so used to responding negatively: *You make some good points, but . . .* But recognizing a source's strengths is a crucial skill for a researcher, because if you can't do that, you can't build on its good ideas in your own work. To read generously, try doing these things:

- Appreciate your source: notice smart lines of reasoning, elegant turns of phrase, clear organization. Look for things you wish that you had said yourself.
- Restate the source's claims in your own words in a way its author would agree with. If you can't, you haven't understood the source on its own terms.
- Reflect on the author's choices: why did she present her evidence or structure her argument in the way that she did?
- Think about the implications of a source: if its claims are true, what else follows?

The more generously you read your sources at the outset, the better you will understand them. And the better you understand them, the more productively you can question them later.

5.1.2   **Read Skeptically to Engage**

In chapter 2 we showed you how to read sources to find potential topics and questions. You can use a similar set of patterns to probe your sources as you read them, to stimulate your thinking, and to find views to acknowledge and respond to in your paper (see 6.4).

No argument is foolproof, so read your source skeptically and look for its shortcomings. Where do its claims need better or different support? Does it overstate or understate its case? Is its reasoning sound?

Likewise, look for *creative* disagreements with your source (see 2.5.1). It's not enough just to disagree. If you do only that, you're only saying *I'm right and you're wrong*. To engage a source effectively, you need to know not just *that* you disagree with it but specifically *where* and *how* and *why*. When reading your sources, look for these types of disagreements:

**Disagreements of Kind**
- Source argues that _____ is a kind of _____, but it's not.
- Source argues that _____ has _____ as one of its features or qualities, but it doesn't.
- Source argues that _____ is normal/good/significant/useful/moral, but it's not.

Source argues that the privatization of public schools benefits students, but it doesn't.

**Disagreements about Parts and Wholes**
- Source argues that _____ is a part of _____, but it's not.
- Source argues that one part of _____ relates to another in a certain way, but it doesn't.
- Source argues that every _____ has _____ as one of its parts, but it doesn't.

Source argues that coding is irrelevant to a twenty-first-century education, but it is essential.

**Disagreements about History or Development**
- Source argues that _____ is changing or developing in some way, but it's not.
- Source argues that _____ originated in _____, but it didn't.

Source argues that grade inflation is increasing, but it isn't.

**Disagreements about Cause and Effect**
- Source argues that _____ causes _____, but it doesn't.

- Source argues that _____ is sufficient to cause _____, but it's not.
- Source argues that _____ causes only _____, but it also causes
  _____.

Source argues that legalizing marijuana will increase its use among teenagers, but it doesn't.

## 5.2   Take Notes Systematically

Once you find and record a source you think you can use, you must read it purposefully and carefully. Then take notes in a way that will help you not only to remember and use what you have read but also to further your own thinking. Careful, systematic note-taking will also protect you from inadvertent plagiarism (see chapter 10). Like the other steps in a research project, note-taking goes better with a plan.

### 5.2.1   Taking Notes on Paper

Years ago, the standard way to take notes on sources was to create a file of index cards. Figure 5.1 offers one example. At the top left is the author, short title, and page number. At the top right are keywords that let the researcher sort and re-sort notes into different categories and orders. The body of the card contains the researcher's notes, not just information from the source itself but also the researcher's questions and responses. A card like this seems old-fashioned, but it provides a template for efficient note-taking:

- Record complete bibliographic information for each source so that you can cite it properly and find it again easily.
- Separate notes on different topics, even if they come from the same source.
- Make sure your notes are accurate, because you need to be able to rely on them later. (If you want to quote more than a few lines, copy or save the passage or the whole document.)
- Record not just the source's claim but also any data or support that you find interesting.
- Note your own agreements, disagreements, speculations, questions, and so on. For example, do you see any complications or contradictions in the source's argument? Did the source raise any questions? That will encourage you to do more than simply record the content of what you read.
- Be sure to clearly distinguish what you quote from a source, what you paraphrase or summarize from a source, and your own thoughts (see chapter 9). If you are writing on paper, use headings or brackets or distinct colors to differentiate these three different kinds of notes.

---

Sharman, <u>Swearing</u>, p. 133.     HISTORY/ECONOMICS (GENDER?)

---

CLAIM: Swearing became economic issue in 18th c.

DATA: Cites <u>Gentleman's Magazine</u>, July 1751 (no page reference) woman sentenced to ten days' hard labor because couldn't pay one-shilling fine for profanity.

"... *one rigid economist entertained the notion of adding to the national resources by preaching a crusade against the opulent class of swearers.*"

SUPPORT: As much about class and money as about morality. Legal treatment the same as for social rather than religious transgressions.

COMPLICATION: ——

Qs: Were men fined as often as women? Not economic earlier?

---

**Figure 5.1. Example of a note card**

## 5.2.2   Taking Notes Electronically

When you take notes electronically, you have some options:

- You can use a word processor. Create a separate file (or at least a separate page) for each source, and be sure to unambiguously distinguish your words from those of your source. Though word processors are easy to use, they also limit your ability to index, organize, sort, and search your notes. For long or complex projects, you might consider other options.
- You can use a dedicated note-taking application to create and organize your notes. Such applications can help you to index, sort, and access your notes. But since they sometimes use proprietary formats, they can make it difficult to share your notes or use them with other programs.
- You can use a full-featured citation management program. In addition to allowing you to make your own notes, these programs can often pull information directly from online library catalogs and databases, and they can format and update your bibliographies as you write. Some will even store full electronic copies of your sources, creating a personal library for your project. But like note-taking applications, these programs sometimes use proprietary formats.

In electronic notes, as in notes on paper, you must clearly distinguish your own words and ideas from those of your source.

- Record quotations from your source in a distinctive color or font size and style so that you can recognize them at a glance. Also enclose them in large quotation marks in case the file loses its formatting.

- Record paraphrases from your source in a second color or font so that you can't possibly mistake them for your own ideas, and enclose them in curly brackets in case the file loses its formatting.
- Record your own thoughts in a third color or font and enclose them in square brackets. Put longer responses in a separate section so there is no chance you will mistake your own ideas for your source's, or vice versa.

---

CAUTION

**Quote Freely in Your Notes**

If you don't record important words now, you can't quote them later. When in doubt, copy or photocopy passages so that you'll have what you need if you decide to quote them in your paper. You should have many more quotations in your notes than in your paper.

---

5.3     **Take Useful Notes**

Readers will judge your paper not just by the quality of your sources and how accurately you report them, but also by how deeply you engage them. To do that, you must take notes in a way that not only reflects but encourages a deeper understanding of your project.

5.3.1   **Take Notes to Advance Your Thinking**

Mechanically recording passages from sources by downloading, copying and pasting, photocopying, or retyping can help you quote or paraphrase accurately, but if you don't *talk back* to your sources, you will simply accumulate inert data. To advance your thinking, annotate key sentences and passages by highlighting or labeling them so you can find them later. Mark ideas or data that you expect to use in your paper. Summarize what you have highlighted or sketch a response to it, or add notes in the margin that help you interpret your highlighting. The more you write about a source now, the better you will understand it later.

5.3.2   **Record the Context**

You can't record everything, but you have to record enough to ensure that you accurately capture the source's meaning. So note not just what your sources say but how they use the information. To guard against misinterpreting or misusing a source, follow these guidelines:

1.   When you quote, paraphrase, or summarize, record the context. When you note an important conclusion, record the author's line of reasoning.

   NOT   Bartolli (p. 123): The war was caused . . . by Z.

   BUT   Bartolli: The war was caused by Y and Z (p. 123), but the most important was Z (p. 123), for two reasons: first, . . . (pp. 124–26); second, . . . (p. 126).

Even if you care only about a conclusion, you'll use it more accurately if you record how a writer reached it.

2.  Record the scope and confidence of a statement. Don't make a claim seem more certain or far-reaching than it is. The second sentence below doesn't accurately or fairly report the first.

**Original:** One study on the perception of risk (Clark, 2008) suggests a correlation between high-stakes gambling and childhood concussions.

**Misleading report:** Clark (2008) says childhood concussions cause high-stakes gambling.

3.  Record how a source uses a statement. Is it an important claim, a minor point, a qualification or concession, and so on? Such distinctions help avoid mistakes like the following.

**Original by Jones:** We cannot conclude that one event causes another because the second follows the first. Nor can statistical correlation prove causation. But no one who has studied the data doubts that smoking is a causal factor in lung cancer.

**Misleading report:** Jones claims "we cannot conclude that one event causes another because the second follows the first. Nor can statistical correlation prove causation." Therefore, statistical evidence is not a reliable indicator that smoking causes lung cancer.

### 5.3.3   Assign Keywords That Categorize Your Notes for Sorting

Finally, a conceptually challenging task: as you take notes, categorize each one under two or more keywords (see the upper right corner of fig. 5.1). Don't mechanically use words from the source; categorize the note by what it implies for your question, by a general idea larger than its specific content. Use the same keywords for related notes; don't create a new one for every new note.

This step is crucial because it forces you to find the central ideas in a note. If you take notes electronically, the keywords let you instantly group related notes with a single Find command. If you use more than one keyword, you can recombine your notes in different ways to discover new relationships (especially important when you feel you are spinning your wheels).

### 5.3.4   State How You Think the Note Is Relevant to Your Argument

If you let your question and hypothesis guide your research, you will choose to record information not just because it is on topic but because it is relevant to the argument you think you can make. Record that information in your notes. Say why you think a source might support or—just as importantly—complicate your argument. At this point, guesses or hunches are okay: you'll have time to reconsider later. But you can't reconsider what you can't remember. So don't rely on your memory to reconstruct what you were thinking when you decided to make a note.

## 5.4   Write as You Read

We've said this before (and will again): writing forces you to think hard, so don't wait to nail down a budding idea before you write it out. Experienced researchers know that the more they write, the sooner and better they understand their project. There is good evidence that successful researchers set a fixed time to write every day—from fifteen minutes to more than an hour. They might write only a paragraph, but they write *something*, not to start a first draft of their paper but to sort out their ideas and maybe discover new ones.

If you write something that seems promising, add it to your storyboard. You will probably revise it for your final draft, maybe even discard it. But no matter how sketchy or rough this early writing might be, it will help you draft more easily later.

---

**CAUTION**

**Don't Expect Too Much of Your Early Writings**

If you're new to a topic, much of your early writing may be just summary and paraphrase. If you see too few of your own ideas, don't feel discouraged at your lack of original thinking. Summarizing and paraphrasing are how we all gain control over new ideas and learn new ways of thinking. Rehashing what we want to understand is a typical, probably even necessary, stage in just about everyone's learning curve.

---

## 5.5   Review Your Progress

Regularly review your notes and storyboard to see where you are and where you have to go. Full storyboard pages indicate reasons with support; empty ones indicate research still to do. Is your hypothesis still plausible? Do you have good reasons supporting it? Good evidence to support those reasons? Can you add new reasons or evidence?

## 5.6   How and When to Start Over

We have urged you to create a storyboard with a hypothesis and a few reasons to guide your research. But some writers start with an idea so vague that it evaporates as they chase it. If that happens to you, search your notes for a generalization that might serve as a working hypothesis, then work backward to find the question it answers.

5.6.1   **Search Your Notes for a Better Answer**

Use the strategies described in 5.1.2 to look for questions, disagreements, or puzzles in your sources and in your reaction to them. What surprises you might surprise others. Try to state it in writing:

> I expected to find that the United States space program originated in scientific curiosity, but it didn't. It was originally motivated by . . .

That surprise suggests a potential claim: the space program was started not primarily because of scientific curiosity but because of the United States' competition with the Soviet Union. Now you have a promising start.

5.6.2   **Invent the Question**

Now comes a tricky part. It's like reverse engineering: you've found the answer to a question that you haven't yet asked, so you have to reason backward to invent the question that it answers. In this case, it might be *Was the space program primarily about the disinterested pursuit of scientific knowledge, or was it an assertion of technical and military superiority motivated by the United States' competition with the Soviet Union?* It may seem paradoxical, but experienced researchers often discover their question only after they answer it.

5.6.3   **Recategorize and Re-sort Your Notes**

If none of that helps, try re-sorting your notes. When you first chose keywords for your notes, you identified general ideas that could organize not just your evidence but also your thinking. Now re-sort your notes in different ways to get a new slant on your material. If your keywords no longer seem relevant, review your notes to create new keywords and reshuffle again.

5.7   **Manage Moments of Uncertainty**

As you shuffle through all of your notes and try to keep straight your different lines of thought, you might start to feel overwhelmed by what seems to be an increasingly complex and unmanageable task. Even the best researchers experience such moments of uncertainty, but they also know that those moments are a normal part of *thinking hard* about their research and arguments. Uncertainty can be uncomfortable, but it is also necessary. You can avoid it by picking a claim before you do your research and then just seeking out sources to back it up—but that isn't research at all. If you have a project that you believe in and a good plan for how to carry it out, you'll get through it. Just start early, break your work into manageable tasks, and set reasonable goals and deadlines, such as a daily page quota when you draft.

# 6 Constructing Your Argument

Most of us would rather read than write. But well before you've done all the research you'd like to do, you have to start thinking about the first draft of your paper. You might be ready when your storyboard is full and you're satisfied with how it looks. But you can't be certain until you start planning that first draft. In this chapter we explain how to assemble the elements of your argument; in the next we will show you how to organize them. As you gain experience, you'll learn to combine those two steps into one process.

## 6.1    What a Research Argument Is and Is Not

The word *argument* has negative associations these days because it evokes images of people shouting at one another. In this kind of argument the goal is to win, to bludgeon or intimidate one's opponent into assent or silence. But a research argument isn't like that. As we suggested in chapter 1, it is more like a conversation with a community of receptive but skeptical peers. Such readers won't necessarily oppose your claims (although they might), but they also won't accept them until they see good reasons based on reliable evidence and until you respond to their questions and reservations.

When you make (not *have*) an argument in a face-to-face conversation, you cooperate with your listeners. You state your reasons and evidence not as a lecturer would to a silent audience but as you would engage friends sitting around a table: you offer a claim and reasons to believe it; they probe for details, raise objections, or offer their points of view; you respond, perhaps with questions of your own; they ask more questions. At its best, it's an amiable but thoughtful back-and-forth that develops and tests the best case that you and they can make *together*.

In writing, even when done collaboratively, that kind of cooperation is harder. You must not only answer your imagined readers' questions but *ask them on their behalf*—as often and as sharply as real readers will. Your aim isn't to think up clever rhetorical strategies that will persuade readers to accept your claim regardless of how good it is. It is to test your claim and especially its support, so that you offer your readers the best case you can make. In a good research paper, readers hear traces of that imagined conversation.

When you make a research argument, therefore, you must lay out your reasons and evidence so that your readers can consider them; then you must imagine both their questions and your answers. Doing all this is hard, but remembering how arguments work in everyday conversations will help you.

## 6.2   Build Your Argument around Answers to Readers' Questions

### 6.2.1   Identify (or Invent) Target Readers Interested in Your Question

You cannot anticipate your readers' questions unless you have a good idea of who they are and what they know. That's a problem for many class papers, since you have no obvious readers but your teacher—who isn't reading as herself (see the Caution below). That's why teachers often set up research papers so that your target readers are your classmates. If not, you have to select at least one target reader for yourself. Your best choice is someone you know who would be interested in your question and who knows as much about it as you did before you started your research. (Even better if you know two or more such people.) Have them in mind when you imagine your readers' questions. If you don't know such a person, invent one. The more you can imagine specific, familiar people asking you questions, the better your argument will be.

---

**CAUTION**

**Write for Target Readers, Not Your Teacher**

Your teacher may be your only reader, but don't write with only your teacher in mind. First of all, teachers generally judge papers not as themselves but from the point of view of your target readers, who know less than they do. Second, you risk making unconscious assumptions that distort your argument: you will fail to explain matters your teacher already understands but readers don't, fail to anticipate questions that readers might have but your teacher won't, and generally produce a paper that is fully suited neither to your teacher nor to your target readers. Once you identify your target readers, write only for them.

6.2.2    **How Arguments Grow from Questions**

Consider the kind of conversation you have every day.

*Abby:* I hear you had a hard time last semester. How do you think this one will go? [Abby *poses a problem in the form of a question.*]

*Brett:* Better, I hope. [Brett *answers the question.*]

*Abby:* Why so? [Abby *asks for a reason to believe* Brett's answer.]

*Brett:* I'm taking courses in my major. [Brett *offers a reason.*]

*Abby:* Like what? [Abby *asks for evidence to back up* Brett's reason.]

*Brett:* History of Art, Intro to Design. [Brett *offers evidence to back up his reason.*]

*Abby:* Why will taking courses in your major make a difference? [Abby *doesn't see the relevance of* Brett's reason to his claim that he will do better.]

*Brett:* When I take courses I'm interested in, I work harder. [Brett *offers a general principle that relates his reason to his claim that he will do better.*]

*Abby:* What about that math course you have to take? [Abby *objects to* Brett's reason.]

*Brett:* I know I had to drop it last time I took it, but I found a good tutor. [Brett *acknowledges* Abby's *objection and responds to it.*]

If you can imagine yourself in that conversation, you'll find nothing strange about assembling a research argument. That's because the five elements of any argument are just answers to the kinds of questions Abby asks Brett—and that you must ask yourself on your reader's behalf.

- Claim: What do you want me to believe? What is your point?
- Reason: Why do you say that? Why should I agree?
- Evidence: How do you know? Can you back it up?
- Acknowledgment and Response: But what about . . . ?
- Warrant: How does that follow? Can you explain your reasoning?

Think of your research as the process of figuring out answers to those questions.

6.3    **Assemble the Core of Your Argument**

At the core of your argument are three elements: your claim, your reasons for accepting it, and the evidence on which those reasons are based. Most students find these elements easy to understand when they think of them in light of the predictable questions they answer. To that core you'll add one and perhaps two more elements: one responds to questions, objections, and alternative points of view; the other answers those who do not understand how your reasons are *relevant* to your claim.

### 6.3.1    Turn Your Hypothesis into a Claim

In the early stages of your research, your job was to find a question and imagine a tentative answer, which we called your *hypothesis*. When you think you can back up your hypothesis with good reasons and evidence, you'll present that hypothesis as your argument's *claim*. A claim is an assertion (which could be one sentence or several) that demands support. Your *main claim* is the assertion supported by your whole research argument. Some call this assertion your *thesis*.

---

**SOME TERMINOLOGY**

**Your Claim's Many Names**

Every good research paper is built around a governing idea, a most important result, a main point that dominates all the rest. It has many names because you have to think about it from many points of view. It is the *answer* to your research question, the *hypothesis* that guides your research, the *main point* or *thesis statement* around which you organize your paper. You need so many names for your claim because it plays so many roles in your research project.

---

### 6.3.2    State and Evaluate Your Claim

Start a new first page of your storyboard or outline. At the bottom, state your claim in a sentence or two. Be as specific as you can, because the words in this claim will help you plan and write your draft. Avoid vague value words like *important*, *interesting*, and *significant*. Compare the following pairs of claims:

Masks play an important role in many religious ceremonies.

In cultures from pre-Columbian America to Africa and Asia, masks allow religious celebrants to bring deities to life so that worshipers experience them directly.

Nursing schools are making significant efforts to attract more male applicants.

To attract more male applicants, nursing schools are challenging the assumption that nursing is an inherently female profession.

Now judge the *significance* of your claim (*So what?* again). A significant claim doesn't make a reader think *I know that*, but rather *Really? How interesting. What makes you think so?* (1.1). Of course what your readers will find interesting depends on what they know, and if you're a beginning researcher, that's something you can't predict. If you're writing one of your first papers, assume that your most important reader is you. It is enough if *you alone* think your answer is significant, if it makes you think, *Well, I didn't know that when I started*. As you become more experienced and come to understand your readers better, you'll learn to frame your arguments in terms of their interests (see chapter 1). If, however, you think your own claim is vague or trivial, you're not yet ready to assemble an argument because you have no reason to make one.

6.3.3   **Support Your Claim with Reasons and Evidence**
It may seem obvious that you must back up a claim with reasons and evidence. But it's easy to confuse those two words, because we often use them as if they mean the same thing:

> What reasons do you base your claim on?
> What evidence do you base your claim on?

But they mean different things. Compare these two sentences:

> On what evidence do you base your reasons?
> On what reasons do you base your evidence?

That second sentence is odd: we don't base evidence on reasons; we base reasons on evidence. We use our minds to *think up* reasons: they are statements that support our claims. We have to *search* for evidence "out there" in the world and then make it available for everyone to see: evidence is the data—statistics, graphs, examples, quotations, images, and so on—that support our reasons. Reasons need the support of evidence; evidence should need no support beyond careful demonstration or a reference to a reliable source.

To be sure, readers may accept a claim based only on a reason, without any evidence at all, if that reason comes from a trusted authority or seems clearly—or *self-evidently*—true:

> We are all created equal,$_{reason}$ so no one has a natural right to govern us.$_{claim}$

But when doing research, you will almost always have to provide evidence as well as reasons. For example, suppose a researcher offers this claim and reason:

> To attract more male applicants, nursing schools are challenging the assumption that nursing is an inherently female profession.$_{claim}$ The admissions literature of many top schools contain more images of male students and fewer images of nurses performing stereotypically feminine tasks than they did a decade ago.$_{reason}$

You might be tempted to stop there, thinking that you have made your case. But skeptical readers will want not just that reason but evidence that it is true. They might ask *What is a "top school"? How many is "many"? How much more is "more"? What tasks are you characterizing as "stereotypically feminine"?* Such readers will accept your reason only when *they* (not *you*) believe that you have given them sufficient evidence for it.

To support this argument, you might compare the websites of three nursing schools to their old admissions brochures, counting the number of men and women they show and analyzing some representative images. But even then, what you consider a true fact and therefore "hard" evidence, your readers might not. For instance, a skeptical reader might disagree that a particular image shows a "stereotypically feminine" task. You won't satisfy every reader; it is almost always possible to raise *some* objection to a reason or piece of evidence. But you should strive to meet the reasonable skepticism you can expect from your best readers.

In introductory courses it is often sufficient to support reasons only by what authoritative sources say: *Wilson says* X, *Yang says* Y, *Schmidt says* Z. Find out from your teacher if you can use the claims of authorities as evidence. But in advanced work, readers expect more: they want evidence drawn not just from secondary sources but from primary sources or your own observations, demonstrations, or experiments.

Review your storyboard: Can you support each reason with what your readers will think is evidence of the right kind, quantity, and quality? Might your readers challenge what you offer as evidence? If so, how? Do you need to offer a better demonstration or a better source? If so, you must produce more or better data or acknowledge the limits of what you have.

Your claim, reasons, and evidence make up the core of your argument, but that argument needs at least one more element, and maybe two.

## 6.4    Acknowledge and Respond to Readers' Questions and Points of View

In our first chapter we encouraged you to think of your argument as a silent conversation in which you speak with and for your readers. No argument is complete that fails to consider its readers' questions and points of view. You must imagine your readers' questions and objections on their behalf and then acknowledge and respond to them. Some teachers call such responses *counterclaims*, but that word can imply that the point of acknowledging other views is to *counter* them, or shoot them down. Sometimes it is, but more often the goal is to demonstrate your own thoughtfulness and carefulness as a researcher by showing that you have carefully considered and responded to the views of others.

### 6.4.1    Imagining Readers' Views

Readers raise two kinds of questions. Try to imagine and respond to both.

1.  The first kind of question points to problems *inside* your argument, usually its evidence.

    Imagine a reader making any of these criticisms of your evidence. If one of them might be reasonable, construct a mini-argument in response:

    · Your evidence is from an unreliable or out-of-date source.
    · Your evidence is inaccurate.
    · You don't have enough evidence.
    · What you report doesn't fairly represent all the evidence available.
    · You have the wrong kind of evidence for our field.

    Then imagine these kinds of objections to your reasons. If one of them might be reasonable, construct a mini-argument in response:

    · Your reasons are inconsistent or contradictory.
    · You don't have enough reasons.
    · They are too weak to support your claim.
    · They are irrelevant to your claim and so do not *count* as reasons (see 6.5).

2.  The second kind of question points to problems *outside* your argument.

    Those who see the world differently from you are likely to define terms differently, reason differently, even to offer evidence that you find irrelevant. Do not treat differing views simply as objections. You will lose readers if you appear to believe that your view is right and those others are simply wrong. Instead, compare your view to those others, so that your readers can understand your argument on its own terms. They still might not agree with you, but if you show them that you respect the views of others, they will be more likely to respect yours.

    If you're a new researcher, you'll find these questions hard to imagine because you might not know how in fact your readers' views differ from your own. Even so, try to think of some plausible questions or objections and then respond to them. It's important to get into the habit of asking yourself, *What could cast doubt on my claim?*

    When you do more advanced work, you will be expected to know the issues that others in your field are likely to raise. So practice imagining and responding to disagreements now. Even if you just go through the motions, you'll cultivate a habit of mind that your readers will respect and that may keep you from jumping to questionable conclusions.

    Add those acknowledgments and responses to your storyboard where you think readers will raise them.

WORKING IN GROUPS

**Ask Friends to Object**

If you cannot imagine objections or alternatives to your argument, enlist help from your friends or writing group. Ask them to read your draft and make the longest list they can of objections, alternative conclusions, different interpretations of evidence, and so on. Ask them not to censor themselves—you want even their nuttiest ideas. You may find in their views a question to acknowledge and respond to; and if not, their list might give you an idea of your own.

## 6.4.2    Acknowledging and Responding

When you acknowledge an anticipated question or objection, you can give it more or less weight. You can mention and dismiss it, summarize it quickly, or address it at length. Do not dismiss a position that your readers take seriously; do not address at length one for which you have no good response.

**Standard Forms for Acknowledging**

We order these expressions from most dismissive to most respectful (brackets and slashes indicate choices).

1.  You can downplay an alternative by summarizing it in a short phrase introduced with *despite*, *regardless of*, or *notwithstanding*:

    [**Despite / Regardless of / Notwithstanding**] the governor's claims that she wants to cut taxes,<sub>acknowledgment</sub> the public believes that . . . <sub>response</sub>

    You can use *although*, *while*, and *even though* in the same way:

    [**Although / While / Even though**] the governor claims that she wants to cut taxes,<sub>acknowledgment</sub> the public believes that . . . <sub>response</sub>

2.  You can signal an alternative with *seem* or *appear*, or with a qualifying adverb, such as *plausibly, reasonably, understandably, surprisingly, foolishly,* or even *certainly.*

    In his letters, Mozart expresses what [**seems / appears**] to be depression.<sub>acknowledgment</sub> But those who observed him . . . <sub>response</sub>
    Liberals [**plausibly / reasonably / foolishly** / etc.] argue that the arts ought to be supported by taxes.<sub>acknowledgment</sub> But we all know . . . <sub>response</sub>

3.  You can acknowledge an alternative without naming its source. This gives it just a little weight.

It is easy to [**think / imagine / say / claim / argue**] that taxes should . . .

There is [**another / alternative / possible / standard**] [**explanation / argument / possibility**] . . .

Some evidence [**might / can / could / would / does**] [**suggest / indicate / lead some to think**] that we should . . .

4.   You can acknowledge an alternative by attributing it to a more or less specific source. This construction gives it more weight.

There are [**some / many / few**] who [**might / could / would**] [**say / think / claim / charge / object**] that climate change is not . . .

[**Most / Many / Some / A few**] administrators [**say / think / claim / charge / object**] that researchers . . .

Jones [**says / thinks / claims / charges / objects**] that students . . .

5.   You can acknowledge an alternative in your own voice or with concessive adverbs such as *admittedly, granted, to be sure*, and so on. This construction concedes that the alternative has some validity, but by changing the words, you can qualify how much validity you acknowledge.

I [**understand / know / realize / appreciate**] that conservatives believe in . . .

It is [**true / possible / likely / certain / must be admitted**] that no good evidence proves that coffee causes cancer . . .

[**Granted / Admittedly / True / To be sure / Certainly / Of course**], Sánchez stated . . .

We [**could / can / might / would**] [**say / argue / claim / think**] that spending on the arts supports subversive . . .

We have to [**consider / raise**] the [**question / possibility / probability**] that further study [**could / might / will**] show crime has not . . .

We cannot [**overlook / ignore / dismiss / reject**] the fact that the Cubs are . . .

Readers use the words of your acknowledgment to judge how seriously you take an objection or alternative. But they will base that judgment even more on the nature of your response. If your readers think an alternative is a serious one, they expect you to respond to it in some detail, including reasons and evidence to support that response. Do not simply dismiss or attack a position that your readers believe strongly; if you cannot make a convincing argument against it, simply show how it differs from yours and explain why you believe as you do.

**Standard Forms for Introducing Responses**

You can respond in ways that range from tactfully indirect to blunt.

1.  You can state that you don't entirely understand:

    But I do not quite understand . . . / I find it difficult to see how . . . / It is not clear to me that . . .

2.  Or you can state that there are unsettled issues:

    But there are other issues . . . / There remains the problem of . . .

3.  You can respond more bluntly by claiming the acknowledged position is irrelevant or unreliable:

    But as insightful as that point may be, it [**ignores / is irrelevant to**] the issue at hand.
    But the evidence is [**unreliable / shaky / thin / not the best available**].
    But the argument is [**untenable / wrong / weak / confused / simplistic**].
    But that view [**overlooks / ignores / misses**] key factors.
    But that position is based on [**unreliable / faulty / weak / confused**] [**reasoning / evidence**].

## 6.5    Explain Your Reasoning If Readers Might Question It

Sometimes readers question an argument not because they object to its evidence or see an alternative interpretation of events, but because they cannot see its logic. Consider this argument, made by the ex–basketball star and TV commentator Charles Barkley:

I should not be held to a higher standard in my behavior,*claim* because I never put myself forward as a role model for kids.*reason*

He was immediately criticized. His critics agreed that his reason was true: in fact, Barkley never claimed to be a role model. But, they said, that reason was irrelevant: he *was* a role model to be held to a higher standard whether he asked for it or not.

Barkley and his critics did not disagree about evidence or reasons: all agreed that Barkley had never asked to be a role model. What they disagreed about was the *warrant*.

A warrant is a general principle stating that if one thing is true, then something else must also be true. It answers those who believe that your reasons are true but still don't see why they should accept your claim: they think your reasons are *irrelevant* to believing your claim because they do not know (or accept) the principle of reasoning that connects them.

For Barkley, the principle was something like this:

Whenever someone does not ask to be a role model, he is not responsible to meet the standard of behavior applied to role models.

But the critics applied a different principle:

Whenever someone willingly engages in an activity that makes him famous and admired, he is a role model whether he asked for it or not.

If we think Barkley's warrant is the right one, then we must accept his claim; if we think the critics have the right warrant, then we must reject his and accept theirs.

All research arguments have warrants, just as they have claims, reasons, and evidence. But unlike those core elements, the warrants are often left unstated. That's because warrants need to be stated only when writers and readers might hold different ones—as in arguments about such topics as politics or morality—or when experts make arguments for general audiences because they have to explain to lay readers how researchers think in their fields.

> **CAUTION**
>
> **Don't Let Warrants Intimidate You**
> If warrants still seem confusing, don't be dismayed. Warrants are most important when you write for readers who think in ways very different from yours. They are least important when your readers are a lot like you. Since you're likely to have target readers who do think more or less as you do, you may not need explicit warrants at all. So if one comes to mind as you draft, include it. But don't try to force yourself to include warrants. As you become more experienced and tackle more advanced research projects, you can revisit the issue of warrants and their uses.

## 6.6   An Argument Assembled

Here is a small argument that pulls together all five parts:

Television aimed at children can aid their intellectual development, but that contribution has been offset by a factor that could damage their emotional development—too much violence.$_{claim}$ Parents agree that example is an important influence on a child's development. That's why parents tell their children stories about heroes. It seems plausible, then, that when children see degrading behavior, they will be affected by it as well.$_{warrant}$ In a single day, children see countless examples of violence.$_{reason}$ Every day the average child watches almost four hours of television and sees about twelve acts of violence (Smith, 2014).$_{evidence}$ Tarnov has shown that children don't confuse cartoon violence with real life (2018). *acknowledgment of alternative point of view* But that may make children more vulnerable to violence in other shows. If they only distinguish between cartoons and people, they may think real actors engaged in graphic violence represent real life. *response* We cannot ignore the possibility that repeated exposure to realistic representations of violence encourages the development of violent adults. *claim restated*

Most of those elements could be expanded to many paragraphs.

Arguments in different fields look different, but again, they all consist of answers to the same five questions.

- Claim: What do you want me to believe? What is your point?
- Reason: Why do you say that? Why should I agree?
- Evidence: How do you know? Can you back it up?
- Acknowledgment and Response: But what about . . . ?
- Warrant: How does that follow? Can you explain your reasoning?

Your storyboard should raise and answer those questions many times. If it does, you'll have an argument that seems rich and—you can hope—convincing.

# 7 Planning a First Draft

Once you assemble your argument, you might be ready to write your draft. But experienced writers know that the time they invest in planning a draft more than pays off when they write it. Some plans, however, are better than others.

---

**WORKING IN GROUPS**

**Organize a Writing Group**

If you haven't done it yet, now is the time to organize a writing group of three to five classmates (no more). If you already have a group, now is the time to get to work seriously. Plan to meet once or, if your deadline is near, twice a week. Have an agenda that reflects your stage in the process of research and writing. Start every meeting with elevator stories (see 3.2.3). If your storyboard is starting to fill up, bring it to the meeting. Although your peers' suggestions are always welcome, your goal early on is to have someone willing to listen and respond to your ideas. The sooner you get those ideas out of your mind and into the light of day, the better you will know how well you really understand them.

---

## 7.1   Avoid Unhelpful Plans

Look out for and avoid plans that resemble these:

1. **Narrative of Discovery.** Do not organize your paper as a story of your research, especially not as a mystery, with your claim revealed at the end. Readers care about what you found, not the steps you took to get there. You see signs of this approach in language like *The first issue was . . . Then I compared . . . Finally, I conclude . . .* If you do this, you are likely still too close to the activity of research to put your readers' needs before your own.

2. **Patchwork of Sources.** Do not patch together a series of quotations, summaries of sources, or downloads from the web. Readers want to see *your* thinking, not a "data dump" of what others have said. If you do this, you are probably overwhelmed by your sources and have not yet developed a controlling claim of your own. *Note*: A paper stitched together from sources, especially one that is copied and pasted from the web, risks a charge of plagiarism (see 10.3).

3. **Mirror of the Assignment.** Do not mechanically organize your paper around the terms of a class assignment. If your assignment lists issues to cover, don't think you must address them in the order given. You owe it to yourself and your teacher to do more. If you do this, you are likely still developing your own ideas and struggling to organize your paper in a way that reflects them. For example, if comparing and contrasting Freud's and Jung's analyses of the imagination, avoid organizing your paper in the two most obvious parts, the first on Freud, the second on Jung. Break those two big topics into their parts, then organize your paper around them.

## 7.2    Consider a Range of Useful Plans

If some plans cause readers to question your credibility, there are many other useful plans from which to choose. In constructing your argument (see chapter 6), you may not have put your reasons in any particular order. But when you plan a draft, you must impose *some* order on them. That's not easy, especially when you're writing on a new topic in a new field.

The best order is the one that best meets your readers' needs. When you're not sure how to order your reasons, consider the following principles.

1. You can organize your paper according to its subject matter:
   • **Chronological.** This is the simplest: earlier-to-later or cause-to-effect.
   • **Part by part.** If you break your topic into its constituent parts, you can deal with each in turn, but you must still order those parts in some way that helps readers understand them: by their functional relationships, hierarchy, similarities and differences, or the like.

2. You can also organize your paper to facilitate your readers' understanding:
   • **Short to long, simple to complex.** Most readers prefer to deal with simpler issues before they work through more complex ones.
   • **More familiar to less familiar.** Most readers prefer to read what they know about before they read what's new.
   • **Most acceptable to most contestable.** Most readers move more easily from what they agree with to what they don't.
   • **Less important to more important (or vice versa).** Most readers prefer to read more important reasons first, but those reasons may have more impact when they come last.
   • **Earlier understanding as a basis for later understanding.** Readers may

have to understand some things—events, principles, definitions, and so on—before they understand another thing.

Often these principles cooperate: what readers agree with and easily understand might also be short and familiar. But these principles may also conflict: readers might reject most quickly reasons that are most important. Whatever your order, it must reflect *your readers'* needs, not the order that the material seems to impose on itself (such as chronology) or, least of all, the order in which those reasons occurred to you.

To test any order, create *one* paragraph that includes just your reasons in the order you want to test. If that paragraph reads like a convincing elevator story (test it on your writing group or a friend), then you have found a usable order.

## 7.3 Create a Plan That Meets Your Readers' Needs

Some fields require a conventional plan for a paper. Readers in the experimental sciences, for example, expect papers to follow some version of this:

Introduction—Methods and Materials—Results—Discussion—Conclusion

If you must follow a conventional plan, find a model in a secondary source or ask your teacher for one. In most fields, however, you have to create a plan of your own, but that plan must make sense to readers. To create it, start with your storyboard or outline.

### 7.3.1 Convert a Storyboard into an Outline

Your best tool for planning a draft is your storyboard (see 3.2 for an example). But if you prefer to work from an outline, you can turn your storyboard into one:

- Start with a sentence numbered *I* that states your claim.
- Add complete sentences under it numbered *II, III,* . . . each of which states a reason supporting your claim (from the top of a reason page in your storyboard).
- Under each reason, use capital letters to list sentences summarizing your evidence; then list by numbers the evidence itself.

For example:

I. Introduction: Educational benefits of writing on laptops are uncertain.
II. Different uses have different effects.
    A. All uses increase number of words produced.
        1. Study 1: 950 vs. 780
        2. Study 2: 1,103 vs. 922
    B. Using laptops encourages writer's block.
III. Studies show limited benefit on revision.

  A. Study A: writers on computers are more wordy.
   1. Average of 2.3 more words per sentence
   2. Average of 20% more words per essay
  B. Study B: writers need hard copy to revise effectively.
   1. 22% fewer typos when done on hard copy vs. computer screen
   2. 2.26% fewer spelling errors
IV. Conclusion: Disadvantages of laptops may outweigh advantages.

A sparer outline just uses phrases, with no formal layers of I, A, 1, and so on.

Introduction: benefits of laptops uncertain
Different uses / different effects
 More words
 Writer's block
Revision studies
 Study 1: longer sentences
 Study 2: longer essays
 Study 3: hardcopy better
Conclusion: disadvantages of laptops may outweigh advantages

As you start a project, a spare outline may be the best you can do. For a short project it may be all you need. But an outline of complete sentences is usually more useful. More useful yet is a storyboard, especially for a long project.

### 7.3.2 Sketch a Working Introduction

Writers are often advised to write their introduction last, but most of us need a working introduction to start us on the right track. Expect to write your introduction twice—first a sketch for yourself and later a final one for your readers. That final introduction will usually have four parts (see chapter 13), so you might as well sketch your working introduction to anticipate them.

> **Create a Four-Part Scheme for Your Introduction**
>
> For now, think of your introduction as having these parts:
>
> 1. Current Situation (what your readers now think or do)
> 2. Research Question (what your readers need to know but don't)
> 3. Significance of the Question (your answer to *So what?*)
> 4. Answer (what your readers should know)
>
> We explain these parts more fully in 13.1. In this section we explain how to sketch them in your storyboard.

  If you followed our earlier suggestion, you have written your main claim at the bottom of the first page of your storyboard. Now fill in the page above it with what leads up to that claim.

1.  At the top of the page state the **Current Situation** that your research question disrupts.

    Since the core of your introduction is your research question, you must first offer readers something for your question to disrupt. Briefly state a belief or condition that you will challenge with your question (you might review the examples in 2.4).

    For example, you might set up a question about the Apollo mission to the moon by asking readers to think about its connection to America's status as a technologically advanced nation. You can state that in terms of

    - what you believed before you began your research (*I used to think . . .*)

      I always thought of the Apollo mission as a sign of American ingenuity.

    - what others believe (*Most people think . . .*)

      The Apollo mission has always been recognized as both a signature achievement in human history and a sign of America's preeminence in technology.

    - an event or situation (*What events seem to show is . . .*)

      Half a century after human beings first set foot on the moon, the Apollo mission remains a sign of American technological skill.

    - what other researchers have found (*Researchers have shown . . .*)

      Virtually everything about the Apollo mission has been extensively researched and documented.

    Of course you could not use *all* of these approaches in one paper; you would choose one or two for your introduction that best motivate your argument. And if you summarize sources at this point, use only those sources whose findings you intend to extend, modify, or correct.

2.  After this, rephrase your **Research Question** as a statement about what we don't know or understand in light of the Current Situation. Start with *but* or *however*.

    **Research Question:**
    How did the Apollo mission become a symbol of American national identity?

    **Motivating Statements:**
    I always thought of the Apollo mission as a sign of America's technological preeminence. A unique moment in human history, the moon landing was also a major moment in American history. But how did it become such a potent symbol of American values and ideals? We know almost everything about *how* Apollo got to the moon, several times over, yet even today we don't fully

understand *why* this particular mission was deemed so central to American national identity.

Writers introduce a motivating statement in many ways. As you read, note how your sources do it, then use them as models.

3.  Next, if you can, explain the **Significance** of your question by answering *So what if we don't find out?*

If we can explain how the Apollo mission became a symbol of American national identity, we can better understand how specific historical events function as symbols of national identity more generally.

You may find any larger significance to your answer hard to imagine. If so, don't dwell on it. We'll return to significance and the *So What?* question in 13.1.3.

4.  Revise your claim as the **Answer** to the question, in terms that match those of the first three parts:

The Apollo mission to land human beings on the moon served as a symbol of national identity not only because it celebrated American ingenuity and technological prowess but because it did so against the Soviet Union, a competitor with the United States in the space race. A successful mission symbolized, for Americans, the superiority of their way of life.

For now, leave that answer at the bottom of the introduction page of your storyboard. You can restate that answer in your conclusion. Most readers prefer to see your main claim at the end of your introduction, because that lets them read what follows faster, understand it better, and remember it longer.

5.  Finally, some writers of longer papers add a "road map" at the end of their introduction:

Part 1 discusses the issue of . . . Part 2 addresses . . . Part 3 examines . . .

Road maps are common in the social sciences, but many in the humanities find them clumsy. You can add a road map to your storyboard to guide your drafting, then cut it from your final draft. If you keep it, make it short.

---

CAUTION

**Don't Fear Giving Away Your Answer**
Some new researchers fear that if they reveal their claim early, in their introduction, readers will be bored and stop reading. Others worry about repeating themselves. Both fears are baseless. If you ask an interesting question, readers will want to see how well you can support its answer.

### 7.3.3   Identify Key Terms That Will Run through Your Paper

For your paper to seem coherent, readers must see a few key concepts running through all its parts. But readers won't recognize those repeated concepts if you refer to them in many different words. Readers need to see specific terms that repeatedly refer to those concepts, not every time you mention them but often enough that readers can't miss them.

You might find them among the terms you used to categorize your notes, but they must include keywords from the sentences stating your claim and its significance. On the introduction page, circle four or five words or phrases that express those concepts. Ignore words that simply refer to your general topic; focus on those relevant to your specific question:

gender, education level, major, choice of profession, wage gap

If you find few words or phrases that can serve as key terms, your topic and point might be too general.

Suppose, for example, you were writing a paper about sampling in electronic music. Your paper might have as one organizing theme the legal concept of fair use. But readers might miss the connection if you use too many different words and phrases to name it: *copyright*, *creativity*, *royalty*, *freedom*, *intellectual property*, *remix*. Although these all relate to your theme of fair use, readers might not make that connection in each case.

For that to happen, your readers need to see one specific term that repeatedly refers to each concept that serves as an organizing theme for your paper, not every time you mention the concept but often enough that readers can't miss the connection.

Before you start drafting, identify the key concepts that you intend to run through your whole paper. For each concept, select one term that you will use most often. As you draft, you may find new themes and drop some old ones, but

> **How to Identify Global Concepts to Unite the Whole Paper**
> 1.  On the introduction and conclusion pages of your storyboard, circle four or five words that name your key concepts. You should find those words in your claim.
>      *   Ignore words obviously connected to your topic: *space, Apollo, United States.*
>      *   Focus on concepts that *you* bring to the argument and intend to develop: *values, national identity, competition,* and so on.
> 2.  For each concept, select one key term that you can run through the body of your paper. It can be one of your circled words or a new one. If you find few words that can serve as key terms, your claim may be too general (review 6.3.2).

you'll write more coherently if you keep your most important terms and concepts in the front of your mind.

As you draft, keep a list of those terms in front of you. They will help you keep yourself—and therefore your readers—on track. If you find yourself drafting two or more pages without those terms, don't just wrench yourself back to using them. You might be discovering a new trail that's worth following.

### 7.3.4    Find the Key Terms Distinctive to Each Section

Now do the same thing for each section: Find the key terms that unify the section and distinguish it from the others. Circle the important words in the reason at the top of each reason page. Some of them should be related to the words circled in the introduction and conclusion. The rest should identify concepts that distinguish that section from all the others. If you cannot find key terms to distinguish a section, think hard about what that section contributes to the whole. Readers may think it repetitive or irrelevant.

We recommend that you use subheads in your drafts to keep yourself on track. Create a subhead for each section out of the key terms you identified in that section. If papers in your field don't use subheads, delete them from your last draft.

### 7.3.5    Sketch a Brief Introduction to Each Section and Subsection

Just as your whole paper needs an introduction that frames what follows, so does each of its sections. If a section is only a page or two, you need just a short paragraph; for a section several pages long, you might need to sketch in two or more paragraphs. This introduction should announce the key terms that are special to the section, ideally in a sentence at its end expressing the section's point, which might be a reason, a response to a different point of view, or a warrant you must explain.

### 7.3.6    Sketch in Evidence, Acknowledgments, Warrants, and Summaries

In their relevant sections, sketch out the parts of your argument. Remember that many of those parts will themselves make points that must be supported by smaller subarguments.

EVIDENCE. Most sections consist primarily of evidence supporting reasons. Sketch the evidence after the reason it supports. If you have different kinds of evidence supporting the same reason, group and order them in a way that will make sense to your readers.

EXPLANATIONS OF EVIDENCE. You may have to explain your evidence—where it came from, why it's reliable, how it supports a reason. Usually these explanations follow the evidence, but you can sketch them before if that seems more logical.

ACKNOWLEDGMENTS AND RESPONSES. Imagine what readers might object to and where, then sketch a response. Responses are typically subarguments with at least a claim and reasons (*Some researchers have said . . . , but I believe* _____ *because . . .*); they often include evidence and maybe even a second response to an imagined objection to your first response.

WARRANTS. If you think you need a warrant to justify the relevance of a reason, develop it before you state the reason. (If you're using a warrant only for emphasis, put it after the reason.) If you think readers will question the truth of the warrant, sketch a subargument to support it. If readers might think that your reason or claim isn't a valid instance of the warrant, sketch a subargument showing that it is.

SUMMARIES. If your paper is long and "fact-heavy" with dates, names, events, or numbers, you might end each major section by briefly summarizing the progress of your argument. What have you established in that section? How does your argument shape up so far? If in your final draft those summaries seem clumsy, cut them.

Writers in different fields arrange these elements in slightly different ways, but the elements themselves and their principles of organization are the same in just about every field or profession. In every paper, regardless of field, you must order the parts of your argument not just to reflect your own thinking but to help your readers understand it.

## 7.3.7   Sketch a Working Conclusion

You should have stated your concluding claim at the top of the conclusion page of your storyboard. If you can add to the significance of that claim (another answer to *So what?*), sketch it after the claim (see 13.2 for more on conclusions).

---

QUICK TIP

**Save the Leftovers**

Once you have a plan, you should discover that you have material that doesn't fit into it. That's a good thing. Research is like diamond mining—you have to dig up a lot of dirt to find a few gems. So be glad about your leftovers. If you don't have any, you haven't done enough research.

But resist the temptation to shoehorn leftovers into your paper just to show your work. File them for future use. They may contain the seeds of another project.

# 8   Drafting Your Paper

Many inexperienced writers think that once they have an outline or storyboard, they can draft by just grinding out sentences. And if you've followed our advice to write as you gather evidence, you may think that you can plug that exploratory writing into your draft. Experienced writers know better. They know that thoughtful drafting is an act of discovery. In fact, most writers don't know what they *can* think until they see it appear on the page before them.

You'll experience one of the most exciting moments in research when you discover yourself writing out ideas that you did not know you had. So don't look at drafting as just translating your storyboard into words. Think of it as an opportunity to discover what your storyboard has missed.

In this chapter we offer advice to turn the early work of your research and planning into a draft that you can share with others as work in progress and later revise.

## 8.1   Draft in a Way That Feels Comfortable

Writers draft in different ways. Some are slow and careful: they have to get every paragraph right before they start the next one. But to do that, they need a specific, complete plan. So if you draft slowly, plan carefully. Other writers let the words flow, skipping ahead when they get stuck, omitting quotations, statistics, and so on that they know they can plug in later. If they get stopped by a stylistic issue like whether to write out a number in words or numerals, rather than lose momentum they insert "[?]" and revisit the issue later. But quick drafters need lots of time to revise. So if you draft quickly, start early. Draft in whatever way works for you, but experienced writers usually draft quickly, then revise extensively.

## 8.2   Picture Your Readers Asking Friendly Questions

We said this before, but it's important enough to say again: you will write better and more easily if you picture yourself talking with a group of friendly readers who have lots of questions. Before you start drafting, imagine the specific readers you hope to address (*not* your teacher!). Imagine their questions, and build your draft around your answers. For now, think of those readers as friendly and supportive: *Why do you say that? I think I see where you are going, but I'm not sure; can you explain it a little more? That's interesting—what's your evidence for it?* While you are drafting, imagine readers whose questions help you move along, who *want* to agree with you if only you will give them the information they need.

Especially if you draft quickly, you need to quiet your own internal naysayer while you draft. Your goal is to get your ideas down as fully and freely as you can. You'll have time and (in chapters 13–16) lots of help to get them right in revision. But if you worry over every detail, you'll spend more time responding to that voice in your head than discovering what you think. So let your imagined friendly readers encourage you as you draft. Later you'll imagine skeptical, even hostile, questions so that you can know where you have to improve your completed draft. But for now, banish the skeptics.

> **WORKING IN GROUPS**
>
> **Avoid Negative Responses**
> There will come a time when you will want your writing group to be as hard on your paper as they can be: better to find out what the problems are before you turn it in. But the drafting stage is not that time. When you meet during the drafting stage, make it a rule that everyone will avoid all but the most obvious criticisms and concentrate on positive suggestions. Too many negative thoughts will only stop up the flow of your writing.

## 8.3  Be Open to Surprises

If you write as you go and plan your argument before you draft, you're unlikely to be totally surprised by how your draft develops. Even so, be open to new directions from beginning to end:

- When your drafting heads off on a tangent, go with it for a bit to see whether you're onto something better than you planned.
- When reporting your evidence leads you to doubt a reason, don't ignore that feeling. Follow it up.
- When the order of your reasons starts to feel awkward, experiment with new ones, even if you thought you were almost done.
- Even when you reach your final conclusion, you may see how to restate your claim more clearly and pointedly.

If you get helpful new ideas early enough, invest the time to make changes. It is a small price to pay for a big improvement.

8.4    **Develop Effective Drafting Habits**

Most of us learn to write in the least efficient way—under pressure, rushing to meet a deadline, doing a quick draft the night before, and maybe a few minutes in the morning for proofreading. That rarely works for a short paper, almost never for a longer one. You need time and a plan that sets small, achievable goals but keeps your eye on the whole.

Most important, draft regularly and often, not in marathon sessions that dull your thinking and kill your interest. Set a small goal and a reasonable quota of words for each session, and stick to it. It's rarely productive to write for more than an hour or so without a break. Get up from the drafting table and do something else for a bit. Once you have reached your quota for that session, honor your plan and only return to drafting in your next scheduled session. The time spent *away* from your paper can be just as productive as the time you spend *on* your paper.

Always draft in a suitable environment. You may not need a particularly quiet place—in fact, many of us prefer a little background noise when we write. But you *must* avoid interruptions. Turn off your phone; don't let friends talk to you while you draft. One of the greatest obstacles to successful drafting is *anything* that forces you to pay attention to something other than what you are writing.

When you start or return to a drafting session, review your storyboard to decide what you're ready to draft that day. *How will it fit into its section and the whole? What reason does this section support? Where does it fit in the overall logic? Which key terms state the concepts that distinguish this section?* If you're blocked, skip to another section.

Whatever you do, don't substitute more reading for writing. Chronic procrastinators are usually so intimidated by the size of their project that it paralyzes them, and they just keep putting off getting started. You can overcome that destructive habit by breaking your project into small, achievable goals (see 8.5).

Before each drafting session, picture your friendly readers and summarize for them (out loud if possible) what has come before the place you plan to start. Then imagine that what you write next simply continues that conversation.

> **CAUTION**
>
> **Avoid Procrastinators' Tricks**
> Don't play procrastinators' tricks on yourself—something *everyone* is prone to do. (We have missed more than one deadline in preparing this book.) You cannot do your best work if you waste the time you have available. Here are the top four mistakes to avoid:
>
> - Don't substitute more reading for writing. Start writing as soon as you have enough evidence to go on. You may have to go back for more, but

don't fool yourself that the writing will be easier if only you do more reading.

- Don't keep revising the same pages over and over. Focus on getting a complete draft that you can then revise.
- Don't focus on how much more you have to do. You will freeze up if you become intimidated by how much you have left. Set small, achievable goals for each day and focus on them.
- Don't allow yourself to do anything else during your writing time. Never spend a few minutes on texting; never tell yourself that a quick computer game will refresh your mind.

Writing is hard. But you won't make it any easier by wasting the time you set aside to write. Put your head down and tell yourself, *Just get it done.*

## 8.5   Stay on Track through Headings and Key Terms

Here are two techniques you can use to keep yourself on track as you draft.

Use headings—ideally full sentences—to break your draft into manageable chunks and to show how your sections are related to one another. Even if your paper won't use headings and subheadings, you can use them as you draft and delete them later. These headings help to map your outline or storyboard onto your draft.

You can also use lists of key terms to keep yourself on track. As you draft, keep in front of you both the terms that should run through your whole paper and those specific to individual sections (see 7.3.3 and 7.3.4). From time to time, check how often you've used those words, both those that run through the whole paper and those that distinguish one section from another. If you find yourself writing something that lacks those terms, pause and reflect: are you just off track, or are you discovering something new? You need not stay yoked to your original plan: you are free to follow a new path to see where it leads, but do that as a choice—not because you got lost along the way.

## 8.6   Stay on Track through Topic Sentences and Transitions

Just as your paper is a series of sections, each section of your paper is a series of paragraphs. Within each section, paragraphs play supporting roles: they introduce claims, offer reasons or evidence, acknowledge counterarguments, and so on. As you draft, keep in mind the purpose of each section and, especially, your readers' needs as they follow your argument.

In early drafts, paragraphs tend to run long or to appear choppy. We don't naturally think in paragraphs but in sentences. As we link sentences together, it's not always clear where one idea ends and another idea begins. That's why it's counterproductive at this stage to worry too much about the structure of paragraphs; save that for revision.

But you can anticipate the final shape of your paper if, as you draft, you keep in mind the two roles that paragraphs play. First, they offer readers brief pauses to take in some point in relation to the whole. Second, they orient readers to the structure of an argument. Each paragraph break is an opportunity to check in with your readers to see that they are still following you. You do so primarily through topic sentences and transition words.

Topic sentences typically lead off a paragraph, forecast its content, and help to hold it together as a set of related sentences. The remaining sentences in a paragraph provide that content. A concluding sentence summarizes that content as the paragraph's major claim or point.

Transition words (and phrases) connect sentences and paragraphs together by signaling some recognizable order: chronological (*First, Second*), cause-to-effect (*As a result*), contrast (*On the other hand*). Transition words are useful as you draft to test your principles of order between sentences and paragraphs, even at the risk of stating the obvious. At this point they are more for your benefit than for your readers'. Later you can delete those that seem unnecessary.

## 8.7    Work Through Procrastination and Writer's Block

If you can't seem to get started on a first draft or struggle to draft more than a few words, you may have writer's block. Some cases arise from anxieties about school and its pressures or other mental health issues; if that sounds like you, seek out the help you need. But most cases of chronic procrastination or writer's block have causes you can address:

- You may be stuck because you have no goals or you've set goals that are too high. If so, set goals that are small and achievable. Then create a routine that helps you achieve them. Use devices to keep yourself moving, such as a progress chart, a timer for writing sessions, or regular meetings with a writing partner or group.
- You may feel so intimidated by the size of your project that you don't know where to begin. If so, break the process into small, achievable tasks; then focus on doing one at a time. Don't dwell on the whole until you've completed several small parts of it. Don't save all the writing until the end; write routinely as you research, not just after.
- You may think that you have to make every sentence or paragraph perfect before you move on to the next one. You don't. Tell yourself you're not writing a final draft but only sketching out some ideas. If you write along the way, you'll be less obsessed with making your draft perfect. And in any event, we all compromise on perfection to get the job done.

QUICK TIP

**Getting Unstuck**

If you have problems like these with most of your writing, go to your school's learning center or writing center. There you will find consultants who have worked with every kind of procrastinator and blocked writer and can tailor their advice to your problem.

On the other hand, some cases of writer's block are opportunities to let your ideas simmer in your subconscious while they combine and recombine into something new and surprising. If you're stuck *and* have time (another reason to start early), do something else for a day or two. Then return to the task to see if you can get back on track.

# 9    Incorporating Your Sources

You should build most of your paper out of your own words that represent your own thinking. But that thinking should be supported by information from various sources. In fact, new researchers typically find most of their evidence in sources. So it is crucial not only that you incorporate information from sources into your argument but that you present it in ways that lead your readers to trust it. For that you must know what readers expect, what choices you have, and how those choices lead readers to draw conclusions about your sources and about you.

## 9.1    When to Quote, Paraphrase, or Summarize?

You can present information from a source in the source's words or in your own. Which you choose depends on how you plan to use the information in your argument but also on the kind of paper you are writing, since different fields use quotation, paraphrase, and summary in different proportions. In general, researchers in the humanities quote most often. Social and natural scientists typically paraphrase and summarize. But you must decide each case for itself.

> **Principles for Choosing Summary, Paraphrase, or Quotation**
>
> **Summarize** when details are irrelevant or a source isn't important enough to warrant the space.
>
> **Paraphrase** when you can state what a source says more clearly or concisely than the source does, or when your argument depends on the details in a source but not on its specific words. (Before you paraphrase, however, read 9.3.)
>
> **Quote** for these purposes:
> - The quoted words themselves are your evidence, and you need to deal with them exactly as they appear in the original.
> - The quoted words are strikingly original, well expressed, odd, or otherwise too useful to lose in paraphrase.

> • The passage states a view that you disagree with, and to be fair you want to state it exactly.
> • The passage is from an authority who backs up your view.
> • The passage expresses your key concepts so clearly that the quotation can frame the rest of your discussion.

You must balance quotations, paraphrases, and summaries with your own fresh ideas. Do not merely repeat or, worse, download words and ideas of others that you then stitch together with a few sentences of your own. Teachers grind their teeth over papers that show so little original thinking.

Readers value research only to the degree that they trust its sources. So when you include a summary, paraphrase, or quotation in your first draft, record its bibliographic data in the appropriate citation style right then and there. (See part 2.)

## 9.2  Creating a Fair Summary

Use a summary to report information from a source when only its main points are relevant to your argument. Because a good summary leaves out details, it is shorter than the original. In some cases, readers expect a summary to cover all the main points, but when you summarize for a research paper, you do not have to cover everything in the source or even in the part you summarize. You can and usually should include only those points relevant to your argument, as long as you do not leave out crucial points that might change how readers understand what the source says.

Suppose, for example, that you were writing a paper on the role of creativity in research. For that paper, the following paragraph would fairly summarize the previous chapter on drafting:

Turabian's *Student's Guide to Writing College Papers* emphasizes that drafting is a process of discovery that can fuel a writer's creative thinking. It acknowledges that some writers have to draft carefully and stick close to their outlines, but it also advises writers to draft as freely and as openly as they can. It encourages even slow and careful drafters to be open to new ideas and surprises and not to be limited by what they do before drafting. It still stresses the value of steady work that follows a plan—for example, writing a little bit every day rather than all at once in a fit of desperate inspiration. But it shows writers how to make the best of a plan while hoping that a better idea will come along.

This summary does not cover the entire chapter; for instance, it ignores the information on key terms, headings, topic sentences and transitions, and procrastination and writer's block. But that's okay, since that information is less relevant to issues of creativity and leaving it out does not distort what the chapter says. The following leaves out so much that it would not be a fair summary:

Turabian's *Student's Guide to Writing College Papers* emphasizes that drafting is a process of discovery that can fuel a writer's creative thinking. It advises writers to draft as freely as they can in order to be open to new ideas and surprises and not to be limited by the plans they make before drafting.

Here the writer gives a false impression of what the chapter says by leaving out something that the chapter emphasizes: the tension between our need to make and follow plans and our need to free our minds to make the most of new ideas.

When you summarize information for a research paper, you should give the summary a slant by focusing on that part of the information most relevant to your argument. But you cannot slant it so much that you misrepresent what the source actually says—which means that you'll have to be sure that *you* understand what the source says. It's another case where you'll have to exercise some judgment.

> **How to Create a Fair and Relevant Summary**
> To be sure that your summary is concise, relevant, and fair, do this:
>
> 1. Summarize only if readers can understand without knowing details. If readers may need more than just the gist of what a source says, don't summarize; quote or paraphrase.
> 2. Decide why the information from the source is relevant to your argument. What reason does it support? What does it add to that support?
> 3. Pick out the most important sentences in the source that are most relevant to a specific part of your argument. In most cases, focus on reasons. But if you will use the summary as evidence, pick out the most important reports of evidence.
> 4. Paraphrase those sentences; list the paraphrases in the order they occur in the original.
> 5. Add any other information that readers might need to understand accurately what the source says.
> 6. Revise to turn the list into a passage that flows.

## 9.3 Creating a Fair Paraphrase

As with a summary, when you paraphrase you report what a source says in your own words. But you don't leave out important details. Don't worry about length: your paraphrase may be a little shorter or a little longer than the original. What's important is that you convey all of the important information from the original.

Some new researchers wonder why they should bother to paraphrase. If a paraphrase has to contain everything important in the original, why not just quote it? That's easier, not to mention safer. Quoting may be easier, but quotations are not always the best way to approach readers. First, when readers see too many quotations, they may suspect that you have just quilted together the ideas of others, with no contribution of your own. Second, when you use your own words, you show readers not only *that* you understand the source but *how* you understand it. Finally, many sources use language that you would never use. For example, how many students would use a phrase like this one from the quotation below: "technology begets more technology"? Your paper will seem more unified and more a product of your own understanding if it sounds more like you than like your sources.

When you paraphrase, read the passage until you think you understand not just its main idea but also its details and complications. Then, without looking back at the source, say out loud what you understand as though you were explaining it to a classmate. (If you stumble, try it again.) When you are happy with an oral version, write it in your draft. Be sure that your paraphrase sounds more like you than like the source:

**Original**

According to Jared Diamond, "Because technology begets more technology, the importance of an invention's diffusion potentially exceeds the importance of the original invention. Technology's history exemplifies what is termed an autocatalytic process: that is, one that speeds up at a rate that increases with time, because the process catalyzes itself" (p. 301).

**Paraphrase**

According to Jared Diamond, technology feeds on itself. One invention leads to another, and then to still more at a rate that increases with time. So what is most important about an invention may not be the invention itself but how quickly it spreads (p. 301).

In most cases, writers introduce a paraphrase in the same way that they introduce a stand-alone quotation, with a phrase or clause that names the source:

According to Jared Diamond, technology feeds on itself . . .

Jared Diamond argues that technology feeds on itself . . .

QUICK TIP

**How to Name Your Sources**

When you refer to a source the first time, use its author's full name. Do not precede it with *Mr., Ms., Professor,* or *Doctor*; you can use titles like *Mayor, Senator, President, Reverend,* or *Bishop*. If you mention the source again, use just the last name:

> According to Steven Pinker, "Claims about a language instinct . . . have virtually nothing to do with possible genetic differences between people." Pinker goes on to argue that "language is not . . ."

## 9.4    Adding Quotations to Your Text

You can insert quotations into your text in two ways:

- For four or fewer lines, use a *run-in quotation* by putting the quoted words on the same line as your text.
- For five or more lines, use a *block quotation* set off as a separate, indented unit.

You can integrate both run-in and block quotations into your text in two ways:

1. Include the quotation as an independent clause, sentence, or passage.

   Jared Diamond reminds us that "circumstances change, and past primacy is no guarantee of future primacy" (p. 417).

   Jared Diamond says, "The histories of the Fertile Crescent and China . . . hold a salutary lesson for the modern world: circumstances change, and past primacy is no guarantee of future primacy" (p. 417).

   According to Jared Diamond,

   > Because technology begets more technology, the importance of an invention's diffusion potentially exceeds the importance of the original invention. Technology's history exemplifies what is termed an autocatalytic process: that is, one that speeds up at a rate that increases with time, because the process catalyzes itself. (p. 301)

2. Weave the quotation into the grammar of your own sentence:

   As Diamond points out, the "lesson for the modern world" in the history of the Fertile Crescent and China is that you can't count on history to repeat itself, because "circumstances change, and past primacy is no guarantee of future primacy" (p. 417).

To make a quotation grammatically mesh with your own sentence, you can modify it, so long as you don't change its meaning and you clearly indicate added or changed words with square brackets and deletions with three dots (called *ellipses*). This sentence quotes the original intact:

Posner focuses on religion not for its spirituality, but for its social functions: "A notable feature of American society is religious pluralism, and we should consider how this relates to the efficacy of governance by social norms in view of the historical importance of religion as both a source and enforcer of such norms" (p. 299).

This version modifies the quotation to fit the grammar of the writer's sentence:

In his discussion of religion, Posner says of American society that "a notable feature . . . is [its] religious pluralism." He argues that to understand how well social norms control what we do, we should consider "the historical importance of religion as both a source and enforcer of such norms" (p. 299).

### 9.5   Introducing Quotations and Paraphrases

You can introduce an independent quotation or paraphrase with a phrase, clause, or sentence *before* the quotation:

In Diamond's view, . . .

Diamond says, . . . *or* Diamond says that . . .

Diamond shows that no society can expect to thrive forever: "The histories . . ." (p. 417).

That introductory part usually names the source, but it does not have to:

As a recent study has shown, "The histories . . ." (Diamond, p. 417).

If there is one thing that America should learn from the past, it's that nothing lasts forever: "The histories . . ." (Diamond, 417).

You can also identify a quotation at its middle or end, although that may feel backward to readers.

"The histories of the Fertile Crescent and China . . . hold a salutary lesson for the modern world," according to Jared Diamond, because "circumstances change, and past primacy is no guarantee of future primacy" (p. 417).

"The histories . . . future primacy," according to Diamond (p. 417).

"The histories . . . future primacy," argues Diamond (p. 417).

Most of those introductory clauses take the form of *Source says*:

Diamond says, "The histories of . . ." (p. 417).

Diamond says that there is a lesson in "the histories of . . ." (p. 417).

Experienced writers use many verbs in place of *says* because the verb that introduces a quotation or paraphrase tells readers how you want them to think about that information and its source. For example, you can indicate whether you think the information is reliable: "Diamond wants to think that" vs. "Diamond proves that." Or you can indicate whether the information is factual or contested: "Diamond reports that" versus "Diamond maintains that." So think carefully about what readers will infer from the verb you use to introduce information from a source.

**Verbs for Introducing a Quotation or Paraphrase**
We can't give you a complete guide to the shades of meaning in the verbs that introduce quotations and paraphrases, but we can give you some ways to use them.

**All-Purpose Verbs**
Use these verbs for claims, facts, opinions, inferences, guesses, or any other kind of information in a source.

These are **neutral**:

Source says that . . .
Also: writes, adds, notes, comments, reports

These indicate **how strongly the source feels** about the information:

Source emphasizes that . . .
Also: affirms, asserts, explains, suggests, hints

These indicate that the information is **a problem for the source**:

Source admits that . . .
Also: acknowledges, grants, allows

**Verbs for Argued Claims**
These are **neutral**:

Source claims that . . .
Also: argues, reasons, contends, maintains, holds

These indicate that you find the claim **convincing**:

Source proves that . . .
Also: shows, demonstrates, determines

**Verbs for Opinions**
These are **neutral**:

Source thinks that . . .
Also: believes, assumes, insists, declares

These indicate that you find the opinion **weak** or **irresponsible**:

Source wants to think that . . .

Also: wants to believe, just assumes, merely takes for granted

**Verbs for Matters of Judgment**
Source judges that . . .
Also: concludes, infers

## 9.6   Mixing Quotation with Summary and Paraphrase

Although we have explained summary, paraphrase, and quotation as though they were entirely distinct, experienced writers often incorporate quotations into the other two. For example, when you weave a quotation into your own sentence, that sentence usually includes some paraphrase (the paraphrase is underlined):

As Diamond points out, the "lesson for the modern world" in the history of the Fertile Crescent and China is that you can't count on history to repeat itself, because "circumstances change, and past primacy is no guarantee of future primacy" (p. 417).

In his discussion of religion, Posner says of American society that "a notable feature . . . is [its] religious pluralism." He argues that to understand how well social norms control what we do, we should consider "the historical importance of religion as both a source and enforcer of such norms" (p. 299).

Similarly, you can include quotations in a summary:

Turabian's *Student's Guide to Writing College Papers* emphasizes that drafting is "an act of discovery" (p. 95) that can fuel a writer's creative thinking. It acknowledges that some writers have to draft carefully and stick close to their outlines, but it also advises writers to draft as freely and as openly as they can. It encourages even slow and careful drafters to be open to new ideas and surprises and not to be limited by what they do before drafting. It still stresses the value of steady work that follows a plan—for example, writing a little bit every day rather than all at once in a fit of desperate inspiration. But it shows writers how to make the best of a plan while hoping that you will "discover what your storyboard has missed" (p. 95).

When you mix a few quotations into your summaries and paraphrases, you seem a more sophisticated writer. You give readers a better sense of the source without quoting so much that your paper seems a copy-and-paste job. You can also take advantage of those places where your source offers an especially interesting or memorable phrase. If you find that you have drafted a couple of pages that are all summary and paraphrase, go back to your notes to find notable phrases or sentences that you can add to liven up your prose.

9.7    **Interpreting Complex Quotations Before You Offer Them**
By the time you add a quotation to your draft, you may have studied it so much
that you think readers can't miss its relevance. But complex evidence never
speaks for itself, especially not a long quotation, image, table, or chart. So when
you quote a passage that is long, difficult to understand, or written in complex
language, you must speak for it by adding a sentence stating what you want your
readers to get out of it.

You have already seen examples of quotations introduced by an introductory
sentence:

> If there is one thing that America should learn from the past, it's that nothing
> lasts forever. "The histories of the Fertile Crescent and China . . . hold a salutary
> lesson for the modern world: circumstances change, and past primacy is no
> guarantee of future primacy" (Diamond, 417).

Such introductory sentences tell readers how the writer wants them to understand the quotation that follows.

You may need even longer introductions when the relationship between the
quotation and the claim it supports is not obvious. For example, it's hard to see
how the quoted lines in this next passage support the claim:

> When Hamlet comes upon his stepfather Claudius at prayer, he coolly and logi-
> cally thinks about whether to kill him on the spot._claim_
>
> > Now might I do it [kill him] pat, now [while] he is praying:
> > And now I'll do't; and so he goes to heaven;
> > And so am I reveng'd . . .
> > [But this] villain kills my father; and for that,
> > I, his sole son, do this same villain send to heaven.
> > Why, this is hire and salary, not revenge. (3.3)_evidence_

It is not clear how that quotation supports the claim because nothing in it specifically refers to Hamlet's cool logic. In contrast, compare this:

> When Hamlet comes upon his stepfather Claudius praying, he logically analyzes
> whether to kill him on the spot._claim_ His impulse is to do it, but he pauses to re-
> flect: if he kills Claudius at prayer, he will send his soul to heaven. But he wants
> Claudius damned to hell, so he coolly decides to kill him later:_interpretive introduction_
>
> > Now might I do it [kill him] pat, . . . _evidence_

Here we see the connection. And note that this kind of explanatory introduction
is especially important when you present evidence in a table or figure (see 11.3.1).

# 10 Avoiding Plagiarism

## 10.1 Guard Against Inadvertent Plagiarism

It is as you draft that you risk the worst mistake a researcher can make: leading readers to think that you're trying to pass off as your own the work of another writer. Do that and you risk an accusation of plagiarism, a charge that, if sustained, could mean, for a professional writer, a damaged reputation or, for a student writer, a failing grade or even expulsion.

Students know they cheat when they put their name on a paper downloaded from the internet. Most also know they cheat when they pass off as their own long passages copied directly from sources. For those cases, there is nothing to say beyond *Don't*. However, even if you don't mean to cheat, you may still have a problem with plagiarism if you fail to follow the rules for using and citing material from sources. More often than not, a charge of plagiarism is the result of being careless or misinformed, not intentionally dishonest. You risk being accused of plagiarism when you do any of the following:

- You quote, paraphrase, or summarize a source but fail to cite it.
- You use ideas from a source but fail to cite it.
- You use the exact words of a source and you do cite it, but you fail to put those words in quotation marks or a block quotation.
- You paraphrase a source and cite it, but you use words so similar to those of the source that anyone can see that you followed the source word by word.

> **Three Principles for Citing Sources**
> When you use any source in any way, readers expect you to follow three principles. You risk a charge of plagiarism if you ignore any one of them.
>
> 1. You must cite the source for any words, ideas, or methods that are not your own.

Writers can avoid paraphrasing too closely if they focus on remembering what they understand from the original, not its actual words. One way to do this is simply to put the original aside as you write the paraphrase (Turabian, p. 104). But a better way is to imagine that you are explaining the idea to someone who hasn't read the original.

2.  When you quote the exact words of a source, you must put those words in quotation marks or a block quotation, *even if you cite the source in your own text*. This would be plagiarism:

    According to Turabian, when you quote the exact words of a source, you must put those words in quotation marks or a block quotation, *even if you cite the source in your own text* (p. 111).

3.  When you paraphrase the words of a source, you must use your own sentences, not sentences so similar to the original that they are almost a quotation. This would be considered plagiarism by many teachers:

    According to Turabian, you risk being charged with plagiarism when you paraphrase a passage from a source not in your own words but in sentences so similar to it that you almost quote them, regardless of whether your own text cites the source (p. 111).

Some students think that they don't have to cite material found online. Not so. These principles apply to sources of any kind—printed, recorded, oral, and online. You risk a charge of plagiarism if you fail to cite *anything* you get from a source, even if it's from a website, a database, or other online source. A source is a source (see part 2).

## 10.2  Take Good Notes

As noted earlier, in 4.4, it is crucial to take good notes from the beginning. It's easy to lose track of which words are yours and which are from your sources. You cannot follow the rules for using and citing information from a source if you don't have the right information in your notes. So, long before you draft, you have to make sure that your notes do the following:

- Record all bibliographic data for each source.
- Clearly distinguish between your words and those of the source.
- Correctly transcribe each quotation, including punctuation.
- If you paraphrase a passage from a source, avoid paraphrasing too closely.
- Record page numbers for each quotation and paraphrase.

In fact, rather than retyping quotations of more than a few lines, download, copy and paste, or photocopy them, labeling them with the name of the source and keywords for sorting.

## 10.3   Signal Every Quotation, Even When You Cite Its Source

Even if you cite your source, readers must know exactly which words are not yours, even if they are as few as a single line. It gets complicated, however, when you copy less than a line. Read this:

"Because technology begets more technology, the importance of an invention's diffusion potentially exceeds the importance of the original invention. Technology's history exemplifies what is termed an autocatalytic process: that is, one that speeds up at a rate that increases with time, because the process catalyzes itself" (Diamond, p. 301).

To write about Diamond's ideas, you would probably use some of his words, such as *the importance of an invention*. But you wouldn't put that short phrase in quotation marks, because it shows no originality of thought or expression. Two of his phrases, however, are so striking that they do need quotation marks: *technology begets more technology* and *autocatalytic process*. For example:

The power of technology goes beyond individual inventions because "technology begets more technology." It is, as Diamond puts it, an "autocatalytic process" (p. 301).

Once you cite those words, you can use them again without quotation marks or citation:

As one invention begets another and that still another, the process becomes a self-sustaining catalysis that spreads across national boundaries.

This is a gray area: words that seem striking to some are not to others. If you put quotation marks around too many ordinary phrases, readers may think you're naive, but if you fail to use them when readers think you should, they may suspect you of plagiarism. It's better to seem naive than dishonest, especially early in your research career, so use quotation marks freely.

## 10.4   Don't Paraphrase Too Closely

You paraphrase appropriately when you represent an idea in your own words more clearly or pointedly than the source does. But readers will think that you plagiarize if they can match most of your words and phrasing with those of your source.

For example, unlike the paraphrase in 10.3, this one plagiarizes the original:

**Original**

Because technology begets more technology, the importance of an invention's diffusion potentially exceeds the importance of the original invention. Technology's history exemplifies what is termed an autocatalytic process: that is, one that speeds up at a rate that increases with time, because the process catalyzes itself (Diamond, p. 301).

**Paraphrase**

According to Diamond, technology gives birth to more technology. As a result, the importance of the spread of an invention may exceed the importance of the invention itself. The history of technology shows what is called an autocatalytic process through which the invention of new technologies speeds up at an increasing rate because the process of change catalyzes itself (p. 301).

The writer of this version may think that she has used her own words: she changes some of Diamond's complex phrases into simpler ones: *begets → gives birth, diffusion → spread, exemplifies → shows*. But the paraphrase follows the original step by step, word by word. That, for most readers, is plagiarism.

---

QUICK TIP

**Safe Paraphrasing**
To avoid unintentionally seeming to be guilty of plagiarism by paraphrase, don't read your source as you paraphrase it. Read the passage, look away, think about it for a moment. *Then, still looking away*, restate it in your own words. Then check whether you can run your finger along your sentence and find the same ideas in the same order as in your source. If you can, so can your readers. Try again.

---

10.5    **(Almost Always) Cite a Source for Ideas Not Your Own**

The basic principle is simple: cite a source for a borrowed idea whenever your readers might think you are claiming that you are its original source. But when you try to apply it, the rule becomes more complicated, because most of our own ideas come from some identifiable sources somewhere in history. Readers don't expect you to find and cite every distant source for every familiar idea. But they do expect you to cite the source for an idea when (1) the idea is associated with a specific person *and* (2) it's new enough not to be part of a field's common knowledge.

For example, psychologists understand that the brain has different functional areas, that it isn't just an undifferentiated lump of gray matter. But no one would expect you to cite the source of that idea, because it's so familiar to psychologists that no reader would think you were taking credit for originating that idea. On the other hand, some psychologists argue that emotions are crucial to rational decision making. You would have to cite the source of that idea because it is fairly new and so closely tied to particular researchers.

QUICK TIP

**When to Cite Ideas**

If you are a new researcher, you have a problem: you can't cite every borrowed idea, but how are you supposed to know which ideas are too familiar to cite? Here are some signs to look for:

· If an idea is a main claim in the source, you should cite it.
· If the source spends time showing how the idea differs from the ideas of others, you should cite it.
· If the source cites an idea, you should too.
· If more than one source uses the idea without citing it, then you don't have to cite it either.

## 10.6    Don't Plead Ignorance, Misunderstanding, or Innocent Intentions

To be sure, what looks like plagiarism is often just ignorance of how to use and cite sources. In those cases, students defend themselves by claiming they didn't *intend* to mislead. The problem is, we read words, not minds. So think of plagiarism not as an act you intend but as one that others *perceive*. Avoid any sign that might give your readers a reason to suspect you of it. Whenever you put your name on a paper, you implicitly promise that you wrote every word that you don't clearly and specifically attribute to someone else.

Here is how to think about this: if someone read your paper immediately after reading your source written by Johnson, would she think, *This sounds just like Johnson* or *I remember these words* or *This idea must have come from Johnson*? If so, you must cite Johnson and set off any sequence of his exact words in quotation marks or a block quotation.

## 10.7    Guard Against Inappropriate Assistance

Before experienced writers turn in their work, they often show drafts to others for criticism and suggestions, and you should too. But teachers differ on how much help is appropriate and what help you should acknowledge. Most teachers encourage students to get general criticism and minor editing, but not detailed rewriting or substantive suggestions. You usually aren't required to acknowledge general criticism, minor editing, or help from a school writing tutor, but you must acknowledge help that's special or extensive. Your teacher, however, sets the rules, so ask.

# 11 Using Tables and Figures

Early in your development as a researcher, you are unlikely to be required to collect and report large sets of numerical data. But if you do include numbers in your paper, your readers will grasp the data most easily if you present them graphically rather than in words. You can present numbers in various graphic forms, but some forms will suit your data and message better than others.

To be sure, papers very often include graphics that are not intended to present quantitative data: photographs of historical events, images of works of art, and so on. But we concentrate in this chapter on tables, graphs, and charts because those are what you must construct for yourself. We show you how to choose the right graphic and to design it so that readers can see both what your data are and how they support your argument.

---

**A NOTE ON TERMINOLOGY**

We use the term *graphics* to name all visual images offered as evidence. Traditionally, graphics are divided into *tables* and *figures*.

- A table is a grid with columns and rows that present data in numbers or words organized by categories.
- Figures are all other graphic forms, including graphs, charts, photographs, drawings, and diagrams.

Figures that present quantitative data are divided into *charts* and *graphs*:

- Charts typically consist of bars, circles, points, or other shapes.
- Graphs typically consist of continuous lines.

---

## 11.1    Choose Verbal or Visual Representations

Few new researchers work with the kinds of data that are best presented graphically. So chances are that you can present your data in sentences rather than in tables or charts. Readers can understand numbers like these without the help of graphics:

In 2015, on average, men earned $50,033 a year, women, $39,157—a difference of $10,876.

You usually need graphics when readers have to deal with more than five or six numbers, particularly if they have to compare them. For example, most readers would struggle to see the important relationships among the numbers in a passage like this:

Between 1970 and 2010, the structure of families changed in two ways. In 1970, 85 percent of families had two parents, but in 1980 that number declined to 77 percent, then to 73 percent in 1990, to 68 percent in 2000, and to 64 percent in 2010. The number of one-parent families rose, particularly families headed by a mother. In 1970, 11 percent of families were headed by a single mother. In 1980, that number rose to 18 percent, in 1990 to 22 percent, to 23 percent in 2000, and to 27 percent in 2010. There were some marginal changes among single fathers (headed 1 percent of the families in 1970, 2 percent in 1980, 3 percent in 1990, and 4 percent in 2000 and 2010). Families headed by no adult have remained stable at 3–4 percent.

Such data are best presented graphically.

Generally our advice is to avoid graphics and stick to words, at least at first. You have enough to keep in mind in learning how to get the words right. But if you do have to present data too complex for words, this chapter will show you how.

11.2    **Choose the Most Effective Graphic**
When you graphically present data as complex as that in the paragraph above, you can choose a table, a bar chart, or a line graph. Each communicates something different to readers.

A **table** seems precise and objective. It emphasizes individual numbers and forces readers to figure out relationships or trends (unless you state them in an introductory sentence):

**Table 11.1. Changes in family structure, 1970–2010**

| Family type | Percentage of total families | | | | |
| --- | --- | --- | --- | --- | --- |
|  | 1970 | 1980 | 1990 | 2000 | 2010 |
| 2 parents | 85 | 77 | 73 | 68 | 64 |
| Mother | 11 | 18 | 22 | 23 | 27 |
| Father | 1 | 2 | 3 | 4 | 4 |
| No adult | 3 | 4 | 3 | 4 | 4 |

**Charts** and **line graphs** communicate specific values less precisely than a table, but their images communicate their message quickly and with greater impact. They also have different effects:

- A bar chart emphasizes comparisons among discrete items that can be seen at a glance.

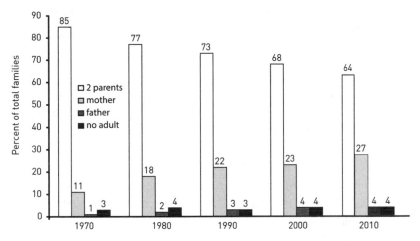

**Figure 11.1. Changes in family structure, 1970–2010**

- A line graph emphasizes the story of trends over time.

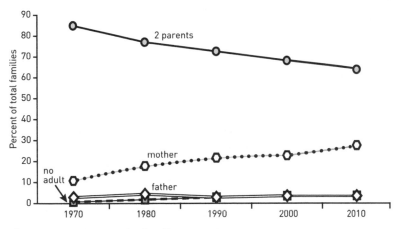

**Figure 11.2. Changes in family structure, 1970–2010**

Decide on the effect you want, then choose the graphic that fits. Do not choose the first form that comes to mind or the one you found in your source.

---

CAUTION

**Your Software Likes Your Graphics Fancy, Your Readers Like Them Simple**
Your computer software will encourage you to use many more graphics than we cover here, but stick to the basics. Unless you have *lots* of experience creating graphics, limit your choices to tables, bar charts, and line graphs.

Even if you have experience, avoid most of the choices your software allows: no merely decorative colors, no 3-D graphics, no fancy graphics when a simple one will do. Graphics that look dazzling but confuse or distract readers will not improve your paper.

## 11.3   Design Tables and Figures

You use graphics to present quantitative data that serve as evidence in support of your reasons. So you must design them to communicate two things: what the data are and how they support your reason.

## 11.3.1   Tell Readers What Your Graphic Shows

A graphic representing complex numbers rarely speaks for itself. You must introduce and label it so that readers know both what to see in it and how it is relevant to your argument.

For example, readers have to study table 11.2 closely to see how it supports its claim:

Most predictions about gasoline consumption have proved wrong.*claim*

**Table 11.2. Gasoline consumption**

|  | 1970 | 1980 | 1990 | 2000 | 2010 |
|---|---|---|---|---|---|
| Annual miles (000) | 9.5 | 10.3 | 10.5 | 11.7 | 12.2 |
| Annual consumption (gal.) | 760 | 760 | 520 | 533 | 515 |

To see the connection, we need a more specific claim, a table title that better identifies what the numbers represent, highlighting that draws our eye to the most important data, *and* another sentence that explains how the numbers relate to the claim:

Gasoline consumption did not grow as many had predicted.*claim* **Even though Americans drove 28 percent more miles in 2010 than in 1970, they used 32 percent less fuel.**

**Table 11.3. Per capita mileage and gasoline consumption, 1970–2010**

|  | 1970 | 1980 | 1990 | 2000 | 2010 |
|---|---|---|---|---|---|
| Annual miles (000) | 9.5 | 10.3 | 10.5 | 11.7 | 12.2 |
| (% change vs. 1970) |  | 8.4% | 10.5% | 23.1% | 28.4% |
| Annual consumption (gal.) | 760 | 760 | 520 | 533 | 515 |
| (% change vs. 1970) |  |  | (31.5%) | (31.6%) | (32.2%) |

That added information tells readers how to interpret the key data in table 11.3.

### How to Set Up a Graphic

1.  Introduce each table or figure with a sentence that states how the data support your point. Include in that sentence any specific number that you want readers to focus on. (That number must also appear in the table or figure, visually highlighted if possible.)
2.  Label every table and figure in a way that describes its data.
    *   For a table, the label is called a *title* and is set flush left above.
    *   For a figure, the label is called a *caption* and is set flush left below.

Keep titles and captions short but descriptive enough to indicate exactly what the data represent and to differentiate each graphic from every other one. Do not use the title or caption to imply a claim about the figure:

> NOT   Weaker effects of counseling on depressed children before professionalization of staff, 1995–2015

> BUT   Effect of counseling on depressed children, 1995–2015

3.  Put into a table or figure information that helps readers see how the data support your point. For example, if numbers in a table show a trend and the size of the change matters, add the change to the final column. Or if a line on a graph changes in response to an influence not mentioned on the graph, add text to the image to explain it.

All of the framing elements work to make figure 11.3 easy to understand: (1) the introductory sentence (see next page) explains what the graph shows and points out not only the trend but what readers should see in it; (2) the label tells readers what the data represent; and (3) the inserted callouts explain the important changes in the data.

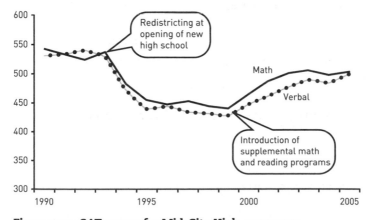

**Figure 11.3. SAT scores for Mid-City High, 1990–2005**

Although reading and math scores initially declined by almost 100 points following redistricting, that trend was substantially reversed by the introduction of supplemental math and reading programs.

## 11.3.2  Keep All Graphics as Simple as Their Content Allows

Some guides encourage you to put as much data as you can into a graphic. But readers want to see only the data relevant to your point, free of distractions. As a new researcher, you can let your software take care of most of the effort in designing your graphics, but you'll have to change several default settings. Follow these guidelines.

**For all graphics:**

- Box a graphic only if you group two or more figures.
- Use caution in employing shading or color to convey meaning. Even if you print your paper on a color printer or submit it as a PDF, shading and color may not reproduce well.
- Plot data on three dimensions only when you cannot display the data in any other way. The added depth can distort how readers judge those data.

**For tables:**

- Never use both horizontal and vertical lines to divide columns and rows. Use light gray lines if you want to direct your reader's eyes in one direction to compare data or if the table is unusually complex.
- For tables with many rows, lightly shading every fifth row (or even every other row) will improve legibility.
- Clearly label rows and columns.
- Order rows and columns by a principle that lets readers quickly find what you want them to see. Do not automatically choose alphabetic order.
- Round numbers to relevant values. If differences of less than 1,000 don't matter, then 2,123,499 and 2,124,886 are irrelevantly precise.
- Sum totals at the bottom of a column or at the end of a row, not at the top or left.

Compare tables 11.4 and 11.5. Table 11.4 looks cluttered and its items aren't helpfully organized:

**Table 11.4. Unemployment in major industrial nations, 2000–2015**

|  | 2000 | 2015 | Change |
|---|---|---|---|
| Australia | 5.2 | 6.2 | 1.0 |
| Canada | 8.0 | 6.9 | (1.1) |
| France | 9.7 | 10.7 | 1.0 |
| Germany | 7.1 | 5.2 | (1.9) |
| Italy | 8.4 | 11.9 | 3.5 |
| Japan | 5.0 | 3.9 | (1.1) |
| Sweden | 8.6 | 7.7 | (0.9) |
| United Kingdom | 7.9 | 6.6 | (1.3) |
| United States | 9.6 | 6.2 | (3.4) |

In contrast, table 11.5 is clearer because its title is more informative, the table has less distracting visual clutter, and its items are sorted to let us see relationships in the data more easily.

**Table 11.5. Changes in unemployment rates of industrial nations, 2000–2015**

|  | 2000 | 2015 | Change |
|---|---|---|---|
| United States | 9.6 | 6.2 | (3.4) |
| Germany | 7.1 | 5.2 | (1.9) |
| United Kingdom | 7.9 | 6.6 | (1.3) |
| Canada | 8.0 | 6.9 | (1.1) |
| Japan | 5.0 | 3.9 | (1.1) |
| Sweden | 8.6 | 7.7 | (0.9) |
| Australia | 5.2 | 6.2 | 1.0 |
| France | 9.7 | 10.7 | 1.0 |
| Italy | 8.4 | 11.9 | 3.5 |

### For bar charts

Because bar charts communicate as much by visual impact as by specific numbers, whenever possible, group and arrange bars to create an image that matches your point.

- Do not use grid lines unless the graphic is complex. Make all grid lines light gray.
- When specific numbers matter, add them to bars or segments.
- Clearly label both axes.
- Color or shade bars only to show a contrast.
- Never use three-dimensional or iconic bars (for example, images of cars to represent automobile production). They add nothing, distort how readers judge values, and look amateurish.
- Group and arrange bars to give readers an image of an order that matches your point.

For example, look at figure 11.4 in the context of the explanatory sentence before it. The items are listed alphabetically, an order that doesn't help readers see the point.

Most of the desert area in the world is concentrated in North Africa and the Middle East.

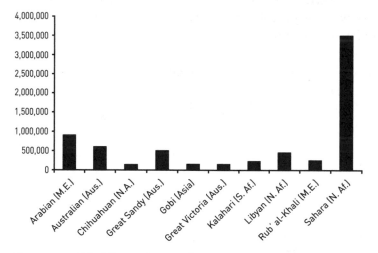

**Figure 11.4. World's ten largest deserts**

In contrast, figure 11.5 supports the claim with a coherent image.

Most of the desert area in the world is concentrated in North Africa and the Middle East.

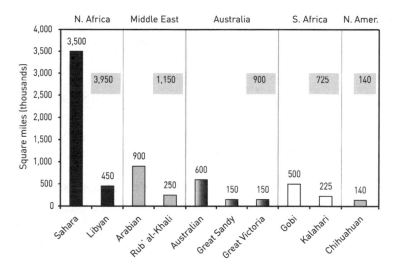

**Figure 11.5. World distribution of large deserts**

---

<br>

> **CAUTION**
>
> **Avoid Pie Charts**
> Most data that fit a bar chart can also be represented in a pie chart. It is a popular choice in magazines, tabloids, and annual reports, but it's harder to read than a bar chart, and it invites misinterpretation because readers must mentally compare proportions of segments whose size is hard to judge accurately. Most researchers consider them amateurish. Use bar charts instead.

**For line graphs:**
Because a line graph emphasizes trends, readers must see a clear image to interpret it correctly. Do the following:

- Use grid lines only if the graphic is complex. Make all grid lines light gray.
- If you plot fewer than ten or so values (called *data points*), indicate each with a dot. If those values are relevant, add numbers above the dots to show their value.
- Choose the variable that makes the line go in the direction, up or down, that supports your point. If the good news is a reduction (down) in high school dropouts, you can more effectively represent the same data as an increase in retention (up). If you want to emphasize bad news, find a way to represent your data as a falling line.
- Plot more than six lines on one graph only if you cannot make your point in any other way.

**Table 11.6. Common graphic forms and their uses**

| | Data | Rhetorical uses |
|---|---|---|
| **Bar chart** | | |
| 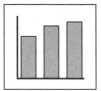 | Compares the value of one variable across a series of items called *cases* (e.g., average salaries for service worker$_{variable}$ in six companies$_{cases}$). | Creates strong visual contrasts among individual cases, emphasizing comparisons. For specific values, add numbers to bars. Can show ranks or trends. Vertical bars (called *columns*) are most common, but bars can be horizontal if cases are numerous or have complex labels. |
| **Bar chart, grouped or split** | | |
| 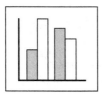 | Compares the value of one variable, divided into subsets, across a series of cases (e.g., average salaries$_{variable}$ for men and women service workers$_{subsets}$ in six companies$_{cases}$). | Contrasts subsets within and across individual cases; not useful for comparing total values for cases. For specific values, add numbers to bars. Grouped bars show ranking or trends poorly; useful for time series only if trends are unimportant. |
| **Bar chart, stacked** | | |
| 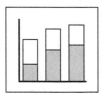 | Compares the value of one variable, divided into two or more subsets, across a series of cases (e.g., harassment complaints$_{variable}$ segmented by region$_{subsets}$ in six industries$_{cases}$). | Best for comparing totals across cases and subsets *within* cases; difficult to compare subsets *across* cases (use grouped bars). For specific values, add numbers to bars and segments. Useful for time series. Can show ranks or trends for total values only. |

**Table 11.6 (continued)**

|  | Data | Rhetorical uses |
|---|---|---|
| **Histogram** | | |
|  | Compares two variables, with one segmented into ranges that function like the cases in a bar graph (e.g., service workers$_{continuous}$ whose salary is $0–5,000, $5,000–10,000, $10,000–15,000, etc.$_{segmented\ variable}$). | Best for comparing segments within continuous data sets. Shows trends but emphasizes segments (e.g., a sudden spike at $5,000–10,000 representing part-time workers). For specific values, add numbers to bars. |
| **Image chart** | | |
| 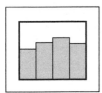 | Shows value of one or more variables for cases displayed on a map, diagram, or other image (e.g., states$_{cases}$ colored red or blue to show voting patterns$_{variable}$). | Shows the distribution of the data in relation to preexisting categories; deemphasizes specific values. Best when the image is familiar, as in a map or diagram of a process. |
| **Pie chart** | | |
| 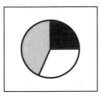 | Shows the proportion of a single variable for a series of cases (e.g., the budget share$_{variable}$ of US cabinet departments$_{cases}$). | Best for comparing one segment to the whole. Useful only with few segments or segments that are very different in size; otherwise comparisons among segments are difficult. For specific values, add numbers to segments. Common in popular venues, frowned on by professionals. |
| **Line graph** | | |
| 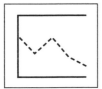 | Compares continuous variables for one or more cases (e.g., temperature$_{variable}$ and viscosity$_{variable}$ in two fluids$_{cases}$). | Best for showing trends; deemphasizes specific values. Useful for time series. To show specific values, add numbers to data points. To show the significance of a trend, segment the grid (e.g., below or above average performance). |

**Table 11.6 (continued)**

|  | Data | Rhetorical uses |
|---|---|---|
| **Area chart** | | |
| 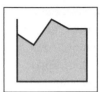 | Compares two continuous variables for one or more cases (e.g., reading test scores$_{variable}$ over time$_{variable}$ in a school district$_{case}$). | Shows trends; deemphasizes specific values. Can be used for time series. To show specific values, add numbers to data points. Areas below the lines add no information and will lead some readers to misjudge values. Confusing with multiple lines/areas. |
| **Area chart, stacked** | | |
| 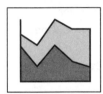 | Compares two continuous variables for two or more cases (e.g., profit$_{variable}$ over time$_{variable}$ for several products$_{cases}$). | Shows the trend for the total of all cases, plus how much each case contributes to that total. Likely to mislead readers on the value or the trend for any individual case. |
| **Scatterplot** | | |
|  | Compares two variables at multiple data points for a single case (e.g., housing sales$_{variable}$ and distance from downtown$_{variable}$ in one city$_{case}$) or at one data point for multiple cases (e.g., brand loyalty$_{variable}$ and repair frequency$_{variable}$ for ten manufacturers$_{cases}$). | Best for showing the distribution of data, especially when there is no clear trend or when the focus is on outlying data points. If only a few data points are plotted, it allows a focus on individual values. |

**Table 11.6 (continued)**

| | Data | Rhetorical uses |
|---|---|---|
| **Bubble chart** | | |

Compares three variables at multiple data points for a single case (e.g., housing sales,$_{variable}$ distance from downtown,$_{variable}$ and prices$_{variable}$ in one city$_{case}$) or at one data point for multiple cases (e.g., image advertising,$_{variable}$ repair frequency,$_{variable}$ and brand loyalty$_{variable}$ for ten manufacturers$_{cases}$).

Emphasizes the relationship between the third variable (bubbles) and the first two; most useful when the question is whether the third variable is a product of the others. Readers easily misjudge relative values shown by bubbles; adding numbers mitigates that problem.

---

QUICK TIP

**Try Out Different Graphics**

If you are new to using graphics, all of these rules and principles can make your choice of graphics confusing. You can cut through that confusion if you try out several ways to represent the same data (your software will usually let you do that quickly). Then ask someone unfamiliar with the data to tell you what they see in each graphic. You might also ask them to judge the alternatives for impact and clarity.

## 11.4    Communicate Data Ethically

Your graphics must be not only clear and accurate but also honest. Do not distort the image of your data to make a point. For example, the two bar charts in figure 11.6 display identical data yet send different messages. The 0–100 scale in the figure on the left creates a fairly flat slope, which makes the drop in pollution seem small. The vertical scale in the figure on the right, however, begins not at 0 but at 80. When a scale is truncated, its sharper slope exaggerates small contrasts.

Graphs can also mislead when the image encourages readers to misjudge values. The two charts in figure 11.7 represent exactly the same data but seem to communicate different messages. These "stacked area" charts represent differences in values not by the *angles* of the lines but by the areas *between* them. In both charts, the bands for south, east, and west are roughly the same width throughout, indicating little change in the values they represent. The band for the north, however, widens sharply, representing a large increase in the value it

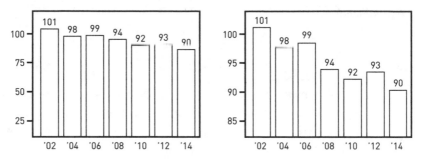

**Figure 11.6. Capitol City pollution index, 2002–2014**

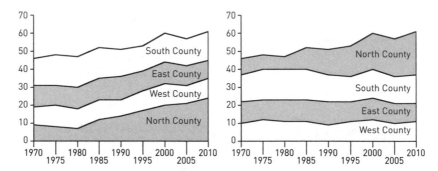

**Figure 11.7. Representation of collar counties among State U. undergraduates (percentage of total)**

represents. In the chart on the left, readers are likely to misjudge the top three bands because they are on top of the rising north band, making those bands seem to rise as well. In the chart on the right, on the other hand, those three bands do not rise because they are on the bottom. Here only the band for the north rises.

Here are four guidelines for avoiding visual misrepresentations:

- Do not manipulate a scale to magnify or reduce a contrast.
- Do not use a figure whose image distorts values.
- Do not make a table or figure unnecessarily complex or misleadingly simple.
- If the table or figure supports a point, state it.

# 12  Organizing Your Paper

Some students think that once they have a draft, they're done. But experienced writers know better. They write a *first* (not necessarily a *rough*) draft to see whether they can make a case to support their answer to their question. Then they revise their draft one or more times until they think they've made that case in a way that meets the needs and expectations of their readers.

That's hard, because we all know our own work too well to read it as others will. To revise effectively, you cannot simply read a draft to see whether it satisfies you. You must know what readers look for and whether your draft helps them find it. To that end, we will give you advice that may seem mechanical. But only when you can analyze your draft objectively can you avoid reading into it what you want your readers to get out of it.

In this chapter we offer advice on *organizing* your paper, now that you have a first draft. We focus here on overall structure, especially the "outer frame" of an introduction and a conclusion. In the next three chapters we focus on *revising* your paper: first revising those crucial introductory and concluding sections (chap. 13), then revising overall, moving from global to local concerns (chap. 14), and finally revising sentences (chap. 15). For guidance on the distinct stage of *editing* your paper, including addressing matters of spelling, punctuation, and the like, see part 3.

Of course no one revises so neatly. All of us fiddle with words as we move paragraphs around and with sentences as we reorganize whole sections. But you're likely to revise best if you revise from whole to part. That's why, before you begin to *fix* anything, you must step back to review the organization of your draft.

## 12.1    Review Your Paper as a Whole

Often the act of drafting takes you in unanticipated directions. As you go from section to section, it's easy to veer off script. Of course, this is not a bad thing. It's *supposed* to happen. As we urge in chapter 8, be open to new discoveries while you draft. You might find new evidence or better reasons to support your claim. You might even discover a need to modify your initial claim in light of efforts to support it. Before you can revise, however, you must review your paper to see what you've actually written, not what you *think* you've written. Almost always you'll be surprised, perhaps even pleasantly, by what you find.

### 12.1.1   Check for Blind Spots in Your Argument

Completing a draft is an accomplishment, but don't move immediately to fine-tuning sentences. After the first draft, parts of your argument will likely still not stand up to a robust challenge. If you spend a lot of time polishing sentences, it can be hard to later accept that whole sections need to be rearranged or even cut. Instead, check your argument's reasoning. Have you considered the strongest relevant counterarguments? Have you looked for evidence that challenges or complicates your reasons? Have you considered alternative interpretations of your evidence? If not, now is the time.

If you find it difficult to think of significant alternatives to your argument now that you have completed a draft, talk with your teacher about where your argument overlooks likely objections. In many cases, this is the time in the process in which you will benefit from a visit to your school's writing center. Consider making an appointment to meet with a writing consultant to review your draft and sketch out a plan for revision.

### 12.1.2   Check Your Introduction, Conclusion, and Claim

Your readers must see three things quickly and unambiguously:

- where your introduction ends
- where your conclusion begins
- what sentences in one or both state your main claim

To make the first two clearly visible, insert a subhead or extra space between your introduction and body and another between the body and conclusion. To make your main claim clear, underline it. We'll come back to it in chapter 13.

### 12.1.3   Make Sure the Body of Your Paper Is Coherent

Once you frame your paper clearly, check its body. Readers will think your paper is coherent when they see the following:

- the key terms that run through your whole paper
- where each section ends and the next begins
- how each section relates to the one before it
- what role each section plays in the whole
- what sentence in each section and subsection states its point
- what distinctive key terms run through each section

To be sure that your readers see those features, check for the following:

1.  Did you repeat key terms through your whole paper?

    If readers don't see key terms on each page, they may think your paper wanders (review 7.3.3, 7.3.4, and 8.5). If you can't find them, neither will your readers.

    - Circle the key terms in the claim in your introduction and in your conclusion.
    - Circle those same terms in the body of your paper.
    - Underline other words related to the ideas named by those circled terms.

    Revise by working those terms into parts that lack them. If you underlined many more words than you circled, change some of them to the circled key terms. If you don't find on every page three or four terms either underlined or circled, you may have strayed too far from your line of reasoning. If so, you have more extensive revising to do.

2.  Did you clearly signal the beginning of each section and subsection?

    If your paper is longer than three or four pages, it will have distinct sections. Even if each section is only two or three paragraphs long, readers must clearly see where one ends and the next begins. For a longer paper, you can use sub-heads or an extra space to signal new sections.

3.  Did you begin each major section with words that signal how that section relates to the one before it?

    Readers must not only recognize where a section begins and ends but also understand why it is where it is (see 7.3.5). Be sure that you signaled the logic of your order with words such as *First, Second, More important, The next issue,* or *Some have objected that.*

4.  Did you make clear how each section is relevant to the whole?

    For each section, ask: *What question does this section answer?* If a section doesn't help answer one of the questions of argument (review 6.2), ask whether it is relevant. Does it create a context, explain a background concept or issue, or help readers in some other way? If you can't explain how a section relates to your claim, cut it.

5.  Did you state the point of each section at the end of a brief opening (or at the end of the section)?

If you have a choice, state the point of a section at the end of its opening. Under no circumstances bury the point of a section in its middle. If a section is longer than three or four pages, you might restate the point at its end.

6.  Did you distinguish each section by running key terms through it?

    Just as some key terms unify your whole paper, other key terms unify its sections. To find those terms, repeat step 1 for each section. Find the sentence that expresses its point, and identify the key terms that distinguish that section from the others. Then check whether those terms run through that section. If you find none, then your readers might not see what distinct ideas that section contributes to the whole. (You can use those key terms in headings.)

## 12.1.4    Check Your Paragraphs

Each paragraph should be relevant to the point of its section. And like sections, each paragraph should have a sentence or two introducing it, usually stating its point and including the key concepts that the rest of the paragraph develops. If the opening sentence or sentences of a paragraph do not state its point, then its last one must. Order your sentences by some principle and make them relevant to the point of the paragraph.

## 12.2    Let Your Draft Cool, Then Paraphrase It

If you start your project early, you'll have time to let your revised draft cool. What seems good one day often looks different the next. When you return to your draft, don't read it straight through. Skim its top-level parts: its introduction, the first paragraph of each major section, and its conclusion. Then, based on what you have read, paraphrase it for someone who hasn't read it. Does the paraphrase hang together? Does it fairly sum up your argument? Even better, ask someone else to read and summarize it: how well that person summarizes your paper will predict how well your readers will understand it.

Finally, be receptive to feedback, especially from more experienced researchers and your teacher or advisor. You don't have to follow every suggestion, but you should consider each carefully. In chapter 16 we tell you how to get the most out of comments on your writing.

Once you've taken these steps to test the organization of your paper and to see what opportunities exist to clarify or strengthen your argument, you are able to turn to the task of revising your paper.

# 13 Writing Your Introduction and Conclusion

Once you have a complete draft and can see what you have in fact written, you can write your final introduction and conclusion. These two parts of your paper strongly influence how readers read and remember the rest, so it's worth your time to make them as clear as you can.

Your introduction has three goals. It should

- put your research in context;
- make your readers think they should read your paper; and
- give them a framework for understanding it.

Most introductions are about 10 percent of the whole. In shorter papers, they may be a single paragraph. In longer papers, they can run to several paragraphs.

Your conclusion has two goals. It should

- leave readers with a clear idea of your claim; and
- reinforce its importance.

Conclusions are typically shorter than introductions; they too may be one or more paragraphs.

## 13.1    Draft Your Final Introduction

In chapter 7 we suggested that you sketch a working introduction with four steps:

1. **Current situation or background.** When this summarizes research, it's called a *literature review*. It puts your project in the context of what is known and thought about your topic and sets up the next step.
2. **A statement of your research question.** This states what isn't known or understood that your paper will answer. It typically begins with *but, however,* or another word signaling a qualification.
3. **The significance of your question.** This answers *So what?* It is key to motivating your readers.
4. **Your claim as an answer.** This answers your research question.

As a way to prepare readers for the rest of your paper, these steps follow a seemingly natural progression:

> Here's what we think we know.
> Here's what we don't know.
> Here's why we need an answer.
> Here's the answer.

But those steps follow another pattern, one that is common not just in research papers but in all types of writing—term papers, essays, business documents, and many others. In most academic and professional writing, the pattern that introductions follow is a familiar dramatic one: stability—disruption and danger—resolution. It's a pattern we learned as toddlers, in the form of fairy tales:

**Once upon a time . . .** Fairy tales begin by "defining a world" so that we know what to expect. When we see Little Red Riding Hood walking through the forest, we know not to expect dragons, and we are not surprised when a woodsman shows up. When we learn in another tale that a wise old king has a beautiful daughter but no sons, we don't look for a fairy godmother but do expect to see knights (and maybe a dragon).

**But then . . .** Once we learn about that stable world, the next step is always trouble—a wolf, a talking fish, an evil stepmother, or one of those dragons.

**And now the dragon's fire . . .** The main body of a fairy tale is, of course, a story of peril for the main character. Here is where the wolf bares his teeth or the dragon shows his fire. It's the dragon's fire that makes him a problem that must be solved.

**And they lived happily ever after.** In the end, all is well. But that happy ending is brought about not through the efforts of the main character but through the work of a helper with special powers: the burly woodsman, a fairy godmother, the valiant knight.

Each move in the fairy tale has a corresponding part in the basic pattern of introductions, and so does each character. The main character is your reader.

The dragon is your research question: it disrupts the stable world you describe in the opening. The dragon's fire is the significance of your question: it shows why that question is a problem by showing readers what they lose by not knowing its answer. The helper with special powers? That's you. Once you show readers that they need an answer to your question, you save the day by offering one.

> **The Dramatic Pattern of Introductions and Fairy Tales**
>
> The typical introduction to a research paper draws some of its ability to motivate readers from the dramatic pattern it shares with fairy tales:
>
> 1. Current Situation / *Once upon a time . . .*
>
>    The fairy tale defines a stable world that it will disrupt; the research paper defines a current way of thinking that it will show to be wrong, or at least inadequate.
>
> 2. Research Question / *But then . . .*
>
>    The fairy tale disrupts its world with a problem creature; the research paper disrupts the current way of thinking with a problem question.
>
> 3. Significance of the Question / *And now the dragon's fire . . .*
>
>    The fairy tale puts its main character in danger; the research paper shows its readers what they will lose without an answer to its question.
>
> 4. Answer / *And they lived happily ever after.*
>
>    In the fairy tale, a helper with special powers steps in to remove the danger, thereby saving the day; in the research paper, the writer with special knowledge (learned from research) steps in to answer the question, thereby saving the day.

You can see how the pattern works in this abbreviated introduction (each sentence could be expanded to a paragraph or more):

Everyone knows that using a cellphone while driving greatly increases the likelihood of a crash. That is because we have all been subjected to years of public-interest informational campaigns intended to make us aware of this behavior's risks and potential consequences.<sub>situation</sub> However, no one has determined why drivers persist in this behavior despite the constant warnings against it: a failure to understand the messaging, personality traits that incline certain people to discount the risks, social influences, or some other factor. <sub>question</sub> If we can determine why some drivers seem to ignore the dangers of cellphone use while driving, we can better understand not only this specific behavior but also the nature of risk-taking in general.<sub>significance</sub> This study compares the self-reported cellphone use of forty-five young-adult drivers to their actual use as documented by a tracking app. Our research suggests that even when drivers are aware of the danger of cellphone use while driving and take it seriously, they may be unaware of the extent to which they habitually engage in this practice.*answer*

Whether they are conscious of it or not, readers look for those four elements, so you should understand them in some detail.

### 13.1.1   Describe the Current Situation

As a rule, writers begin with the ideas that their own work will extend, modify, or correct. For the kind of projects most beginners undertake, the current situation can be described in a few sentences:

Everyone knows that using a cellphone while driving greatly increases the likelihood of a crash. That is because we have all been subjected to years of public-interest informational campaigns intended to make us aware of this behavior's risks and potential consequences. Which of us can't recall seeing at least one advertisement or billboard warning of the dangers of texting and driving? To offer just one statistic, . . .

When advanced students write a paper for other researchers, this opening describes more fully a line of research studies that the paper will extend or modify.

Zhang and Constantine (2013) have demonstrated that public-service announcements about distracted driving have succeeded in fostering a broad awareness of the seriousness of this issue. More recently, Jackson (2016) examined the degree to which this awareness affects the behavior of drivers in different age groups, showing that . . .

Some advanced researchers go on like that for pages, citing scores of books, reports, and articles.

---

QUICK TIP

**Two Alternatives to the Literature Review**

Early in your career, you may not feel confident writing a review of the prior research on your topic. But you have two easy alternatives.

1.  Use one source as your prior research.

    If you have found one source that can set up your research question, use it as your current situation. You might copy one of the patterns in section 2.5.

2.  Use *your* prior understanding.

> Imagine your reader as someone like yourself *before* you started your research. Make your current situation what you thought then. This is where you can use a working hypothesis that you rejected: *It might seem that X is so, but* . . .

No one expects a beginner to provide an extensive review of the prior research. But you do have to define *some* stable context, a way of thinking about your issue that your research question will disrupt, improve, or amplify. The four most common sources of this context are these:

- what you believed before you began your research (*I used to think* . . .)
- what others believe (*Most people think* . . .)
- an event or situation (*What events seem to show is* . . .)
- what other researchers have found (*Researchers have shown* . . .)

You have other options. If you find a good one in your reading, use it. But these four are reliable ways to get your paper started.

---

**WRITING IN GROUPS**

**Use Your Colleagues' Misunderstandings**

If you cannot think of any reasonable stable context to lay out as your current situation, turn to your writing group. Ask them what they think of your topic: *Why do you think drivers persist in using cellphones while driving?* If their answer is wrong or misleading, that is the current thinking your paper will correct: "Many drivers think that . . . , but . . ."

---

### 13.1.2  Restate Your Question as Something Not Known or Fully Understood

After establishing the context, state what is wrong or missing in that current way of thinking. Introduce that statement with *but*, *however*, or some other term indicating that you're about to modify the received knowledge and understanding that you just described:

Everyone knows that using a cellphone while driving greatly increases the likelihood of a crash . . . <sub>situation</sub> **However,** no one has determined why drivers persist in this behavior despite the constant warnings against it: a failure to understand the messaging, personality traits that incline certain people to discount the risks, social influences, or some other factor.<sub>question</sub>

Although you must build your paper around a research *question*, you should state it not as a direct question—*Why do drivers use cellphones while driving despite the warnings?*—but as an assertion that we don't know something: *We don't know why people use cellphones while driving despite the warnings.*

### 13.1.3   State the Significance of Your Question

Now you must show your readers the *significance* of answering your research question. Imagine a reader asking *So what?*, and then answer it. Frame your response as the consequence of not knowing the answer to your research question, as the answer to *So what?*

> Everyone knows that using a cellphone while driving greatly increases the likelihood of a crash . . . <sub>situation</sub> However, no one has determined why . . . <sub>question</sub> [*So what?*] If we can determine why some drivers seem to ignore the dangers of cellphone use while driving, we can better understand not only this specific behavior but also the nature of risk-taking in general. <sub>significance</sub>

Especially if you are addressing a practical problem (see 2.3.1), you should consider phrasing your significance negatively, not as a benefit but as a cost:

> [*So what?*] Unless we can better understand why some drivers seem to ignore the dangers of cellphone use while driving, we will be unable to intervene effectively to curtail this destructive behavior. <sub>significance</sub>

Alternatively, you can phrase the significance as a benefit:

> [*So what?*] If we can better understand why some drivers seem to ignore the dangers of cellphone use while driving, we will be able to intervene more effectively to curtail this destructive behavior. <sub>significance</sub>

You may struggle to answer that *So what?* because you don't know enough about the larger context of your research question. It is a problem that only experience can solve, but the fact is, even experienced researchers can be vexed by it. If no larger context is available, state your question and its significance in terms of the research community of your class:

> [*So what?*] If we can determine why some drivers seem to ignore the dangers of cellphone use while driving, we can better understand the psychology of risky behavior, which has been a major topic of our class. <sub>significance</sub>

### 13.1.4   State Your Claim

Once you state what isn't known or understood and why readers need to know it, readers want an answer:

> Everyone knows that using a cellphone while driving greatly increases the likelihood of a crash . . . <sub>situation</sub> However, no one has determined why . . . <sub>question</sub> [*So what?*] If we can determine why some drivers seem to ignore the dangers of cellphone use while driving, we can better understand . . . <sub>significance</sub> This study

compares the self-reported cellphone use of forty-five young-adult drivers to their actual use as documented by a tracking app. Our research suggests that even when drivers are aware of the risk of using their cellphones while driving and take it seriously, they may be unaware of the extent to which they habitually engage in this practice.*answer*

In most cases, your readers expect you to locate your claim at or near the end of your introduction. They will be more likely to follow your argument if they know from the beginning what claim your evidence and reasoning will support. If you have reason to hold your claim until the end of your paper, write a sentence to end your introduction that uses your key terms to frame what follows without completely revealing your claim:

This study compares the self-reported cellphone use of forty-five young-adult drivers to their actual use as documented by a tracking app. Specifically, it explores the question of whether drivers intentionally discount the dangers of cellphone use while driving or whether the behavior persists for some other reason.*promise of a claim*

Those four steps may seem mechanical, but they constitute the introductions to most research papers in every field, both inside the academic world and out.

QUICK TIP

**Model Your Work on What You Read**
As you read your sources, especially journal articles, watch for that four-part framework. You will not only learn a range of strategies for writing your own introductions but better understand the ones you read.

### 13.1.5    Draft a New First Sentence
Some writers find it so hard to write the first sentence of a paper that they fall into clichés. Avoid these common ones:

- Do not repeat the language of your assignment.
- Do not quote a dictionary definition: Webster's *defines risk as* . . .
- Do not try to be grand: *For centuries, philosophers have debated the burning question of* . . . (Good questions convey their own importance.)

The last example, especially, reflects a striving for significance that has the opposite effect. There's no need to oversell your research. If you want to begin with something livelier than prior research, try one or more of these openers (but note the warning that follows).

1. A pithy quotation:

   "Honk if you love Jesus. Text while driving if you want to meet him."

2. A relevant anecdote:

   When Jenny S. glanced at the text message from her boss, she didn't expect to become the fiftieth distracted driving fatality in her state this year.

3. A striking fact:

   The National Highway Traffic Safety Administration reports that in 2014, approximately 7 percent of drivers on the road were using a cellphone at any given moment.

   The National Safety Council reports that in 2014, over a quarter of all motor vehicle crashes involved either talking on a cellphone or texting.

   You can combine all three:

   One of the pleasures of Jenny S.'s morning commute was reading the words of wisdom offered on a sign on the side of a local church. Last Friday that sign read, "Honk if you love Jesus. Text while driving if you want to meet him." *quotation* Tragically, when Jenny S. glanced at a text message from her boss that morning, she became her state's fiftieth distracted driving fatality. *anecdote* Jenny S. is not alone. One recent study reports that approximately 7 percent of drivers on the road at any given moment are using a cellphone; another reports over a quarter of all motor vehicle crashes involved some form of cellphone use. *striking fact*

   Be sure to include in these opening sentences terms that anticipate key concepts you'll use when you write the rest of the introduction (and the rest of the paper). In this case they include *texting*, *driving*, *distracted driving*, *fatality*, *cellphone use*, *crash*.

## 13.2 Draft Your Final Conclusion

Your conclusion sums up your argument, but just as important, it offers an opportunity to raise new questions suggested by your research. You can build your conclusion around the elements of your introduction, only in reverse order.

### 13.2.1 Restate Your Claim

Restate your claim early in your conclusion, but more fully than in your introduction:

For years, efforts by public-interest organizations to curtail cellphone use while driving have focused on informing people of the practice's dangers, but much evidence exists to show that cellphone use remains common on our roadways. My study, however, challenges the assumption that risky behaviors are primarily a matter of choice by showing that even when people are aware of the dangers of cellphone use, they may be unaware of actually using their cellphones in the moment. I conclude that cellphone use while driving might be better understood as a habitual activity that occurs below the threshold of conscious attention.

Take this last chance to make your claim as specific and complete as you can. You may find it useful to rephrase the language of your claim from the introduction in light of the argument you present in your paper.

### 13.2.2    Point Out a New Significance, a Practical Application, or New Research

After stating your claim, remind readers of its significance or, better, state a new significance or a practical application:

> If my conclusion is correct, it suggests that we might productively change the focus of our efforts to reduce cellphone use by drivers. Rather than attempting to influence drivers' decisions through information campaigns or legal prohibitions, we ought to pursue technological solutions that make it difficult or impossible for drivers to engage unconsciously in this unsafe behavior.

Finally, suggest other questions that your research might raise. This gesture suggests how other researchers can continue the conversation. And it mirrors the opening context:

> My research improves our understanding of the causes of cellphone use while driving and risky behavior generally, but these findings are nevertheless preliminary. This study focused exclusively on young-adult drivers, and so it is possible that drivers of other ages may display different behaviors. Likewise, I did not consider the influence of gender. Moreover, my findings do not indicate which sorts of technological interventions might be most effective in curtailing the behavior, nor do they tell us how these interventions might be combined with other prevention efforts. Additional research is thus needed before we can know how to apply these results effectively at the level of policy.

When you state what remains to do, you keep the conversation alive. So before you write your final words, imagine other researchers who are intrigued by your work and want to follow it up. What more would *you* like to know, as *their* reader? What research would you suggest they do?

### 13.3    Write Your Title Last

Your title is the first thing your readers read, but it should be the last thing you write. It should both announce your topic and communicate its important concepts, so build it out of the key terms that you earlier circled and underlined (review 12.1.3). Compare these three titles:

Cellphone Use and Driving

Preventing Cellphone Use while Driving

Choice or Habit: Cellphone Use while Driving as an Unconscious Activity

The first title is accurate but too general to give much guidance about what is to come. The second is more specific but doesn't go as far as it could in signaling the paper's contribution. The third uses both a title and a subtitle to give advance notice of the paper's keywords. When readers see the keywords in a title turn up in an introduction and again throughout a paper, they are more likely to think the paper holds together. Two-part titles—a main title followed by a colon and a subtitle—can be useful. They give you more room for key terms and let you display some personal flair.

# 14 Revising Your Paper

Beginning writers think of revising in terms of making corrections to a paper, often in response to comments from readers, especially teachers. However, experienced writers know that revising is not merely reworking the surface level of the text with a bit of rewording here and there. They know that revising is its own necessary stage of the writing process, one that follows not only from completing an early draft but also from a prior stage of reviewing a paper's overall organization (see chapter 12). Once you have let your draft cool and taken note of where it does (and doesn't) meet your readers' needs and expectations, you are ready to revisit specific sections of your draft and make needed changes.

In chapter 13 we offered advice on how to draft your final introduction and conclusion. In this chapter we give more general advice on the process of revision with an emphasis on working from whole to part. In the next chapter we look at revising for style at the sentence level.

## 14.1   Plan Your Time (No One-Draft Wonders)

Have you heard of the one-draft wonder? That's the student who starts writing a paper at midnight on the day it's due, knocks out a quick yet perfect draft, and receives the best grade in the class. The one-draft wonder is an enduring school-based urban legend. We couldn't pull it off when we were in school, and we've never taught a student who could do it either—though we have taught many students who hoped they could fool us with weak drafts all too obviously written the night before.

Let's face it: you can't write a decent research paper if you begin the night or even the week before it's due. This is confirmed not only by thousands of students we've known but by studies of successful and unsuccessful writers. Research shows that the most successful writers tend to share some certain habits:

- They start drafting as soon as possible, before they think they have all the evidence they might need.

- They write in regular short periods rather than in marathon bursts that dull their thinking and kill their interest.
- They set a goal to produce a small number of pages every time they write, even if those pages are not very good.
- They report their progress to someone else if possible, or on a chart if not.
- They anticipate that everything will take longer than they think it should.

To make these insights work for you, you'll have to work backwards from your due date to set interim goals with specific deadlines. Plan your working sessions, periods of time that you can manage in a single sitting when you will focus on specific tasks. Start by giving yourself at least one working session to proofread; then set aside time for a final revision—at least two working sessions for a paper under seven pages, up to twice that for a longer one. Depending on how long your paper is and how quickly you draft, set aside enough time to complete a draft; then add 20 percent. You'll need at least a day before that to review and revise your argument. Next, set aside the time you'll need for finding and reading sources; again, add 20 percent. Finally, you'll need a day or two to find and test your research question. Plot these interim deadlines on a calendar, and keep track of your progress as you go. If you need a deadline to motivate you to work, find someone who will get on your case if you miss one of these interim deadlines.

One of the pleasures of a research project is the opportunity to discover something new, at least to you, perhaps to everyone else. It's a *thoughtful* process that requires you to consider and reconsider what you learn, both when you first find it out and again when you pull everything together. That kind of reflection takes time. To get the time you need, you need a plan that lets you start early, progress steadily, and reflect regularly.

## 14.2    Revise Globally, Then Locally

It's tempting to tinker with words and sentences in your draft without gaining a bird's-eye view of opportunities for revision. As you read your draft, perhaps for the first time, you will find things that you don't like and wish to change them immediately. Avoid this temptation. It does little good to rewrite sentences or even whole paragraphs only to cut them later. Better to revise first globally, then locally.

The review process for organizing your paper (see chapter 12) will give you ideas for where to begin based on gaps or flaws you identify in your argument. Based on what you learn in reviewing your draft, you can return to the outer frame of your introduction and conclusion to more clearly state your claim and address its significance. Or return to the body of your paper in light of reasons and evidence you provide or should provide. You might discover that your argument benefits from additional reasons or evidence or from a reordering of your supporting claims. If you decide that your basic argument is sound, you might address issues of coherence through the presence or absence of key terms across your paper or in specific sections. Only then will it be useful to revise sentences or paragraphs to address the flow and clarity of your ideas.

Here again it's useful to diagnose problems, not just fix isolated instances. Read your paper a few times over and you'll likely notice recurring issues, perhaps a problem with incorporating sources or with your use of transition words. Note global issues as you find them, and use these discoveries to guide local revision.

Note the length of your paragraphs. Avoid strings of short paragraphs (fewer than five lines) or very long ones (for most fields, more than half a page). Reserve the use of two- or three-sentence paragraphs for lists, transitions, introductions and conclusions to sections, and statements that you want to emphasize. (We use short paragraphs here because our readers sometime need to skim sections—not a consideration in research writing.) If you find multiple short or long paragraphs, that's a good sign that you have further work to do to structure your argument.

Look at the first few words of your sentences within and across paragraphs. Many of us unconsciously begin multiple sentences in the same way, for example with pronouns like *It* and *There* or with conjunctions like *And* and *But*. What is natural to us as writers can be a distraction to readers, so try to break up obvious patterns of repetition as you revise.

## 14.3   Use a Range of Revising Strategies to Meet Your Readers' Needs

Experienced writers return to a draft differently from less experienced writers. For one thing, they have learned to shift from thinking like a writer in putting ideas on the page to thinking like a reader in seeing where an argument might be difficult to follow. This is something that comes with practice, but you can develop your ability to anticipate and meet your readers' needs through some tested revising strategies.

### 14.3.1   Revise on Hard Copy

One secret to successful revising is to get a fresh look at your work. You can do that if you revise on hard copy (paper), especially when you want to catch the small details. So edit early drafts on screen, if you prefer, but you will catch more errors and get a better sense of the structure of your paper if you read at least one version of it on paper.

This shift from a writing space to a reading space has the added benefit of slowing you down when you move from keyboard and screen to pen and paper. Reading at a different pace allows you to see your argument unfold in a different way. Simply spreading out the pages on a desk (or a floor) can help you to visualize the flow of your argument in a way that is difficult to do on a computer screen.

14.3.2    **Exchange Papers with Other Writers or Meet with a Writing Consultant**

One of your greatest obstacles to revising well is your memory. By the time you are ready to revise, you know your paper so well that you can't really read it; you can only remember what you meant when you wrote it. That's why our suggestions for revision are so mechanical: they help you bypass your too-good memory of your paper.

But your group provides an even better way to circumvent your memory. For the revision steps here and in chapter 15, trade papers with another student. Each of you should mark up the other's paper. We guarantee that you'll be far better at finding what needs improving in the paper you read than in your own.

But don't just read and make suggestions. Suggestions are welcome, but what is far more valuable is for each of you to go through those steps for revising (14.2) with the other's paper. You can't fix a problem you can't find.

You might also benefit from talking with a writing consultant. Most colleges have a writing center with trained consultants ready to assist writers at every stage of a paper's development.

14.3.3    **Welcome Your Teacher's Advice (but Do So Prudently)**

If your teacher has commented on your draft, always revise in light of that advice. Otherwise you will miss an opportunity to improve your paper. And you will annoy someone who took time to read your work to help you, only to see you ignore those efforts. You don't have to follow all or even most of the suggestions, but your revision should show that you considered each one seriously. (We offer additional advice on benefiting from a returned paper in chapter 16.)

Almost as irritating as students who ignore a teacher's suggestions, however, are those who follow the minor editorial suggestions (grammar, spelling, etc.) but ignore all comments that ask them to rethink larger issues. No teacher wants to be treated as a proofreader.

# 15 Revising Sentences

Your last big task is to make your sentences as clear as you can for your readers. On some occasions you may know your writing is awkward, especially if you're writing about an unfamiliar and complex topic. But too often you won't recognize when your sentences need help. You need a reliable way to revise sentences that you know are problematic, but even more, you need a way to identify those that you think are fine but that readers will think are not.

We can't tell you how to fix every problem in every sentence, but we can tell you how to deal with those that most often affect writers struggling to sound like "serious scholars," a style that most experienced readers find just pretentious. Here is a short example:

1a. A better understanding of student learning could achieve improvement in teaching effectiveness.

However impressive that sounds, the student who wrote it meant only this:

1b. If we better understood how students learn, we could teach them more effectively.

To analyze 1a and revise it into 1b, however, you must know a few grammatical terms: *noun, verb, active verb, passive verb, whole subject, simple subject, main clause, subordinate clause*. If they're only a dim memory, skim a grammar guide before you go on.

15.1    **Focus on the First Seven or Eight Words of a Sentence**
Just as the key to a clearly written paper is in its first few paragraphs, so the key to a clearly written sentence is in its first few words. When readers grasp those first seven or eight words easily, they read what follows faster, understand it better, and remember it longer. It is the difference between these two sentences:

2a. The United Nations' insistence on acceptance by all nations of the principles of equal rights and self-determination of peoples is a product of its recognition that maintenance of stability in the world order requires that nations be guided by values beyond narrow self-interest.

2b. The United Nations insists that all nations accept the principles of equal rights and self-determination of peoples, because it recognizes that maintaining a stable world order requires that nations be guided by values beyond narrow self-interest.

In this section we will show you how to write a sentence like 2b—or to revise one like 2a into 2b.

> **Five Principles for Clear Sentences**
> To draft clear sentences or revise unclear ones, follow these five principles:
>
> 1.  Make subjects short and concrete, ideally naming the character that performs the action expressed by the verb that follows.
> 2.  Avoid interrupting the subject and verb with more than a word or two.
> 3.  Put key actions in verbs, not in nouns.
> 4.  Put information familiar to readers at the beginning of a sentence, new information at the end.
> 5.  Avoid long introductory phrases: get to a short, familiar subject quickly.

Those principles add up to this: readers want sentences that let them get past a short, concrete, familiar subject quickly and easily to a verb expressing a specific action. When the beginning of your sentence does that, the rest of your sentence will usually take care of itself. To analyze your own writing, skim the first seven or eight words of every sentence. Look for sentences in which you don't follow our five principles, and then revise them as follows.

15.1.1   **Make Subjects Short and Concrete**
Readers need to grasp the subject of a sentence easily, but they can't when the subject is long, complex, and abstract. Compare these two sentences (the whole subjects in each are underlined; the one-word simple subject is boldfaced):

3a. A school system's successful **implementation** of a new reading curriculum for its elementary schools depends on the demonstration in each school of the commitment of its principal and the cooperation of teachers in setting reasonable goals.

3b. A school **system** will successfully implement a new reading curriculum for elementary schools only when each **principal** demonstrates that **she** is committed to it and **teachers** cooperate to set reasonable goals.

In 3a the whole subject is fourteen words long, and its simple subject is an abstraction—*implementation*. In 3b, the clearer version, the whole subject of every verb is short, and each simple subject is relatively concrete: *school system, each principal, she, teachers*. Moreover, each of those subjects performs the action in its verb: ***system** will implement,* ***principal** demonstrates,* ***she** is committed,* ***teachers** cooperate.*

Think of sentences like stories. Readers tend to find a sentence readable when the subject of its verb names the main *character* in a few concrete words, ideally a character that is also the "doer" of the action expressed by the verb that follows.

But there's a complication: we are not saying that to be clear you must write only about people and concrete things. In fact, writers often tell clear stories about abstract characters. Those characters can be entities such as "school system" in 3b or "athletics" in 4:

4. Athletics debases a college's educational mission only when it overstimulates the passions of alumni and others who no longer need an education but do need a source of meaning in their lives.

Or they can be purely abstract characters:

5. No skill is more valued in the professional world than problem solving. Solving problems quickly requires us to frame situations in different ways and to find more than one solution. In fact, effective problem solving may define general intelligence.

Few readers have trouble with those abstract subjects, because they're short and familiar: *no skill, solving problems quickly,* and *effective problem solving.* What gives readers trouble is an abstract subject that is long and unfamiliar.

To fix sentences with long, abstract subjects, revise in three steps:

- Identify the main character in the sentence.
- Find its key action, and if it is buried in an abstract noun, make it a verb.
- Make the main character the subject of that new verb.

For example, compare 6a and 6b (actions are boldfaced; verbs are capitalized):

6a. Without a means for **analyzing interactions** between social class and education in regard to the **creation** of more job opportunities, success in **understanding** economic mobility will REMAIN limited.

6b. Economists do not entirely **UNDERSTAND** economic mobility, because they cannot **ANALYZE** how social class and education **INTERACT** to **CREATE** job opportunities.

In both sentences the main character is *economists*, but in 6a that character isn't the subject of any verb; in fact, it's not in the sentence at all: we must infer it from actions buried in nouns: *analyzing* and *understanding* (what economists do). We revise 6a into 6b by making the main characters (*economists, social class*, and *education*) subjects of action verbs (*understand, analyze, interact*, and *create*).

Readers want subjects to name the main characters in your story, ideally flesh-and-blood characters, and verbs to name their key actions.

## 15.1.2    Avoid Interrupting Subjects and Verbs with More Than a Word or Two

Once past a short subject, readers want to get to a verb quickly, so avoid splitting a verb from its subject with long phrases and clauses:

7a. Some economists, because they write in a style that is impersonal and objective, do not communicate with laypeople easily.

In 7a the *because* clause separates the subject *some economists* from the verb *do not communicate*, forcing us to suspend our mental breath. To revise, move the interrupting clause to the beginning or end of its sentence, depending on whether it connects more closely to the sentence before or after. When in doubt, put it at the end (for more on this see 15.1.4).

7b. Because some economists write in a style that is impersonal and objective, they do not communicate with laypeople easily. This inability to communicate . . .

7c. Some economists do not communicate with laypeople easily because they write in a style that is impersonal and objective. They use passive verbs and . . .

Readers manage short interruptions more easily:

8. Few economists deliberately write in a style that is impersonal and objective.

## 15.1.3    Put Key Actions in Verbs, Not in Nouns

Readers want to get to a verb quickly, but they also want that verb to express a key action. So avoid using an empty verb such as *have, do, make*, or *be* to introduce an action buried in an abstract noun. Make the noun a verb.

Compare these sentences (action nouns are boldfaced; action verbs are capitalized; verbs with little action are italicized):

9a. During the early years of the First World War, the Great Powers' **attempt** at enlisting the United States on their side *was met* with **failure.**

9b. During the early years of the First World War, the Great Powers ATTEMPTED to ENLIST the United States on their side but FAILED.

In 9a two important actions aren't verbs but nouns: *attempt* and *failure*. The third action, *enlisting*, also functions like a noun in the sentence. Sentence 9b seems more direct because it expresses those actions in verbs: *attempted, enlist, failed*.

## 15.1.4    Put Familiar Information at the Beginning of a Sentence, New at the End

Readers understand a sentence most readily when they grasp its subject easily, and the easiest subject to grasp is not just short and concrete but *familiar*. Compare how the second sentence in each of the following passages does or doesn't "flow":

10a. New insights into global weather patterns are emerging from recent research on the large low-pressure zones rotating over the Earth's poles known as the polar vortices. Rising temperatures associated with the recession of the ice caps at both poles are weakening the vortices. These temperature changes are causing the vortices to deviate toward the equator, bringing with them the frigid air responsible for our recent colder winters.

10b. New insights into global weather patterns are emerging from recent research on the large, low-pressure zones rotating above the Earth's poles known as the polar vortices. The vortices are being weakened by rising temperatures associated with the recession of the ice caps at both poles. These temperature changes are causing the vortices to deviate toward the equator, bringing with them the frigid air responsible for our recent colder winters.

Most readers think 10b flows better than 10a, partly because the subject of the second sentence, *The vortices*, is shorter than the longer subject of 10a: *Rising temperatures associated with the recession of the ice caps at both poles*. But 10b also flows better because the order of its ideas is different.

In 10a the first words of the second sentence express new information:

10a. . . . the polar vortices. Rising temperatures associated with the recession of the ice caps at both poles . . .

Those words about rising temperatures seem to come out of nowhere. But in 10b the first words echo the end of the previous sentence:

10b. . . . the polar vortices. The vortices . . .

Moreover, once we make that change, the end of that second sentence introduces the third more cohesively:

10b. . . . by rising temperatures associated with the recession of the ice caps at both poles. These temperature changes . . .

Contrast 10a; the end of its second sentence doesn't flow into the beginning of the third as smoothly:

10a. ... the vortices. These temperature changes ...

That is why readers think that passage 10a feels choppier than 10b: the end of one sentence does not flow smoothly into the beginning of the next. No principle of writing is more important than this: use familiar information to introduce unfamiliar information. That is, put old before new.

## 15.1.5   Avoid Long Introductory Phrases

Compare these two sentences (introductory phrases are boldfaced, whole subjects underlined):

11a. **In view of findings by researchers on higher education indicating at least one change by most undergraduate students of their major field of study,** first-year students seem not well informed about choosing a major field of study.

11b. Researchers on higher education have found that most students change their major field of study at least once during their undergraduate careers. **If that is so,** then first-year students seem not well informed when they choose a major.

Most readers find 11a harder to read than 11b, because it makes them work through a twenty-four-word phrase before they reach its subject (*first-year students*). In the two sentences in 11b, readers start with a subject either immediately, *Researchers...*, or after a very short delay, *If that is so, ...*

The principle is this: start most of your sentences directly with their subject. Begin only a few sentences with introductory phrases longer than ten or so words. You can usually revise long introductory phrases and subordinate clauses into their own independent sentences, as in 11b.

## 15.2   Understand Two Common Prohibitions

To help their students develop as writers, some teachers tell students not to use certain grammatical constructions. You may have heard these two rules:

- Do not use the passive voice.
- Do not use the first person in an academic paper.

Neither of these rules is absolute: sometimes a passive verb can make your writing more rather than less clear, and the first person is used regularly by professional scholars and researchers in almost every field. (We just used a passive verb in that last sentence.) But these rules do have a good purpose for student writers: they can help you avoid common pitfalls in academic writing and develop a mature writing style. You need to understand the spirit of these rules so that you can choose wisely when to follow them and when they can be ignored.

15.2.1    **Choose Active or Passive Verbs to Reflect the Previous Principles**
Student writers sometimes overuse the passive voice when trying to sound "academic." That's why some teachers ban it. You should avoid passive verbs when they would cause your sentences to violate our five principles for clear writing, as in the second sentence here:

12a. Climate change may have many catastrophic effects. Tropical diseases and destructive insect life even north of the Canadian border could be increased<sub>pas-</sub> _sive verb_ by it.

That second sentence opens with a twelve-word subject conveying new information: *Tropical diseases . . . Canadian border.* It is the subject of a passive verb, *be increased*, and that verb is followed by a short, familiar bit of information from the sentence before: *by [this climatic change].* That sentence would be clearer if its verb were active:

12b. Climate change may have many catastrophic effects. It could increase<sub>active</sub> _verb_ tropical diseases and destructive insect life even north of the Canadian border.

Now the subject is familiar, and the new information in the longer phrase is at the end. In this case, the active verb is the right choice.

But if you never make a verb passive, you'll write sentences that contradict the old-new principle. We saw an example in 10a:

10a. New insights into global weather patterns are emerging from recent research on the large low-pressure zones rotating over the Earth's poles known as the polar vortices. Rising temperatures associated with the recession of the ice caps at both poles are weakening<sub>active verb</sub> these vortices.

The verb in the second sentence is active, but the passage flows better when it's passive:

10b. New insights into global weather patterns are emerging from recent research on the large low-pressure zones rotating above the Earth's poles known as the polar vortices. The vortices are being weakened<sub>passive verb</sub> by rising temperatures associated with the recession of the ice caps at both poles.

Readers prefer a subject that is short, concrete, and familiar, even if you must use a passive verb. So choose active *or* passive depending on which gives you that kind of subject.

## 15.2.2   Use First-Person Pronouns Appropriately

Almost everyone has heard the advice to avoid using *I* or *we* in academic writing. In fact, opinions differ on this. Some teachers tell students never to use *I* because it makes their writing "subjective." Others encourage using *I* as a way to make writing more lively and personal.

Most teachers and editors do agree that two uses of *I* should be avoided:

- Insecure writers begin too many sentences with *I think* or *I believe* (or their equivalent, *In my opinion*). Readers assume that you think and believe what you write, so you don't have to say so.
- Inexperienced writers too often narrate their research: *First, I consulted . . . , Then I examined . . .* , and so on. Readers care less about the story of your research than about its results.

But we believe, and most professionals agree, that the first person is appropriate on two occasions. That last sentence illustrates one of them: *we believe . . . that the first person . . .*

- An occasional introductory *I* (or *we*) *believe* can soften the dogmatic edge of a statement.

Compare this blunter, less qualified version:

13. But ~~we believe, and most professionals agree, that~~ the first person is appropriate on two occasions.

The trick is not to hedge so often that you sound uncertain or so rarely that you sound smug.

The second occasion depends on the action in the verb:

- A first-person *I* or *we* is also appropriate as the subject of a verb naming an action unique to you as the writer of your argument.

14. In this paper I will show that social distinctions at this university are . . .

Verbs referring to such actions typically appear in introductions: *I will show/ argue/prove/claim that X*, and in conclusions: *I have demonstrated/concluded/ . . .* Since only you can show, prove, or claim what's in your argument, only you can say so with *I*.

On the other hand, researchers rarely use the first person for an action that others must repeat to replicate the reported research. Those words include *divide*, *measure*, *weigh*, *examine*, and so on. Researchers rarely write sentences with active verbs like this:

15a. I *calculated* the coefficient of X.

Instead they're likely to write in the passive, because anyone can repeat this calculation:

15b. The coefficient of X *was calculated.*

Those same principles apply to *we*, if you're one of two or more authors. But many teachers and editors do object to two other uses of *we*:

- the royal *we* used to refer reflexively to the writer
- the all-purpose *we* that refers to people in general

Not this:

16. We must be careful to cite sources when we use data from them. When we read writers who fail to do that, we tend to distrust them.

We know that some teachers flatly forbid the first person in papers, just as some editors discourage it in their journals. If your teacher won't let you use *I* or *we*, you should ask why. There might be a very good reason—perhaps because your teacher knows that students often overuse the first person or because it's good for you to try other kinds of sentences. In the long run, that will help you write better. You have to take seriously the preferences of those with authority over your writing, but ultimately it's your choice.

---

QUICK TIP

**Read Drafts Aloud**

You can best judge how your readers will respond to your writing if you read it aloud—or better, have someone read it back to you. If that person stumbles over certain phrases or sentences or seems to drone, you should trust your reader's ear and look for opportunities to revise.

---

15.3    **Analyze the Sentences in What You Read**

Once you understand how readers judge what they read, you know not only how to write clearly but also why so much of what you must read seems so dense. Sometimes you struggle to understand a reading because its content is difficult. But sometimes you struggle because the writer didn't write clearly. This next passage, for example, is the sort that might be found in any textbook:

17a. Recognition of the fact that grammars differ from one language to another can serve as the basis for serious consideration of the problems confronting translators of the great works of world literature originally written in a language other than English.

But in half as many words, it means only this:

17b. Once we recognize that languages have different grammars, we can consider the problems of those who translate great works of literature into English.

So when you struggle to understand some academic writing (and you will), don't blame yourself, at least not at first. Analyze its sentences. If they have long subjects stuffed with abstract nouns expressing new information, the problem is probably not your inability to read easily but the writer's inability to write clearly. If that is the case, then the tools we've given you for writing clearly will also help you unpack such dense prose.

## 15.4   Choose the Right Word

Another bit of standard advice is *Choose the right word*. It has two aspects:

1.  Choose the word with the right meaning.

    *Affect* doesn't mean *effect*, *elicit* doesn't mean *illicit*. Many handbooks list commonly confused words. If you're an inexperienced writer, invest in one.

2.  Choose the word with the right level of diction.

    If you draft quickly, you risk choosing words that mean roughly what you think they do but that are too casual for your paper. Someone can *criticize* another writer or *knock* him; a risk can seem *frightening* or *scary*. Those pairs have similar meanings, but most readers judge the second to be too casual for academic writing.
    On the other hand, if you try too hard to sound "academic," you risk using words that are too formal. You can *think* or *cogitate*, *drink* or *imbibe*. Those pairs are also close in meaning, but the second in each is too fancy for a paper written in ordinary English. Whenever you're tempted to use a word that you think especially fine, look for a more familiar one.
    The obvious advice is to look up words you're not sure of. But they're not the problem; the problem is the ones you *are* sure of. Worse, no dictionary tells you that a word like *visage* or *perambulate* is too fancy for just about anyone to write. The short-term solution is to ask someone to read your paper before you turn it in. The long-term solution is to read a lot, write a lot, endure a lot of criticism, and learn from it.

## 15.5   Polish Your Paper

Before you submit your paper, proofread it one last time to catch errors in grammar, spelling, and punctuation (see part 3 for a refresher course on such matters). Many experienced writers proofread from the last sentence back to the first to keep from getting caught up in the flow of ideas and missing the words. Do not rely solely on your word-processing program's spelling and grammar checker. It will sometimes miss words that are spelled correctly but used incorrectly— *their/there/they're, it's/its, too/to, accept/except, affect/effect, already / all ready, complement/compliment, principal/principle, discrete/discreet,* and so on—and it will flag constructions like the passive voice even when they may be the best choice. If you know you have mixed up a pair of words before, do a global search to check on both words.

Some students think they have to worry about the quality of their writing only in English or writing courses. That's not true. Teachers of every subject appreciate clear and coherent writing, and every course in which you write is an opportunity for you to practice writing better.

# 16 Learning from Readers' Comments

Whether you're a beginning researcher writing a paper for a class or an advanced scholar submitting a manuscript for publication in a peer-reviewed journal, you can learn much from the feedback of careful readers. But to get the most benefit from such comments—whether they are on a draft or a final version—you need to know how to use them.

As you develop as a writer and researcher, you will receive feedback from many different readers, some (like teachers and editors) having authority over you and others being people whose responses you seek out. Experienced writers know that nothing is more valuable than comments from a trusted reader. None of us can accurately judge the way readers will respond to our writing, for the simple reason that we are too close to it. We need readers to show us, through their responses, what we got right and where we went wrong.

## 16.1    Two Kinds of Feedback: Advice and Data

Commenting on a paper is hard (even if a reader is being paid to do it). When giving feedback, that reader's responsibility is to be honest and to try to be helpful. Your responsibility as a writer is to make the most of the comments you receive.

To do that, you must decide whether to treat a reader's comments as *advice*—language identifying things you could do (or should have done) to make the paper better—or as *data* documenting a particular reader's response. When you treat comments as advice, you must decide whether to accept or reject them. Good advice, especially from a trusted reader, can be invaluable to new and experienced researchers alike. Sometimes you might feel a strong obligation to accept a reader's advice, such as when it comes from a teacher, advisor, or editor. But even in those instances you are not obligated to accept it wholesale; as a writer, you are responsible for not only your ideas but the choices you make in expressing them.

When you treat comments as data, you don't accept or reject them but analyze them to understand why your reader responded to your paper as she did. And when you understand that, you can revise or make a different decision the next time. As a writer, you might know what you wanted your paper to *say*, but only your reader can tell you what it in fact *said*—at least to her. Again, the writer is ultimately responsible: if a careful reader misunderstood your paper, you should not blame her for that misunderstanding but use the data of her feedback to figure out how and why that misunderstanding occurred.

In this sense, bad advice can be great data. Even the most dedicated and careful reader is not infallible. She might misunderstand your intentions or argument, or give you wrongheaded advice (even if she is a teacher). In that case, ignore the advice, but ask yourself, "What about my paper created that misunderstanding? How did I lead my reader astray?" If you can answer those questions, you can still improve your paper, or the next one.

Here are some tips for making the most of the comments you receive, however you choose to interpret them.

## 16.2    Find General Principles in Specific Comments

When you review your reader's comments, focus on those that you can apply to your next project.

- Look for a pattern of errors in spelling, punctuation, and grammar. If you see one, you know what to work on.
- If your reader says you made factual errors, check your notes. Did you take bad notes or misreport them? Were you misled by an unreliable source? Whatever you find, you know what to do in your next project.
- If your reader reports only her judgments of your writing, look for what causes them. If she says your writing is choppy, dense, or awkward, check your sentences using the steps in chapter 15. If she says it's disorganized or wandering, check it against chapter 12. You won't always find what caused the complaints, but when you do you'll know what to work on next time.

As most teachers recognize, feedback itself can be either *formative* or *summative*, depending on where it comes in the cycle of a writing assignment. Formative feedback on a work in progress is meant to help you *form* your ideas and express them in your paper. Its purpose is to help you revise. Summative feedback on a finished paper *sums up* that reader's evaluation of it. This is the kind of feedback you receive on a graded paper. But don't just look at the grade: even if you can't change that paper, you can still learn from the comments and apply those lessons to future efforts.

Increasingly, teachers employ rubrics as a tool to assess writing and to communicate standards. A rubric can be a useful form of feedback if it helps place individual efforts into a larger context rather than as a local response to one paper.

## 16.3    Talk with Your Reader

If you receive comments that include words like *disorganized, illogical,* and *unsupported* and you cannot find what triggered them, ask your reader. Such words are not descriptions of your paper but descriptions of the reader's impressions of it. You need to find out what it is in the paper itself that provoked those impressions. Following these guidelines will help that conversation go well:

- If your reader marked up your spelling, punctuation, and grammar, correct those errors *before* your meeting to show that you took his comments seriously. You might also jot down responses to more substantive comments so that you can discuss them.
- If your reader is your teacher, don't complain about your grade. Be clear that you want to understand the comments so that you can do better next time.
- Prioritize: focus on those comments that address the most important issues, like your paper's argument and organization. It's tempting to zero in on local concerns that can be quickly corrected, especially if your reader has done a lot of line editing, or to quibble over minor points of disagreement.
- Rehearse your questions so that they'll seem amiable—not "You say this is disorganized but you don't say why," but rather "Can you help me see where I went wrong with my organization so I can do better next time?"
- Ask your reader to point to passages that illustrate her judgments and what those passages should have looked like. Don't ask "What didn't you like?" but rather "Where exactly did I go wrong, and what could I have done to fix it?"

A final word for students: you might think that meeting with your teacher is helpful only when a paper of yours receives a low grade. But that would be wrong. Even after a high grade, it's useful to know how you earned it. Your next project will likely be more challenging, so it's good to know what successful practices you can build on. Of course, in that new project you might again feel like a beginner. That's the way it goes with research.

# 17 Delivering Your Research as a Presentation

It may be too early in your career to think about publishing your research, but it's not too early to present it. Researchers at all stages communicate their work to others in live presentations, an oral report or discussion supplemented with slides and a handout. Increasingly undergraduate and even secondary school researchers also share their work in this way with audiences in and beyond the classroom, including at local research fairs and conferences. Indeed, the ability to stand and talk about your research clearly and confidently is a crucial skill for any career.

In this chapter we show you how to use your plan for a written text to plan for and deliver a presentation, both as you draft your paper and after you have completed it. Our focus is not on your presentation's supplements—your handout or slides—but on what you must do to deliver your work to a live audience. A presentation may be easier to prepare than a written paper, but to benefit from delivering it, you must plan just as carefully. In giving a talk, you get immediate feedback that is often very helpful when testing new ideas or new data. There's nothing like a face-to-face audience, able to respond in real time, to help you clarify your thinking.

## 17.1    Give a Presentation as You Draft

It won't be until you are ready to draft that you can even think of presenting your work to your class, let alone an audience beyond the classroom. Before then, you will have too little to say and you will be too unsure of what you do have. But you can learn a great deal from reporting on your work as you draft. It cannot be the same kind of presentation you give after you have completed your paper (see 17.2), but it can be a very useful exercise.

Your presentation should have two goals: (1) to forecast what your final paper will say, so that you can discover whether it makes as much sense when you *say* it as when you *think* it; and (2) to test your ideas through the responses of your peers. In particular, your presentation at this stage should do three things:

- present your research question and answer/claim
- outline your reasons supporting that claim
- preview the kind of evidence you will use to support those reasons

### 17.1.1   Prepare Notes, Not a Script

Most of us are anxious at the idea of speaking before a group, and you're likely to be more anxious when presenting on research ahead of a completed paper. Many students think that the cure for that anxiety is to write out a script they can just read rather than remember. That's generally a bad idea. Few will want to sit while you read it.

Instead of a script to be read aloud, prepare good notes that include the following:

- a complete introduction and conclusion
- your reasons, in order, preferably in large bold type
- for each reason, a list of your two or three best bits of evidence, named but not explained

### 17.1.2   Write Out a Complete Introduction and Conclusion

There are two parts of your presentation that you must get right: your introduction, which prepares listeners for what's coming, and your conclusion, which tells them what to remember. Because they are so important, these are the only two parts for which you should fully prepare in advance. You don't need to memorize them, but you should rehearse enough that you can deliver them with only a few glances at your notes. That way you get off to a confident start, which will improve the rest of your performance, and you end confidently, which will color how your audience remembers your presentation.

If you have been storyboarding your paper, you already have a sketch of an introduction and notes on a conclusion. Write them out in language *to be spoken*. Except for technical terms you may need, don't use words that make you feel uncomfortable to say or make you sound like a textbook. State your research question clearly, and be sure to end with your answer. In between, do what you can to explain the significance of your research question.

17.1.3    **Make the Body of Your Notes an Outline**
In the body of your presentation, concentrate on your reasons. Use them to organize your notes, in bold type. These are the sentences you must be sure to say. For everything else, adapt to your audience: spend time on what seems to engage them; skip what doesn't. But do cover each reason. And just before you conclude, run through your main reasons in order: this is the best summary of your argument.

If you have time, present some of your best evidence, especially for any reasons that your audience is unlikely to accept right off. But at this stage your presentation should be focused on your problem, its answer, and your reasons supporting that claim. Communicate them clearly, and you will have done a fine job.

17.2    **Give a Presentation of Your Completed Paper**
There are at least two relevant differences between a preliminary and a final presentation: before you were guessing what your argument might be; now you know. That should make your presentation more confident, but not different in structure. Also, you now know how your evidence supports each reason. Accordingly, you should give more attention to evidence in a final presentation than in a preliminary one. *Do not walk readers through every scrap of evidence.* If you do, you will run out of time. Instead, present one best bit of evidence for each reason. This will assure your audience that you can back up your claims without their having to listen to your entire argument.

17.2.1    **Narrow Your Focus**
Typically a talk can cover only a fraction of what a paper can. A major, if common, mistake that even seasoned researchers make is to cram too many words into the allotted time. In a twenty-minute talk, plan on eight to ten double-spaced pages for text to be read aloud. This isn't much time to communicate your ideas, so you must boil down your work to its essence or present just a part of it. Here are two common options:

- *Claim with a sketch of your argument.* If your claim is new, focus on its originality. Start with a short introduction (review chapter 13), then explain your reasons, summarizing your evidence for each.
- *Summary of a subargument.* If your argument is too big for a brief presentation, focus on a key subargument. Mention your larger claim in your introduction and conclusion, but be clear that you're addressing only part of it.

17.2.2    **Understand the Differences between Listeners and Readers**
Unless you know and respect the difference between listening and reading, your audience will find your presentation tiring or hard to follow. When we read, we can stop to reflect and puzzle over difficult passages. To stay on track, we can

look at headings and even paragraph indentations. If our minds wander, we can always reread. But as listeners in an audience, we can do none of these things. We must be motivated to pay attention, and we need help to follow any complicated line of thought.

That's why it is important to not simply read your paper with little or no eye contact or, if presenting slides, merely introduce them and repeat their content. You must engage your audience as in a conversation but with extra care for what listeners need. So when speaking, you have to be explicit about your purpose and your organization. If you're reading a paper aloud, you have to make your sentence structure far simpler than in a written paper. So favor shorter sentences with consistent subjects (see 15.1.2). Use "I," "we," and "you" a lot. What may seem repetitive to readers will be welcomed by listeners.

### 17.2.3  Design Your Presentation to Be Listened To

To hold your listeners' attention, you must seem to be not lecturing *at* but conversing *with* them. This is a skill that does not come easily. Few of us can write as we would speak, and most of us need notes to stay on track. If you do read your paper, read no faster than two minutes per page (at 300 words a page). This is faster than you speak ordinarily, so time yourself. Inexperienced presenters tend to read more quickly than their listeners can comfortably hear and digest.

It's also important that your audience see you, and not just the top of your head; so build in moments when you look directly at your audience, especially when you say something important. Do so at least once or twice per page, ideally at the end of each paragraph.

It's always better to talk from notes, as we have said, but doing that well takes a lot of practice. In the next section we advise on how to structure your talk based on notes rather than a text to be read aloud.

### 17.2.4  Sketch Your Introduction

For a short talk, you get only one shot at motivating your audience before they tune out, so prepare your introduction more carefully than any other part of your talk. Base it on the four-part problem statement described in section 13.1, plus a road map that previews the direction your presentation will take. (Below we suggest times for a talk lasting twenty minutes.)

Use notes only to remind yourself of the four parts, not as a word-for-word script. If you can't remember the content, you're not ready to give your talk. Sketch enough in your notes to *remind* yourself of the following:

1. what research you extend, modify, or correct (no more than a minute)
2. what question your research addresses—the gap in knowledge or understanding (thirty seconds or less)
3. why your research matters—an answer to *So what?* (thirty seconds)

Those three steps, as you know by now, are crucial in motivating your listeners. If your question is new or controversial, give it more time. If your listeners recognize its significance, mention it quickly and go on.

4.  your claim, the answer to your research question (thirty seconds or less)

Listeners want to know your answer up front, even more than readers do. So unless you have a compelling reason to wait, state your answer up front. If you must wait, at least preview it.

5.  a forecast of the structure of your presentation (ten to twenty seconds)

Most useful is an oral table of contents: "First, I will discuss . . ." That may seem clumsy in print, but listeners need more help than readers. Repeat that structure through the body of your talk.

Rehearse your introduction, not only to get it right but also to be able to look your audience in the eye as you give it. You can look down at notes later.

All told, spend no more than three minutes or so on your introduction.

## 17.2.5  Design Notes You Can Understand at a Glance

Do not write your notes as complete sentences (much less paragraphs) that you then read aloud. Notes should help you see at a glance only the structure of your talk and cue what to say at crucial points. *So do not copy and paste sentences from a written text; create your notes from scratch.*

Use a separate page for each main point. On each page, write out your main point not as a topic but as claims, either in shortened form or (if you must) in complete sentences. Above each point, you might add an explicit transition as the oral equivalent of a subhead: "The first issue is . . ."

Visually highlight those main points so that you spot them instantly. Under them list the evidence that supports them. If your evidence consists of numbers or quotations, you'll probably have to write them out. Otherwise, know your evidence well enough to be able to talk about it directly to your audience.

Organize your points so that you cover the most important ones first. If you run long (most of us do), you can skip a later section or even jump to your conclusion without losing anything crucial to your argument. Never build up to a climax that you might not reach. If you must skip something, use the question-and-answer period to return to it.

## 17.2.6  Model Your Conclusion on Your Introduction

Make your conclusion memorable, because listeners will repeat it when asked, *What did Jones say?* Learn it well enough to present it looking at your audience, without reading from notes. It should have these three parts:

- your claim, in more detail than in your introduction (if listeners are mostly interested in your reasons or data, summarize them as well)
- your answer to *So what?* (you can restate an answer from your introduction, but try to add a new one, even if it's speculative)
- suggestions for more research, what's still to be done

Rehearse your conclusion so that you know exactly how long it takes (no more than a minute or two). Then when you have that much time remaining, conclude, even if you haven't finished your last (relatively unimportant) points. If you had to skip one or two points, work them into an answer during any question-and-answer period. If your talk runs short, don't ad lib. You're finished.

### 17.2.7    Anticipate Questions

If you're lucky, you'll get questions after your talk, so prepare answers for predictable ones. Expect questions about your data or sources, especially if you didn't cover them much in your talk. Also be prepared for questions about a source you never heard of. The best policy is to acknowledge that you haven't but that you'll check it out. If the question seems friendly, ask why the source is relevant.

Listen to every question carefully; then to be sure you understand the question, *pause before you respond and think about it for a moment*. If you don't understand the question, ask the questioner to rephrase it. Good questions are invaluable, even when they seem to be a challenge. Use them to refine your thinking.

### 17.2.8    Create Handouts

If your evidence is suitable for it, prepare a handout: you can share key slides from your presentation, a list of quotations, important graphics or tables, illustrations, questions for discussion, and so on. However, never simply parrot your slides or your handout. Nothing is more tedious for an audience than that.

# 18  On the Spirit of Research

As we've said, we can reach good conclusions in many ways other than research. But the truths we reach in those ways are personal. We can't present our intuitions and feelings as evidence to convince others of our claims; we can ask only that they take our report of our inner experience—and our claims—on faith.

In contrast, the truths of research and how we reached them must be available for public scrutiny. We base research claims on evidence available to everyone and on principles of reasoning that, we hope, our readers accept as sound. And then those readers test all of that in all the ways that they and others can imagine. That may be a high standard, but it must be if we expect others to base their understanding and actions, even their lives, on what we ask them to believe.

When you accept the principles that shape public, evidence-based belief, you accept two more that can be hard to live by. One concerns our relationship to authority. No more than five centuries ago, the search for better understanding based on *evidence* was often regarded as a threat. Among the powerful, many believed that all the important truths were already known and that the scholar's job was to preserve and transmit them, certainly not to challenge them. If new facts cast doubt on an old belief, the belief usually trumped the facts. Many who dared to follow evidence to conclusions that challenged authority were banished or imprisoned, and some were even killed.

Even today, those who reason from evidence can anger those who hold a cherished belief. For example, DNA evidence has proved that Thomas Jefferson had multiple children with his slave Sally Hemings. But for many years, some refused to accept this possibility, despite its likelihood based on the sum of the available historical evidence, not because they had better counterevidence but because of a fiercely held belief: *a person of Jefferson's stature couldn't do such a thing* (see 5.5). However, in the world of research, both academic and professional, good evidence and sound reasoning beat out belief every time, or at least they should.

In some parts of the world it's still considered more important to guard settled beliefs than to test them. But in places informed by the values of research, we think differently: we believe not only that we *may* question settled beliefs but that we *must*, no matter how much authority cherishes them—so long as we support our answers with sound reasons based on reliable evidence.

But that principle requires another. When we make a claim, we must expect, even encourage, others to question not just our claim but how we reached it, to ask, *Why do you believe that?* It's often hard to welcome such questions, but we're obliged to listen with goodwill to objections, reservations, and qualifications that collectively imply *I don't agree, at least not yet*. And the more we challenge old ideas, the more we must be ready to acknowledge and answer those questions, because we may be asking others to give up deeply held beliefs.

When some students encounter these values, they find it difficult, even painful, to live by them. Some feel that a challenge to what they believe isn't a lively search for truth but a personal attack on their deepest values. Others retreat to a cynical skepticism that doubts everything and believes nothing. Others fall into mindless relativism: *We're all entitled to our own beliefs, and so all beliefs are right for those who hold them!* Many turn away from an active life of the mind, rejecting not only answers that might disturb their settled beliefs but even the questions that inspired them.

But in our worlds of work, scholarship, civic action, and even politics, we can't replace tested knowledge and hard-won understanding with personal opinion, a relativistic view of truth, or the comfortable, settled knowledge of "authority."

That does not mean we reject long-held and time-tested beliefs lightly. We replace them only after we're persuaded by sound arguments backed by good reasons based on the best evidence available, and after an amiable but searching give-and-take that tests those arguments as severely as we can. In short, we become *responsible* believers when we can make our own sound arguments that test and evaluate those of others.

You may find it difficult to see all of this at work in a paper written for a class, but as we've emphasized since the beginning of this book, a research paper written for any audience is a conversation—imagined to be sure, but still a cooperative but rigorous inquiry into what we should and should not believe.

# PART II  *Citing Sources*

In part 2 we show you how to create citations that your readers will trust because they are complete, accurate, and in the correct format. Much of the time, your job is simply to collect some basic information about the sources you encounter as you do your research and insert it into your paper in the correct format later on.

Still, citing your sources can seem like a lot of extra work. So we understand if you'd rather just skip it. But there are good reasons to cite your sources. If you fail to cite what you should, you open yourself to a charge of plagiarism (see chapter 10). And if your citations are inaccurate or incomplete, you risk losing credibility. If your readers notice mistakes or, worse, can't find what you've cited, they have less reason to trust your research. Of course, at this stage in your career as a researcher, you can't harm anyone with a bad citation; you do not yet have readers whose well-being depends on the results of your research. But you will. And your most important reader at this stage—your teacher—will be every bit as demanding as any of your future readers might be.

**Read Me First: How to Use Part 2**
Citing your sources means extra work, but it's really not all that hard. (Writing your paper is the hard part.) Start by reviewing the steps outlined here.

**Before you start to research**
Read chapter 19: it will help you guide your research and drafting. It will also help you understand how source citations work, which will help you make better decisions as you do your research and draft your paper. If you are interested, you might also read the introductory sections of the chapter that explains the citation style you plan to use. Don't try to study and remember all the models—you will consult them as you add and double-check individual citations.

**As you research**
Record all the bibliographical data on each source as you find it, *before* you do anything else with the source. Be disciplined about this job and you will avoid much trouble later (see 4.4). If you use software to manage your citations—for example, a program like EndNote or EasyBib—record all the data there. Even if you're not using citation software, you can still take advantage of the citations offered by library catalogs and other websites whenever they are available.

**As you draft**

First, read the section that explains how to cite sources in your text (for Chicago 20.1, for MLA 21.1, or for APA 22.1). If you are using MLA or APA, add the in-text citations as you draft. If you are using Chicago style, you don't need to create full notes as you draft if doing so will disrupt the flow of your writing. Instead record just the basic information for each source—for example, author, title, and page numbers—so that you can come back later to create proper notes.

If you use citation software, you can use it to insert citations as you draft, but only if you have already entered or imported the bibliographic data for each of your sources. (Do not disrupt your writing to enter bibliographic data as you go.) If you take advantage of this convenience, *do not think that you can leave it all to the software.* Even the best citation tools make mistakes, so be prepared to double-check your citations for accuracy and proper format.

**After you draft**

Once you are sure that your in-text citations are correct, create notes and a bibliography for Chicago style (20.1–2), a works cited list for MLA (21.2), or a reference list for APA (22.2). For each source, find the model for that kind of source and make sure your entry is formatted like the example. Pay close attention to the details, including capitalization, punctuation, and abbreviations. You can let your software create a draft of bibliographical entries, but you still must check each one against the appropriate model.

Before you turn in your paper, make sure you can answer yes to these two questions: Is the information for each source that you cite accurate and complete? Is each citation formatted correctly according to one of the styles in this book?

# 19 Citations

In this chapter we explain what you need to know about citations, no matter which kind of citations you plan to use: why researchers cite sources, the general form of citations, and a plan for collecting information for your citations. You'll find models for your specific citations in chapters 20–22. But first read this chapter for an overview that will help you make better decisions when you use the models.

## 19.1    Why Cite Sources?

There are four main reasons to cite your sources:

1. **To be honest about what you did and what you borrowed.** With every citation, you give credit to the person(s) behind a source for the hard work that went into finding and reporting the information you used. You also avoid seeming to take credit for work you did not do, which protects you against a charge of plagiarism (see chapter 10).

2. **To assure readers that they can trust your evidence.** You can't expect readers to accept evidence simply on your own say-so. They want to know where it came from and why they should trust it. For evidence you gathered yourself, they want to know how and where you found it. For evidence gathered by others, they want to know its source so that they can judge its reliability, perhaps even check it out for themselves. Readers do not trust a source they do not know and cannot find; if they do not trust your sources, they will not trust your evidence; if they do not trust your evidence, they will not trust your paper—or you. You establish the first link in that chain of trust by citing sources fully and properly.

3. **To tell readers which earlier research informed your work.** Researchers cite some sources for the data they use as evidence, but they also cite sources for the ideas or methods that influenced how they thought about their problem and its

solution. When you cite sources that influenced your thinking, you show readers how your work connects to that of others.

4. **To help readers follow or extend your research.** Just as you used the references in your sources to find other useful works on your question (see 4.2.5), so your readers may use your sources to guide their research.

All of these reasons share the same goal: to help your readers understand and trust your research.

As a student, you also have a more immediate reason to cite your sources: because you want to succeed, and to do that, you have to cite your sources. Unless your teacher tells you otherwise, assume that every research assignment requires proper citations for all sources.

## 19.2 When You Must Cite a Source

You must include a citation every time you use the words, ideas, or distinctive methods of a source (see 10.3). In particular, include a citation every time you use a source in any of these three ways:

- You quote the exact words of a source, including single words or phrases if they are distinctive enough. You must also indicate every quotation with quotation marks or a block indent.
- You paraphrase the words of a source.
- You use distinctive ideas or methods you found in a source.

## 19.3 Three Citation Styles

Researchers have been publishing their work for more than four centuries. In that long tradition of citing sources, they have developed many distinctive citation systems. Here we will cover the three most popular citation styles for academic research:

- Chicago style (also known as Turabian style), from the University of Chicago Press. This style is widely used in the humanities and qualitative social sciences.
- MLA style, from the Modern Language Association. This style is widely used in literary studies.
- APA style, from the American Psychological Association. This style is widely used in the quantitative social sciences.

The distinctive features of these styles are described in chapters 20–22.

In all three styles you must identify citations in two places: in your text and in a separate list of sources at the end. First you must indicate in your text where you used a source and what parts of a source you used.

For Chicago style, you do that with notes: insert a raised (superscript) note number in the text to show where you used the source, and identify the source and the page(s) you used in the corresponding note.

**Chicago**

Thirty years before Wonder Woman would make her first appearance, an Amazon was "any woman rebel—which, to a lot of people, meant any girl who left home and went to college."[1] By this time, women like Holloway were not only going to college in greater numbers and gaining crucial momentum toward attaining the right to vote . . .

    1. Jill Lepore, *The Secret History of Wonder Woman* (New York: Vintage Books, 2015), 17.

For MLA and APA style you do not use notes but insert a brief parenthetical reference with the page number(s) and just enough information to find the source in your list at the end:

**MLA**

Thirty years before Wonder Woman would make her first appearance, an Amazon was "any woman rebel—which, to a lot of people, meant any girl who left home and went to college" (Lepore 17). By this time . . .

**APA**

Thirty years before Wonder Woman would make her first appearance, an Amazon was "any woman rebel—which, to a lot of people, meant any girl who left home and went to college" (Lepore 2015, p. 17). By this time . . .

Then at the end of your paper, you include an alphabetical list of all your sources with complete bibliographical information for each.

Don't let yourself become overwhelmed by all the details. Few researchers try to remember even half of them. Experienced researchers learn the basic form for common citations and then consult a book like this one to double-check the details. This book will also help you as you navigate the options for each style in your preferred citation software.

19.4    **What to Include in a Citation**

Although Chicago, MLA, and APA styles format citations differently, they have the same goal: to give readers the information they need to identify and find a source. For most sources, that information must answer three questions:

1.   *Who created or is otherwise responsible for the text?*

This is usually the author, but it might also be an editor, a translator, or an organization.

2. *What is it called?*

This includes the title and subtitle of the work itself.

3. *Who published it, where, and when?*

These are known as the facts of publication. For a book, the facts of publication include the publisher and (except in MLA style) the place of publication. For an article in a journal, they include the title of the journal as well as a volume and issue number and the page numbers of the article. For sources consulted online, they include a URL. For all sources, the facts of publication include the date of publication, posting, or revision; for an undated source consulted online, you must include the date you accessed the source.

With this information, readers can almost always identify and find the specific source in your citation.

19.5     **Collect Bibliographical Data as You Research and Draft**

As you go through the early stages of your project, you may be tempted to put off collecting citations. Resist. Not only will you have to find each source twice— once to read it and again to get data for a citation—but you may not always be able to find the source again. And if you're like most people, you'll have more time for citations at the beginning than at the end, when your deadline is looming. So record *all* the bibliographical data the first time you locate a source (whether or not you are using a program like EndNote or EasyBib to manage your citations). You'll be glad you did.

19.5.1     **What Bibliographical Data You Should Save**

You won't need to memorize the details of each citation format, but you will need to know what information to save. Even if you plan on getting most of your citations online, copy this checklist and keep it handy as you do your research.

| For books, record | For articles, record |
|---|---|
| ☐ author(s) | ☐ author(s) |
| ☐ title (including subtitle) | ☐ title (including subtitle) |
| ☐ edition or volume number (if any) | ☐ title of journal, magazine, website, etc. |
| ☐ title of multivolume work or series (if any) | ☐ volume and issue number (if any) |
| ☐ city and publisher | ☐ date published |
| ☐ year published | ☐ pages for article (if any) |
| ☐ title and pages for chapter (if relevant) | ☐ URL (for articles read online) |
| ☐ URL (for books read online) | |

For other types of sources, the information will vary. Record as much of the above as applies, along with anything else that might help readers locate the source.

**A Cautionary Tale**

**The scholar who misplaced his source**

Many years ago, a young Professor Williams made an important discovery about the history of the English language because he found some old church records that no one had thought to connect to how people spoke in Shakespeare's time. But when it came time to publish his discovery, he came to an awful realization: he had not recorded all of the bibliographical data on the source, and he could not remember exactly where he had found it. For more than a year he could not publish his paper, while he searched for that source. Then it came to him one night in his sleep: he had been looking in the wrong library!

Professor Williams was happy to report that he never made that mistake again.

19.5.2    **How to Find the Data You Need**

For the most part, you will find all of the bibliographic data you need at the beginning of books and journals and on the title page of articles. For websites, you may have to look around. Here are some examples of where to find data for books and journal articles, two of the most common kinds of sources used by researchers. It is a good idea to become familiar with how to look for these things even if you copy most of your citation data directly from a library catalog or Google Books.

# The University of Chicago

— Title of book

✳

## A HISTORY

— Subtitle of book

## John W. Boyer

— Author's name

The University of Chicago Press    CHICAGO AND LONDON

Publisher's name        City of publication
(cite first-named city only)

JOHN W. BOYER is the Martin A. Ryerson Distinguished Service
Professor in History at the University of Chicago. In 2012 he was
appointed to a fifth term as Dean of the College. A specialist in the
history of the Habsburg Empire, he has written three books on
Austrian history, including, most recently, *Karl Lueger (1844–1910):
Christlichsoziale Politik als Beruf.*

The University of Chicago Press, Chicago 60637
The University of Chicago Press, Ltd., London
© 2015 by The University of Chicago
All rights reserved. Published 2015.
Printed in the United States of America

Year of publication ———
(use copyright date)

24  23  22  21  20  19  18  17  16  15      1  2  3  4  5

ISBN-13: 978-0-226-38120-6 (cloth: limited edition)
ISBN-13: 978-0-226-24251-4 (cloth)
ISBN-13: 978-0-226-24265-1 (e-book)
DOI: 10.7208/chicago/9780226242651.001.0001

Library of Congress Control Number: 2015021573

♾ This paper meets the requirements of ANSI/NISO Z39.48-1992
(Permanence of Paper).

# Economic Analysis of the Digital Economy

Title of book

Edited by **Avi Goldfarb, Shane M. Greenstein, and Catherine E. Tucker**

Editors' names (*not* authors)

REVISED EDITION

# BLACK PICKET FENCES

— Title of book

*Privilege and Peril among
the Black Middle Class*

— Subtitle of book

SECOND EDITION

— Edition number

# MARY PATTILLO

— Author's name

Year of publication
(cite only the year of
the revised edition)

The University of Chicago Press, Chicago 60637
The University of Chicago Press, Ltd., London
© 1999, 2013 by The University of Chicago

# Sergei Eisenstein's *Ivan the Terrible* as History*

Article title

Joan Neuberger ——— Author's name
*University of Texas at Austin*

Film scholars have long known that the great Soviet director Sergei Eisenstein read extensively in historical sources while preparing to make his epic 1940s film, *Ivan the Terrible*.[1] But no one has asked what he did with this material, how it shaped his understanding of Ivan IV and the Russian past, or how it shaped his ideas about artistic production and political reality in the Soviet present. Professional historians tend to be suspicious of historical films, and for good reason. Filmmakers do not share our concerns with evidence, and their goals as well as their audiences differ from ours. *Ivan the Terrible* will never be mistaken for a historian's rendering of the past, and Eisenstein never claimed to match historians' standards for accuracy. His immersion in the primary and secondary sources on Ivan's Muscovy, however, indicates an approach that is far from cavalier. Eisenstein did more than skim the main books in the field. He read a substantial number of the major works on Ivan and sixteenth-century Muscovy and many minor ones as well. He took detailed notes and linked what he read with works on psychology, ethnography, and literature to compose his portrait of the tsar and develop his approach to history. His notes on sources, his attempt to accompany the publication of his screenplay with an exhaustive "Historical Commentary,"[2] and the choices that we ultimately see in his screenplay and film

*Research for this article was generously supported by the University of Texas at Austin, the Humanities Institute and the Institute for Historical Studies at University of Texas at Austin, the National Council for Eurasian and East European Research, and the International Research and Exchanges Board (IREX). I wish to thank Valerie Kivelson, Sabine Hake, and the *JMH* anonymous reviewers for their helpful comments. I am also grateful to the fellows of the Humanities Institute and the Institute for Historical Studies, to Gleb Tsipursky, Nicholas Breyfogle, David Hoffman, and the members of their seminar at the Ohio State University, and to Yana Skorobogatov and the Berkeley *kruzhok* for stimulating discussions on the material presented here.

[1] R. Iurenev, *Sergei Eizenshtein: Zamysly, Fil'my, Metod*, 2 vols. (Moscow, 1988), 2:211–13; Naum Kleiman, "Kommentariia," in Sergei Eizenshtein, *Izbrannye proizvdeniia v shesti tomakh*, 6 vols. (Moscow, 1964–71), 6:548; M. I. Andronikova, *Ot prototipa k obrazu: K probleme portreta v literature i v kino* (Moscow, 1974), 55–58; Viktor Shklovskii, *Eizenshtein* (Moscow, 1973), 251–52.

[2] The "Historical Commentary" is a compendium of more than 300 quotations from the screenplay annotated with citations of the original text from scores of historical sources; Sergei Eizenshtein, "Istoricheskii kommentarii k fil'mu *Ivan Groznyi*," *Kinovedcheskie zapiski* 38 (1998): 177–245.

Pages of article

*The Journal of Modern History* 86 (June 2014): 295–334

Journal title   Volume number   Date of publication

Title of journal +
volume, issue, and date

The Journal of Modern History

The Journal of Modern History

Volume 86, Number 2 | June 2014

SUBSCRIBE/RENEW ⌄     BROWSE ISSUES ⌄     CONTRIBUTORS ⌄     ABOUT ⌄

‹ Previous Article                          ⎯ Article title   Next Article ›

# Sergei Eisenstein's *Ivan the Terrible* as History*

Joan Neuberger ⎯⎯⎯⎯ Author's name
University of Texas at Austin

First Page     **Full Text**     PDF

Film scholars have long known that the great Soviet director Sergei Eisenstein read extensively in historical sources while preparing to make his epic 1940s film, *Ivan the Terrible*.[1] But no one has asked what he did with this material, how it shaped his understanding of Ivan IV and the Russian past, or how it shaped his ideas about artistic production and political reality in the Soviet present. Professional historians tend to be suspicious of historical films, and for good reason. Filmmakers do not share our concerns with evidence, and their goals as well as their audiences differ from ours. *Ivan the Terrible* will never be mistaken for a historian's rendering of the past, and Eisenstein never claimed to match historians' standards for accuracy. His immersion in the primary and secondary sources on Ivan's Muscovy, however, indicates an approach that is far from cavalier. Eisenstein did more than skim the main books in the field. He read a substantial number of the major works on Ivan and sixteenth-century Muscovy and many minor ones as well. He took detailed notes and linked what he read with works on psychology, ethnography, and literature to compose his portrait of the tsar and develop his approach to history. His notes on sources, his attempt to accompany the publication of his screenplay with an exhaustive "Historical Commentary,"[2] and the choices that we ultimately see in his screenplay and film

**TOOLS**

◰ Export Citation        ◉ Track Citation

✉ Email A Friend         ☆ Add To Favorites

🔓 Permissions           ◈ Reprints

**SHARE**

f  G+  𝕐  in  ✉  +

**RECOMMEND THIS JOURNAL**
*to your library.*

*Sign up for eTOC alerts.*

**ARTICLE CITATION**

Joan Neuberger, "Sergei Eisenstein's *Ivan the Terrible* as History," *The Journal of Modern History* 86, no. 2 (June 2014): 295-334.

DOI: 10.1086/675483

Basic citation data
(in Chicago style) +
DOI for article

19.5.3    **How to Record Bibliographical Data as You Go**

Your best method for recording bibliographical data depends on where and how you do your research. But no matter your circumstances, always record everything you might need the first time you encounter a source.

*If you are reading online*

1.   Before you finish with a source, copy its citation data. If you are using citation software, enter the data there. Otherwise, enter the data in a document that you've created for this purpose, leaving room for any notes about the source and why you need it (create a template for this).
2.   Double-check your data against the source while it's in front of you—so you don't have to return to the source later just to finish your citation.
3.   Save links to any web page that has material you may use. If you plan on citing the page, enter its citation data and save a copy of the page in case you need to refer to it later.
4.   You might also consider making copies of title pages, copyright pages, and others with bibliographical information you might need. (This is also good advice for pages with long quotations.)

*If you are reading in a library but away from your computer*

1.   Before you head for the library, use your word processor to create a template for the information you will record. Print more copies than you expect to need. (Or, if you use your phone to take notes, plan on creating a separate note for each source.)
2.   Before you finish with a source, record its citation data on a template page (or in a note). Check twice so that you only have to find the source once. Consider making copies of pages with the information you need.
3.   Back at your computer, enter the information from your template pages (or notes) either into your citation database or in the template file.

19.5.4    **What to Do When You Can't Find the Data You Need**

You can expect little trouble in finding the bibliographical data you need for most sources. But if your source lacks the usual information or doesn't seem to fit any pattern, you can almost always find information that will substitute. Be flexible and think about *why* readers might need each kind of information. For example, if you cite a TV show or a film, you probably won't include an author, but readers will be happy if you cite the director instead. For a song, the songwriter or the performer is most like an author and the record company is most like the publisher.

　　　　If all else fails, make sure to answer these three basic questions about your source: *Who created it? What is it called? Who published it, where, and when?* (See also 19.4.) Then test your citation. Does it give enough information to lead your readers back to the same exact source that you consulted? If so, it's probably good enough. Just make sure to format it in a logical way, according to one of the three styles covered in this book.

# 20 Chicago Style

This chapter shows you how to use the Chicago notes-bibliography style. In Chicago style, you use numbered *notes* for the citations in your text. Whenever you use the words or ideas of a source, you mark the place in your text with a raised number called a superscript and give the information about the source in a correspondingly numbered note. You then collect all the sources you have cited into an alphabetical listing called a *bibliography*. This list should also include any works that you did not cite but that influenced your thinking. In special cases you may include all sources you consulted, even if you did not use them in any way; but ask your teacher before you do so.

The forms for notes and bibliography entries are different for different kinds of sources, but for each kind of source a note and bibliography entry are similar.

**NOTE FOR JOURNAL ARTICLE**

1. Santosh Anagol and Thomas Fujiwara, "The Runner-Up Effect," *Journal of Political Economy* 124, no. 4 (August 2016): 950.

**BIBLIOGRAPHY ENTRY FOR JOURNAL ARTICLE**

Anagol, Santosh, and Thomas Fujiwara. "The Runner-Up Effect." *Journal of Political Economy* 124, no. 4 (August 2016): 927–991.

**NOTE FOR BOOK**

  2. Jill Lepore, *The Secret History of Wonder Woman* (New York: Vintage Books, 2015), 17.

**BIBLIOGRAPHY ENTRY FOR BOOK**

Lepore, Jill. *The Secret History of Wonder Woman.* New York: Vintage Books, 2015.

Although they look similar, these forms vary in small but important details, such as order of elements and how they're punctuated. In some cases they will also vary in how the elements are capitalized or abbreviated. So be sure you use the right kind of example and pay close attention to these details. To help you avoid confusing the note form with the form for the bibliography entry, we've listed them in different sections (20.1 Notes and 20.2 Bibliography).

---

## How to Use This Chapter

This chapter presents models for the most common kinds of sources, starting with articles and ending with books. You will find models for notes in section 20.1 and for bibliography entries in 20.2. Within each section, the models are listed by category: articles; websites, blogs, and social media; reference works; personal communications and interviews; and books. Whether you are double-checking your citations or creating them from scratch, follow these steps:

1. **Find a model.**
   - Find the model that matches your kind of source. For instance, if you need to cite a scholarly journal article in an online database, find the example under "Journal."
   - If your source does not match any of the examples in this chapter, find one that is similar. Or consult a more comprehensive guide, such as Kate. L. Turabian, *A Manual for Writers of Research Papers, Theses, and Dissertations*, 9th ed. (Chicago: University of Chicago Press, 2018).

2. **Match the model.**
   - Make sure your citation matches the bibliographical details in the model. Pay close attention to punctuation, capitalization, and abbreviations.
   - If your source has multiple authors, consult the information on authors' names in section 20.1.2.1 (notes) or 20.2.1.1 (bibliography).

3. **Adjust as needed.**
   - You may make reasonable small adjustments if your source is the same kind as a model but its bibliographic information is slightly different. For example, if the person who put together a book of collected material is called a "compiler" rather than an editor, you may

> use the form for an edited volume and use the word "compiler" or the abbreviation "comp." wherever the example uses "editor" or "ed.":
> 68. Henry Jones, compiler, *The Oxford Book of* . . .
> - If your source is different from any of the models, make sure your citation answers these three questions: *Who created the source? What is it called? Who published it, where, and when?*

You will likely get many of your citations from a library or website. And you may use software that formats citations for you automatically. It's okay to let your software create a first draft of your citations, *but do not trust it to produce the correct form in every case.* Always double-check each note and bibliographic entry against the appropriate model. (By the time you do this, you should have already checked your data for accuracy against the sources themselves.) It's easy to miss small but important details when a citation is already formatted for you, so go slowly and be careful.

## 20.1   Notes

### 20.1.1   When and How to Add Notes

You must indicate in your text every place where you use the words or ideas of a source. In most cases you should cite a source in a numbered note, with a corresponding number inserted in your text. The exact form of the note depends on the kind of source you cite: book, journal article, information from a website, and so on. For sources you cite often, you can use parenthetical references.

For a quotation or paraphrase, insert the note number or parenthetical reference at the end of the quotation or at the end of the sentence that includes it:

The founding fathers' commitment to religious freedom was based on their commitment to the freedom of ideas. They were adamant that the "coercion of the laws" cannot apply to "the operations of the mind" in the way that they must apply to "the acts of the body."[3]

For ideas or methods, insert the note number at the end of the sentence in which you first introduce or explain the borrowed material. *Be sure to cite every source that influenced your thinking, even if you do not quote or paraphrase from it.* A reader might think you're guilty of plagiarism if you seem to reflect the ideas of a text that you do not cite. (See chapter 10.)

Notes are called *footnotes* if you put them at the bottom of the page or *endnotes* if they are in a separate list at the end. Most readers find footnotes easier to use because they can see the text and the note at the same time, without turning to the end of the paper. Find out what your teacher prefers, but if you have a choice, use footnotes.

20.1.1.1   *Numbered Notes*

Most citations in your paper should be in numbered notes. Use your word processor to insert a number into your text that directs readers to a correspondingly numbered note.

Thirty years before Wonder Woman would make her first appearance, an Amazon was "any woman rebel—which, to a lot of people, meant any girl who left home and went to college."[1] By this time . . .

> 1. Jill Lepore, *The Secret History of Wonder Woman* (New York: Vintage Books, 2015), 17.

The note number in your text must be placed *after* any punctuation:

NOT . . . equality[2]. Supporters . . .   BUT . . . equality.[2] Supporters . . .

Your word processor should format the note for you. In some cases you may need to adjust the settings. Follow these guidelines:

- Number each note with a superscript in both the text and at the beginning of the corresponding note. In the note, however, it is okay to instead use a regular number followed by a period: 1. Jill Lepore, *The Secret History* . . .
- Indent each note like a paragraph.
- Single-space notes with a blank line between notes.
- For footnotes, put a line between the body text and the first footnote on each page.
- For endnotes, list all notes starting on a new page after the text but before the bibliography; center the heading "Notes" at the top.

20.1.1.2   *Shortened Notes*

If you refer to the same source more than once, you can use a short form after the first note. The first note must give the full citation. After that, give enough information to identify the source, usually the author's last name and a word or two from the title. If you add page numbers, put a comma after the title and then the pages (but do not use "p." or "pp.").

Thirty years before Wonder Woman would make her first appearance, an Amazon was "any woman rebel—which, to a lot of people, meant any girl who left home and went to college."[1] By this time, women like Holloway were not only going to college in greater numbers and gaining crucial momentum toward attaining the right to vote but also embracing a new feminist ideal of political equality.[2] Supporters of women's rights . . .

> 1. Jill Lepore, *The Secret History of Wonder Woman* (New York: Vintage Books, 2015), 17.
> 2. Lepore, *Wonder Woman*, 21.

20.1.1.3    *Parenthetical References in the Text*
Although most citations should be in notes, you can use parenthetical references if you have several citations of the same source. This is common when your paper analyzes one or two texts, as in many literary, philosophical, or historical essays.
In these cases, the first reference to the source should be a complete note:

> 3. Thomas Jefferson, *Notes on the State of Virginia*, ed. William Peden (New York: W. W. Norton, 1954), 16.

After that you can use a short parenthetical reference inserted into your text each time you cite this source. Give just enough information to match the reference to the full citation given in the note. In most cases you should include only the author's last name and the page number, separated by a comma:

> The founding fathers' commitment to religious freedom was based on their commitment to the freedom of ideas. They were adamant that the "coercion of the laws" cannot apply to "the operations of the mind" in the way that they must apply to "the acts of the body" (Jefferson, 159).

If you mention the author's name in your text, you can give just the page number in parentheses:

> . . . their commitment to the freedom of ideas. As Thomas Jefferson put it, the "coercion of the laws" cannot apply to "the operations of the mind" in the way that they must apply to "the acts of the body" (159).

If, however, your paper cites two works by the same author, you need to give both the author's name and a keyword or two from the title so that readers will know which work you are citing:

> . . . the "coercion of the laws" cannot apply to "the operations of the mind" in the way that they must apply to "the acts of the body" (Jefferson, *Notes*, 159).

20.1.2    **Elements Common to All Notes**
When you create a note, you have to pay attention to the kind of source you are citing, because many elements of notes are different for different kinds of sources. But almost all notes consist of four basic elements—author's name, title of the work, publication facts, and page numbers.

20.1.2.1    *Author's Name*
The first element in a note is always the name of the author or authors. You should give the full name of the author *exactly* as it is shown in the source; use initials only if that's how the name appears. Do not include titles such as *Sir, Saint, Sister, Reverend*, and *Doctor*. List all authors' names in regular order: first-middle-last. (*Note*: Authors are listed differently in bibliography entries; see 20.2.1.1.)

**SINGLE AUTHOR**

> 4. Atul Gawande, *Being Mortal* . . .
> 5. J. K. Rowling, *Harry Potter and* . . .

**MULTIPLE AUTHORS**

If there is more than one author, list them in the order shown in the source. For three authors, put a comma between names and add *and* before the last name.

> 6. Steven D. Levitt and Stephen J. Dubner, *Freakonomics* . . .
> 7. Joyce Heatherton, James Fitzgilroy, and Jackson Hsu, *Meteors and Mudslides* . . .

If there are four or more authors listed in the bibliography, include only the first one, followed by "et al." (and others).

> 8. Barry Eichengreen et al., *The Korean Economy* . . .

If there is no author listed in the source, begin the note with the title of the work.

20.1.2.2   *Title*

Give the title *exactly* as it is shown in the source, including a subtitle if there is one. For articles and other short works, you will need both the article title and the title of the book, journal, website, or other work in which it appears.

Capitalize titles headline-style: capitalize the first and last words of the title and subtitle and all other words *except* articles (*a, an, the*), coordinating conjunctions (*and, but, or, nor, for*), prepositions (*of, in, at, above, under,* and so forth), and the words *to* and *as*. If a title includes a subtitle, put a colon between the main title and the subtitle. With few exceptions, titles are set off in quotation marks or italics.

Put the titles of short works that are part of longer ones in regular type, enclosed in quotation marks. These include articles, chapters in books, and other shorter works or parts of longer works. Put the titles of longer works in italics. These include books, journals, magazines, newspapers, and blogs. For additional categories, including examples, see 25.1. *Note*: Except for blogs and news sites, Chicago style does not put the titles of websites in italics.

20.1.2.3   *Publication Facts*

In addition to the author's name and title of the work, a note usually includes facts that identify *who* published the source, *where*, and *when*. Publication facts vary from one kind of source to another, so check each model carefully.

*Note*: The publication facts for books include the city of publication. For well-known cities like New York or London, you don't have to include a state or country. For all other cities, add the state or country unless it's included in the publisher's name.

For sources consulted online, you must include a complete online address, or URL (uniform resource locator). In most cases you should copy the URL from your browser's address bar. For online sources that do not list a date of publication or posting or revision, you must also include an access date. For examples, see 20.1.4 and 20.1.6.

*Note*: If you consult a library database like LexisNexis Academic or one of the databases offered by EBSCOhost, you can list the name of the database instead of a URL, especially if the URL for the specific item is very long. For examples, see 20.1.3 (newspaper article) and 20.1.7.1 (book).

20.1.2.4    *Page Numbers*

If you cite a specific passage in a source, you must indicate where readers can find that passage, usually by adding a page number. Do not include the word "page" or the abbreviation "p." or "pp." before the number. For books and most other types of sources, the number is preceded by a comma. For journal articles, the number is preceded by a colon.

> 9. Santosh Anagol and Thomas Fujiwara, "The Runner-Up Effect," *Journal of Political Economy* 124, no. 4 (August 2016): 950.

If you cite a range of pages, include all the digits in both numbers: do not abbreviate the second (*not* 127–32). (This is a departure from strict Chicago style, for the sake of simplicity.)

> 10. Jill Lepore, *The Secret History of Wonder Woman* (New York: Vintage Books, 2015), 124–125.

If you cite material from a table or lines from a poem, use the word *table* or *line(s)* and an identifying number(s).

> 11. Kenneth T. Jackson, *Crabgrass Frontier: The Suburbanization of the United States* (New York: Oxford University Press, 1985), table 1.
> 12. Ogden Nash, "Song for Ditherers," lines 1–4.

Sources published online or as an e-book often lack fixed page numbers. For articles and other shorter sources, you can skip this element. For a book, you can cite by chapter or section—or find a version that includes page numbers and cite that instead.

20.1.3    **Notes for Periodical Articles**

Most of the articles you will consult will be found in *periodicals*—journals, magazines, newspapers, and other works published at periodic intervals in print form, online, or both.

- **Journals** are scholarly, literary, or professional periodicals written for experts and available primarily through academic libraries. Journals often include the word *journal* in their title (*Journal of Modern History*) but not always (*Ethics*).

- **Magazines** are not scholarly publications; they are designed for more general readers in both their content and their availability outside of academic settings. If you are unsure whether a periodical is a journal or a magazine, see whether its articles include citations; if so, treat it as a journal.
- **Newspapers and news sites** are generally daily or weekly publications whose articles are closely tied to recent events.

### THE BASIC PATTERN

**Chicago note format for a journal article:** Commas between most elements, but no comma before volume number and colon before page number. End with a period.

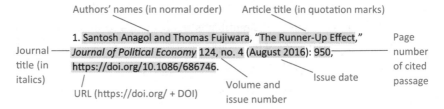

Authors' names (in normal order)    Article title (in quotation marks)

1. Santosh Anagol and Thomas Fujiwara, "The Runner-Up Effect,"    Page
Journal — *Journal of Political Economy* 124, no. 4 (August 2016): 950,    number
title (in    https://doi.org/10.1086/686746.    of cited
italics)    /    Issue date    passage
URL (https://doi.org/ + DOI)    Volume and
issue number

### JOURNAL

If a journal lists both a volume and issue number, include both; give the date in parentheses. If you consult the article online, include a URL. If the article comes with a suggested form of the URL, use that. If it lists a DOI (a type of permanent identifier), add the DOI to "https://doi.org/" to create the URL.

*Note*: If the article title includes a term in quotation marks, use single quotation marks for the term. If it includes a term in italics, retain the italics.

13. Mónica Domínguez Torres, "Havana's Fortunes: 'Entangled Histories' in Copley's *Watson and the Shark*," *American Art* 30, no. 2 (Summer 2016): 9.

14. Abadir M. Ibrahim, "A Not-So-Radical Approach to Human Rights in Islam," *Journal of Religion* 96, no. 3 (July 2016): 351–352, https://doi.org/10.1086 /686568.

15. Alexander Ivashkin. "Who's Afraid of Socialist Realism?," *Slavonic and East European Review* 92, no. 3 (2014): 435, http://www.jstor.org/stable/10.5699 /slaveasteurorev2.92.3.0430.

16. Barbara Novak, "Church, Humboldt, and the Politics of Display," *Getty Research Journal* 8 (2016): 75.

### MAGAZINE

You can include page numbers for articles in printed magazines; omit them for online articles that do not have page numbers. If the article is part of a "department" (a recurring section with the same title in each issue), add the department name in regular type without quotation marks between the article and magazine titles.

17. David Dempsey, "How to Get Published, More or Less," *Harper's Magazine*, July 1, 1955, 77.
18. Patricia Marx, "Big Skyline," Talk of the Town, *New Yorker*, April 27, 2015, http://www.newyorker.com/magazine/2015/04/27/big-skyline.
19. Stefan Fatsis, "The Definition of a Dictionary," *Slate*, January 12, 2015, http://www.slate.com/articles/life/culturebox/2015/01/merriam_webster _dictionary_what_should_an_online_dictionary_look_like.html.

NEWSPAPER OR NEWS SITE
Omit page numbers, even for a printed edition. You may clarify which edition you consulted by adding "final edition," "Midwest edition," or whatever applies.

20. Bishop, Greg. "Favre Wins in Debut for Jets." *New York Times*, September 7, 2008, late edition.
21. "Donald Trump Is Now Hiring," editorial, *New York Times*, November 14, 2016, LexisNexis Academic.
22. Libby Nelson, "Why Trigger Warnings Are Really So Controversial, Explained," *Vox*, September 26, 2016, http://www.vox.com/2015/9/10/9298577 /trigger-warnings-college.
23. "Edward Snowden Explains How to Reclaim Your Privacy," interview by Micah Lee, *The Intercept*, November 12, 2015, https://theintercept.com/2015/11 /12/edward-snowden-explains-how-to-reclaim-your-privacy/.

*Note*: Interviews are cited like ordinary articles, except the author is listed after the title of the interview. In the bibliography, the entry is listed under the name of the interviewee (see 20.2.2). Unpublished interviews are cited as a form of personal communication (see 20.1.5).

## 20.1.4   Notes for Websites, Blogs, and Social Media
You must cite *all* material you find online, even if you did not find it through your library, and even if it is not published by a journal, magazine, or newspaper. In a note, cite the specific item that you consulted (https://www.nasa.gov/mission _pages/juno/), not the website as a whole (https://www.nasa.gov/). Similarly, do not cite an entire blog or social media account in a note; instead, cite the particular post or comment that you use in your paper.

WEBSITE CONTENT
To cite website content, including webpages, articles, and videos, include the following information in a note:

- author, if any
- title of page, article, video, etc. (in quotation marks)
- website title, if any (in regular type)
- owner or sponsor of the content or site (if different from website title)
- date of publication or posting or revision, if any; otherwise, include an access date
- format, if relevant (e.g., "YouTube video")
- URL for the page

24. "Privacy Policy," Privacy & Terms, Google, last modified March 25, 2016, http://www.google.com/policies/privacy/.

25. Bill de Blasio, "Mayor de Blasio Delivers the State of the City Address," NYC Mayor's Office, February 13, 2018, YouTube video, https://youtu.be/yp3ggth d8ho.

26. "History," Columbia University, accessed July 1, 2016, http://www .columbia.edu/content/history.html.

### BLOG POST

Blog posts (or entries) are cited like articles from newspapers or news sites (see 20.1.3). If the blog is part of a larger publication such as a newspaper or website, give the name of the publication after the title of the blog.

27. Sharon Jayson, "Is Selfie Culture Making Our Kids Selfish?," *Well* (blog), *New York Times*, June 23, 2016, http://well.blogs.nytimes.com/2016/06/23/is-selfie -culture-making-our-kids-selfish/.

28. Lindy West, "Sweden Introduces New Gender-Neutral Pronoun, Makes Being a Man ILLEGAL," *Jezebel*, April 11, 2013, http://jezebel.com/sweden -introduces-new-gender-neutral-pronoun-makes-bei-472492079.

### SOCIAL MEDIA CONTENT

Content shared over social media and available to the public can usually be cited by identifying the following elements:

- The author of the post. List a screen name in addition to the name of the person or group on the account, if known. Otherwise just use the screen name.
- In place of a title, the text of the post. Quote up to the first 160 characters (enough to capture the typical text message), capitalized as in the original. (*Note*: If you quoted the post in your text, there is no need to repeat it in a note.)
- The type of post. This can include a description (*photo*, *video*, etc.).
- The date, including month, day, and year. You can also include a time stamp to help differentiate a post from others on the same day.
- A URL. The URL can often be found via the date stamp for the item.

29. Conan O'Brien (@ConanOBrien), "In honor of Earth Day, I'm recycling my tweets," Twitter, April 22, 2015, 11:10 a.m., https://twitter.com/ConanOBrien /status/590940792967016448.

30. Chicago Manual of Style, "Is the world ready for singular they? We thought so back in 1993," Facebook, April 17, 2015, https://www.facebook.com /ChicagoManual/posts/10152906193679151.

31. Pete Souza (@petesouza), "President Obama bids farewell to President Xi of China at the conclusion of the Nuclear Security Summit," Instagram photo, April 1, 2016, https://www.instagram.com/p/BDrmfXTtNCt/.

A direct message or other private content shared with you through social media and not available for others to consult is cited as a form of personal communication. See 20.1.5 for examples.

READERS' COMMENTS

To cite a reader's comment, begin with the identity of the commenter (as listed with the comment), the date (and time, if listed) of the comment, and the words "comment on," followed by the information for the original article or post.

32. Francois (Chicago), June 24, 2016, comment on Sharon Jayson, "Is Selfie Culture Making Our Kids Selfish?," *Well* (blog), *New York Times*, June 23, 2016, http://well.blogs.nytimes.com/2016/06/23/is-selfie-culture-making-our-kids -selfish/.
   *or, if you've already cited the original post,*
33. Francois (Chicago), June 24, 2016, comment on Jayson, "Selfie Culture."

*Note*: If you identify the comment in the text, you don't need to also include it in a note. Just be sure to cite the original article or post that the comment refers to.

## 20.1.5    Notes for Personal Communications and Interviews

Unpublished interviews, conversations, email, direct messages, texts, and other forms of personal communications with the author are cited in the notes as shown here. If the name of the interviewee or correspondent has been mentioned in the text, it may be omitted from the note. Unless the communication is conducted in person, include the medium.

34. Emma Fenton, Instagram direct message to author, March 25, 2018.

35. Retired US Army Captain Adam J. Reid, interview by author, November 1, 2018.

36. Home health aide, interview by author via Facebook Messenger, April 2, 2018.
   *or, if you've mentioned the interviewee in the text,*
37. Interview by author via Facebook Messenger, April 2, 2018.

For an example of a published interview, see 20.1.3 (under "Newspaper or News Site").

20.1.6   **Notes for Reference Works**

Reference works are sources such as encyclopedias and dictionaries; their entries usually do not have authors. (Cite an entry with an author as you would a chapter of a book; see 20.1.7.2.)

Most reference works are arranged by alphabetical or searchable entries and are cited by entry, not by page number. List the entry in quotation marks, preceded by "s.v." (for the Latin *sub verbo*, or "under the word"). If you list more than one entry in the same note, use "s.vv."

For entries found online, include a URL; if the entry does not include a date of publication or revision, add an access date.

*Note*: Titles of websites like Wikipedia are usually in regular type in Chicago style, not italics.

**ENCYCLOPEDIA**

38. Wikipedia, s.v. "Muhammad Ali," last modified September 25, 2016, https://en.wikipedia.org/wiki/Muhammad_Ali.

39. *Britannica Academic*, s.v. "Olympic Games," last modified September 9, 2016, http://academic.eb.com/levels/collegiate/article/108519.

If an encyclopedia has an edition number, include it.

40. *Encyclopaedia Britannica*, 15th ed. (1980), s.v. "Sibelius, Jean."

**DICTIONARY**

41. *Oxford English Dictionary*, s.v. "ROFL," accessed June 26, 2016, http://www.oed.com/view/Entry/156942#eid1211161030.

42. *Merriam-Webster*, s.v. "mondegreen," accessed September 27, 2016, http://www.merriam-webster.com/dictionary/mondegreen.

20.1.7   **Notes for Books**

**THE BASIC PATTERN**

Chicago note format for a book: Commas between most elements, but publisher info in parentheses and colon between city of publication and publisher's name. End with a period.

Author's name (in normal order)        Title of book (in italics)

1. Jill Lepore, *The Secret History of Wonder Woman* (New York: Vintage Books, 2015), 17.

Publisher's name     Year of publication     Page number of cited passage     City of publication

20.1.7.1   *Whole Books*

**BOOK, GENERAL FORMAT**

43. Herman Melville, *Moby-Dick; or, The Whale* (New York: Harper & Brothers, 1851), 627.

44. Janice M. McCabe, *Connecting in College: How Friendship Networks Matter for Academic and Social Success* (Chicago: University of Chicago Press, 2016), 112.

If the book is produced by an organization rather than a person, list the organization as the author:

45. United Nations, *Basic Facts about the United Nations, 2014* (New York: UN Department of Public Information, 2014), 211.

**ONLINE BOOK**

Most online books have page numbers. If the version you want to cite does not, find one that does (or identify the pages by section or chapter number). Use the URL for the main page (if there is more than one). If you consulted the book through a library database, you can list that instead of a URL.

46. Herman Melville, *Moby-Dick; or, The Whale* (New York: Harper & Brothers, 1851), 627, http://mel.hofstra.edu/moby-dick-the-whale-proofs.html.

47. John David Skrentny, *After Civil Rights: Racial Realism in the New American Workplace* (Princeton, NJ: Princeton University Press, 2014), 267–268, eBook Academic Collection, EBSCOhost.

**E-BOOK**

Instead of page numbers, many e-book formats use location or screen numbers, which change depending on a user's settings. In that case, cite chapters or sections instead, or find an edition that includes page numbers. Identify the e-book format as the last element.

48. Jane Austen, *Pride and Prejudice* (New York: Penguin Classics, 2007), chap. 23, iBooks.

49. Lin-Manuel Miranda and Jeremy McCarter, *Hamilton: The Revolution* (New York: Grand Central Publishing, 2016), act 2, chap. 22, Kindle.

**EDITED OR TRANSLATED BOOK**

If a book has an editor or translator but no author, put the editor or translator in place of the author, followed by the abbreviation "ed." or "trans."

50. Gian Carlo Delgado-Ramos, ed., *Inequality and Climate Change: Perspectives from the South* (Dakar, Senegal: CODESRIA, 2015), 88.

51. Theodore Silverstein, trans., *Sir Gawain and the Green Knight* (Chicago: University of Chicago Press, 1974), 34.

If a book has an author as well as an editor or a translator, identify the editor or translator between the title and the publication facts.

52. Yves Bonnefoy, *New and Selected Poems*, ed. John Naughton and Anthony Rudolf (Chicago: University of Chicago Press, 1995), 64.

53. Georges Feydeau, *Four Farces by Georges Feydeau*, trans. Norman R. Shapiro (Chicago: University of Chicago Press, 1970), 122.

### REVISED EDITION

If you consult a book labeled as a "revised" edition or a "second" (or subsequent) edition, place this information between the title and the publication facts, using abbreviations.

54. Mary Kinzie, *A Poet's Guide to Poetry*, 2nd ed. (Chicago: University of Chicago Press, 2013), 83.

55. Steven D. Levitt and Stephen J. Dubner, *Freakonomics: A Rogue Economist Explores the Hidden Side of Everything*, rev. ed. (New York: HarperCollins, 2006), 47.

### MULTIVOLUME WORK OR SERIES

If you cite one book from a group of books with the same title (known as a *multivolume work*), give the total number of volumes after the title. Indicate the specific volume number immediately before the page number, with the two numbers separated by a colon (do not include the word "volume" or the abbreviation "vol.").

56. Muriel St. Clare Byrne, ed., *The Lisle Letters*, 6 vols. (Chicago: University of Chicago Press, 1981), 4:243.

If the volume you cite has a different title from that of the whole group, give the volume title after the title of the group as a whole.

57. Clayborne Carson, ed., *The Papers of Martin Luther King, Jr.*, vol. 7, *To Save the Soul of America, January 1961–August 1962*, ed. Tenisha Armstrong (Berkeley: University of California Press, 2014), 182.

If you cite a book that belongs to a named series, you can give the series title after the book title, in regular type.

58. Blake M. Hausman, *Riding the Trail of Tears*, Native Storiers: A Series of American Narratives (Lincoln: University of Nebraska Press, 2011), 25.

## 20.1.7.2  *Parts of Books*

### CHAPTER IN AN EDITED BOOK

If a book consists of chapters written by several different authors, cite the chapter you consulted.

59. Kelly Gillespie, "Before the Commission: Ethnography as Public Testimony," in *If Truth Be Told: The Politics of Public Ethnography*, ed. Didier Fassin (Durham, NC: Duke University Press, 2017), 72.

**INTRODUCTION, PREFACE, OR AFTERWORD**

If someone other than the author has written a supplemental part of a book, such as an introduction, foreword, afterword, or epilogue, cite it separately. If the part has a title, include it in quotation marks.

60. Susan McClary, "Humanizing the Humanities," foreword to *Just Vibrations: The Purpose of Sounding Good*, by William Cheng (Ann Arbor: University of Michigan Press, 2016), xvii.

**LETTER IN A COLLECTION**

61. Adams to Charles Milnes Gaskell, London, March 30, 1868, in *Letters of Henry Adams, 1858–1891*, ed. Worthington Chauncey Ford (Boston: Houghton Mifflin, 1930), 141.

**SHORT STORY OR POEM IN A COLLECTION**

Put the title of a short story or a poem in regular type with quotation marks. (*Exception*: The title of a very long poem that was first published separately as a book can be put in italics: Milton, *Paradise Lost*.)

62. Jhumpa Lahiri, "This Blessed House," in *Interpreter of Maladies* (Boston: Houghton Mifflin Harcourt, 1999), 138.

63. Seamus Heaney, "To George Seferis in the Underworld," in *District and Circle: Poems* (New York: Farrar, Straus and Giroux, 2006), 23.

## 20.2    Bibliography

If you have notes to more than four or five sources, you must list each source at the end of your paper in a section called a bibliography. You should also list other works you read but did not cite, if they influenced your thinking; a reader might think you're guilty of plagiarism if you seem to reflect the ideas of a text that you do not include in your bibliography (see chapter 10). Normally you should not include sources you consulted but did not use in any way, but your teacher may ask you to include them in order to see the scope of your research.

Start your list of sources on a new page. Center the heading "Bibliography" at the top of the first page. Skip two lines and list all entries in alphabetical order, single-spaced, with an extra line space after each entry. Format each entry with a half-inch hanging indent. Alphabetize the sources according to the last names of the authors or editors. You can use your word processor to do this. If you do it yourself, follow the order of the letters:

Macally, Mack, Madden, McArthur, Mecks . . .
Saint-Beuve, Schwab, Selleck, Skillen, St. Helena, Stricker . . .

If you have to list more than one source by the same author, order those sources alphabetically by their titles. If a source does not have an author or editor, the first element in the bibliography entry will be the title, so use that to place the entry alphabetically among the authors' names.

See the sample bibliography in Chicago style at the end of this chapter.

### 20.2.1   Elements Common to All Bibliography Entries

When you create a bibliography entry, you have to pay attention to the kind of source you are citing, because many elements are different for different kinds of sources. But most bibliography entries consist of three basic elements—author's name, title of the work, and publication facts.

### 20.2.1.1   *Author's Name*

Whenever possible, begin each bibliography entry with the name of the author(s). Spell out the full name of the author *exactly* as it is shown in the source: use initials only if that's how the name appears. Do not include titles such as *Sir*, *Saint*, *Sister*, *Reverend*, and *Doctor*. However, list the author's name in *inverted* order: last name–comma–first name–middle name (if any). (*Note*: Authors are listed differently in notes; see 20.1.2.1.)

**SINGLE AUTHOR**

Gawande, Atul. *Being Mortal* . . .
Rowling, J. K. *Harry Potter and* . . .

**MULTIPLE AUTHORS**

List authors in the order they appear on the title page. To allow the authors to line up in alphabetical order by last name, invert the name of the *first* author. List all other authors in regular order. Separate the names by commas and put *and* before the last author. A period follows the name of the last author.

Levitt, Steven D., and Stephen J. Dubner. *Freakonomics* . . .
Heatherton, Joyce, James Fitzgilroy, and Jackson Hsu. *Meteors and Mudslides* . . .

If there is no author listed, begin the entry with the title of the work.

**MULTIPLE WORKS BY ONE AUTHOR**

If you cite multiple works by the same author or group of authors, you will have several entries that begin the same. For all entries after the first, replace the name(s) with three long dashes (em dashes). If the work is edited or translated, add the corresponding designation after the three em dashes and a comma. *Add these dashes only after you have sorted your final bibliography.* Note that the "ed." or "trans." is ignored in alphabetizing.

| NOT | BUT |
|---|---|
| Schank, Roger C. *Dynamic Memory* . . . | Schank, Roger C. *Dynamic Memory* . . . |
| Schank, Roger C., ed. *Inside Multi-media* . . . | ———, ed. *Inside Multi-media* . . . |
| Schank, Roger C. *Reading and* . . . | ———. *Reading and* . . . |
| Schank, Roger C. *Tell Me a Story* . . . | ———. *Tell Me a Story* . . . |

### 20.2.1.2    Title

Give the title *exactly* as it is shown in the source, including a subtitle if there is one. For articles and other short works, you will need both the article title and the title of the book, journal, website, or other work in which it appears.

Capitalize titles headline-style: capitalize the first and last words of the title and subtitle and all other words *except* articles (*a, an, the*), coordinating conjunctions (*and, but, or, nor, for*), prepositions (*of, in, at, above, under*, and so forth), and the words *to* and *as*. If a title includes a subtitle, put a colon between the main title and the subtitle. With few exceptions, titles are set off in quotation marks or italics.

Put the titles of short works that are part of longer ones in regular type, enclosed in quotation marks. These include articles, chapters in books, and other shorter works or parts of longer works. Put the titles of longer works in italics. These include books, journals, magazines, newspapers, and blogs. For additional categories, including examples, see 25.1. *Note*: Except for blogs and news sites, Chicago style does not put the titles of websites in italics.

### 20.2.1.3    Publication Facts

In addition to author's name and title, a bibliographic citation usually includes facts that identify *who* published the source, *where*, and *when*. Publication facts vary from one kind of source to another, so check each model carefully.

*Note*: The publication facts for books include the city of publication. For well-known cities like New York or London, you don't have to include a state or country. For all other cities, add the state or country unless it's included in the publisher's name.

For sources consulted online, you must include a complete online address, or URL (uniform resource locator). In most cases you should copy the URL from your browser's address bar. For online sources that do not list a date of publication or posting or revision, you must also include an access date. For an example, see 20.2.3.

*Note*: If you consult a library database like LexisNexis Academic or one of the databases offered by EBSCOhost, you can list the name of the database instead of a URL, especially if the URL for the specific item is very long. For examples, see 20.2.2 (newspaper article) and 20.2.6.1 (book).

### 20.2.2   Bibliography Entries for Periodical Articles

Most of the articles you will consult will be found in *periodicals*—journals, magazines, newspapers, and other works published at periodic intervals in print form, online, or both.

- **Journals** are scholarly, literary, or professional periodicals written for experts and available primarily through academic libraries. Journals often include the word *journal* in their titles (*Journal of Modern History*) but not always (*Ethics*).
- **Magazines** are not scholarly publications; they are designed for more general readers in both their content and their availability outside of academic settings. If you are unsure whether a periodical is a journal or a magazine, see whether its articles include citations; if so, treat it as a journal.
- **Newspapers and news sites** are generally daily or weekly publications whose articles are closely tied to recent events.

**THE BASIC PATTERN**

**Chicago bibliography entry for a journal article:** Periods between most elements, but no punctuation before volume number and colon before page numbers. End with a period.

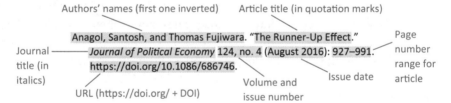

**JOURNAL**

If a journal lists both a volume and an issue number, include both; give the date in parentheses. If you consult the article online, include a URL. If the article comes with a suggested form of the URL, use that. If it lists a DOI (a type of permanent identifier), add the DOI to "https://doi.org/" to create the URL.

*Note*: If the article title includes a term in quotation marks, use single quotation marks for the term. If it includes a term in italics, retain the italics.

Domínguez Torres, Mónica. "Havana's Fortunes: 'Entangled Histories' in Copley's *Watson and the Shark*." *American Art* 30, no. 2 (Summer 2016): 8–13.

Ibrahim, Abadir M. "A Not-So-Radical Approach to Human Rights in Islam." *Journal of Religion* 96, no. 3 (July 2016): 346–377. https://doi.org/10.1086/686568.

Ivashkin, Alexander. "Who's Afraid of Socialist Realism?" *Slavonic and East European Review* 92, no. 3 (2014): 430–448. http://www.jstor.org/stable/10.5699 /slaveasteurorev2.92.3.0430.

Novak, Barbara. "Church, Humboldt, and the Politics of Display." *Getty Research Journal* 8 (2016): 73–92.

**MAGAZINE**

Magazine articles often jump across many pages with unrelated material, so do not include page numbers. If the article is part of a "department" (a recurring section with the same title in each issue), add the department name in regular type without quotation marks between the article and magazine titles.

Dempsey, David. "How to Get Published, More or Less." *Harper's Magazine*, July 1, 1955.

Fatsis, Stefan. "The Definition of a Dictionary." *Slate*, January 12, 2015. http:// www.slate.com/articles/life/culturebox/2015/01/merriam_webster _dictionary_what_should_an_online_dictionary_look_like.html.

Marx, Patricia. "Big Skyline." Talk of the Town. *New Yorker*, April 27, 2015. http:// www.newyorker.com/magazine/2015/04/27/big-skyline.

**NEWSPAPER OR NEWS SITE**

Omit page numbers, even for a printed edition. You may clarify which edition you consulted by adding "final edition," "Midwest edition," or whatever applies.

Bishop, Greg. "Favre Wins in Debut for Jets." *New York Times*, September 7, 2008, late edition.

Nelson, Libby. "Why Trigger Warnings Are Really So Controversial, Explained." *Vox*, September 26, 2016. http://www.vox.com/2015/9/10/9298577/trigger -warnings-college.

*New York Times*. "Donald Trump Is Now Hiring." Editorial. November 14, 2016. LexisNexis Academic.

Snowden, Edward. "Edward Snowden Explains How to Reclaim Your Privacy." Interview by Micah Lee. *The Intercept*, November 12, 2015. https://theintercept .com/2015/11/12/edward-snowden-explains-how-to-reclaim-your-privacy/.

*Note*: If a news article has no author, list it under the name of the newspaper or news site in the bibliography.

*Note*: Interviews are listed under the name of the interviewee; the name of the interviewer follows the title of the interview. Unpublished interviews are cited as a form of personal communication (see 20.2.4).

20.2.3   **Bibliography Entries for Websites, Blogs, and Social Media**
To cite website content, blog posts, and content shared via social media in a bibliography, adapt the recommendations and examples for notes at 20.1.4.

WEBSITE CONTENT

List under the author, if any, or under the main website or sponsoring organization. For undated content, include an access date.

Columbia University. "History." Accessed July 1, 2016. http://www.columbia.edu /content/history.html.

de Blasio, Bill. "Mayor de Blasio Delivers the State of the City Address." NYC Mayor's Office, February 13, 2018. YouTube video. https://youtu.be/yp3ggth d8ho.

Google. "Privacy Policy," Privacy & Terms. Last modified March 25, 2016. http:// www.google.com/policies/privacy/.

BLOG POST

Jayson, Sharon. "Is Selfie Culture Making Our Kids Selfish?" *Well* (blog). *New York Times*, June 23, 2016. http://well.blogs.nytimes.com/2016/06/23/is-selfie -culture-making-our-kids-selfish/.

West, Lindy. "Sweden Introduces New Gender-Neutral Pronoun, Makes Being a Man ILLEGAL." *Jezebel*, April 11, 2013. http://jezebel.com/sweden-introduces -new-gender-neutral-pronoun-makes-bei-472492079.

If you have cited more than two posts from the same blog in your notes, cite the blog as a whole in your bibliography, not the individual posts.

Carmichael, Emma, ed. *Jezebel*. http://jezebel.com/.

SOCIAL MEDIA CONTENT

Cite social media content under the name of the account holder, including screen name. (If only a screen name is known, list under that; ignore an @ in alphabetizing the name.)

Chicago Manual of Style. "Is the world ready for singular they? We thought so back in 1993." Facebook, April 17, 2015. https://www.facebook.com /ChicagoManual/posts/10152906193679151.

O'Brien, Conan (@ConanOBrien). "In honor of Earth Day, I'm recycling my tweets." Twitter, April 22, 2015, 11:10 a.m. https://twitter.com/ConanOBrien /status/590940792967016448.

Souza, Pete (@petesouza). "President Obama bids farewell to President Xi of China at the conclusion of the Nuclear Security Summit." Instagram photo, April 1, 2016. https://www.instagram.com/p/BDrmfXTtNCt/.

If you cite more than two posts from a single account in your notes, cite the account as a whole in your bibliography, not the individual posts.

Chicago Manual of Style. Facebook. https://www.facebook.com/ChicagoManual.

A direct message or other private content shared with you through social media is cited as a form of personal communication. See 20.2.4 for examples.

READERS' COMMENTS
Readers' comments are cited only in the text or in the notes, not in the bibliography. See 20.1.4.

20.2.4  **Bibliography Entries for Personal Communications and Interviews**
Unpublished interviews, conversations, email, direct messages, texts, and other forms of personal communications are cited under the name of the interviewee or conversation partner. If the name is withheld, use a description in place of a name. Text messages and other brief forms of correspondence can often be omitted from the bibliography but should be cited in the text or in a note (see 20.1.5).

Fenton, Emma. Instagram direct message to author, March 25, 2018.
Home health aide. Interview by author. Facebook Messenger, April 2, 2018.
Reid, Adam J., US Army Captain, Retired. Interview by author, November 1, 2018.

For an example of a published interview, see 20.2.2 (under "Newspaper or News Site").

20.2.5  **Bibliography Entries for Reference Works**
Bibliography entries for general reference works such as the *Encyclopaedia Britannica* and the *Oxford English Dictionary* should cite the work as a whole, not specific entries as in notes (see 20.1.6). List the title of the work, the edition number (if any), and for online works the URL for the home page. Do not include an access date.

*Britannica Academic.* http://academic.eb.com/.
*Merriam-Webster.* http://www.merriam-webster.com/.
*Oxford English Dictionary.* 2nd ed. 1989.

If your teacher allows, a longer article in a general reference work may be included in your bibliography, under the name of the article:

"Muhammad Ali." Wikipedia. Last modified September 25, 2016. https://en
      .wikipedia.org/wiki/Muhammad_Ali.

Specialized reference works are usually cited like books (see 20.2.6); an article in such a work is cited like a chapter in a book (see 20.2.6.2).

## 20.2.6   Bibliography Entries for Books

**THE BASIC PATTERN**

**Chicago bibliography entry for a book:** Periods between most elements, but colon between city of publication and publisher's name and comma before year of publication. End with a period.

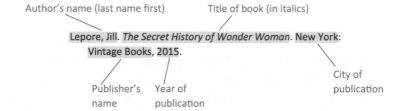

Author's name (last name first)      Title of book (in italics)

Lepore, Jill. *The Secret History of Wonder Woman*. New York: Vintage Books, 2015.

Publisher's   Year of            City of
name          publication        publication

### 20.2.6.1   Whole Books

**BOOK, GENERAL FORMAT**

McCabe, Janice M. *Connecting in College: How Friendship Networks Matter for Academic and Social Success*. Chicago: University of Chicago Press, 2016.

Melville, Herman. *Moby-Dick; or, The Whale*. New York: Harper & Brothers, 1851.

If the book is produced by an organization rather than a person, list the organization as the author:

United Nations. *Basic Facts about the United Nations, 2014*. New York: UN Department of Public Information, 2014.

**ONLINE BOOK**

Use the URL for the main page (if there is more than one). If you consulted the book through a library database, you can list that instead of a URL.

Melville, Herman. *Moby-Dick; or, The Whale*. New York: Harper & Brothers, 1851. http://mel.hofstra.edu/moby-dick-the-whale-proofs.html.

Skrentny, John David. *After Civil Rights: Racial Realism in the New American Workplace*. Princeton, NJ: Princeton University Press, 2014. eBook Academic Collection, EBSCOhost.

**E-BOOK**

Identify the e-book format as the last element.

Austen, Jane. *Pride and Prejudice*. New York: Penguin Classics, 2007. iBooks.

Miranda, Lin-Manuel, and Jeremy McCarter. *Hamilton: The Revolution*. New York: Grand Central Publishing, 2016. Kindle.

### EDITED OR TRANSLATED BOOK

If a book has an editor or translator instead of an author, put the name of the editor or translator in place of the author's, followed by the abbreviation "ed." or "trans."

Delgado-Ramos, Gian Carlo, ed. *Inequality and Climate Change: Perspectives from the South*. Dakar, Senegal: CODESRIA, 2015.

Silverstein, Theodore, trans. *Sir Gawain and the Green Knight*. Chicago: University of Chicago Press, 1974.

If a book has an author as well as an editor or a translator, identify the editor or translator between the title and the publication facts. Do not abbreviate the words "Edited by" or "Translated by."

Bonnefoy, Yves. *New and Selected Poems*. Edited by John Naughton and Anthony Rudolf. Chicago: University of Chicago Press, 1995.

Feydeau, Georges. *Four Farces by Georges Feydeau*. Translated by Norman R. Shapiro. Chicago: University of Chicago Press, 1970.

### REVISED EDITION

If you consult a book labeled as a "revised" edition or a "2nd" (or subsequent) edition, place this information between the title and the publication facts, using abbreviations as in the following examples.

Kinzie, Mary. *A Poet's Guide to Poetry*. 2nd ed. Chicago: University of Chicago Press, 2013.

Levitt, Steven D., and Stephen J. Dubner. *Freakonomics: A Rogue Economist Explores the Hidden Side of Everything*. Rev. ed. New York: HarperCollins, 2006.

### MULTIVOLUME WORK OR SERIES

If you cite one book from a group of books in a multivolume work, list only the specific volume you consulted. Identify the volume number ("Vol. X").

Byrne, Muriel St. Clare, ed. *The Lisle Letters*. Vol. 4. Chicago: University of Chicago Press, 1981.

If you consulted more than one volume in a group, list the whole group in a single entry. State the number of volumes after the title ("X vols.").

Byrne, Muriel St. Clare, ed. *The Lisle Letters*. 6 vols. Chicago: University of Chicago Press, 1981.

Carson, Clayborne, ed. *The Papers of Martin Luther King, Jr.* 7 vols. Berkeley: University of California Press, 1992–.

If you cite a single volume with a distinct title, use both titles, starting with the
title of the work as a whole.

Carson, Clayborne, ed. *The Papers of Martin Luther King, Jr.* Vol. 7, *To Save the Soul
of America, January 1961–August 1962*, edited by Tenisha Armstrong. Berkeley: University of California Press, 2014.

If you cite a book that belongs to a named series, you can give the series title
after the book title, in regular type.

Hausman, Blake M. *Riding the Trail of Tears*. Native Storiers: A Series of American
Narratives. Lincoln: University of Nebraska Press, 2011.

## 20.2.6.2   *Parts of Books*

### CHAPTER IN AN EDITED BOOK

Cite the specific chapter, not the whole book, if you refer only to that one chapter
in your notes. You may cite two specific chapters separately, if you specifically
compare them in your text. Otherwise cite the edited book as a whole.

Gillespie, Kelly. "Before the Commission: Ethnography as Public Testimony." In *If
Truth Be Told: The Politics of Public Ethnography*, edited by Didier Fassin, 69–95.
Durham, NC: Duke University Press, 2017.

### INTRODUCTION, PREFACE, OR AFTERWORD

If you have a note to a supplemental part of a book that was written by someone
other than the book author, cite it separately. If the part has a title, include it in
quotation marks.

McClary, Susan. "Humanizing the Humanities." Foreword to *Just Vibrations: The
Purpose of Sounding Good*, by William Cheng, xvii–xix. Ann Arbor: University
of Michigan Press, 2016.

### LETTER IN A COLLECTION

Cite individual letters from a collection in the text or notes only (see 20.1.7.2); the
collection as a whole is included in the bibliography.

Adams, Henry. *Letters of Henry Adams, 1858–1891*. Edited by Worthington
Chauncey Ford. Boston: Houghton Mifflin, 1930.

**SHORT STORY OR POEM IN A COLLECTION**

Cite the specific work, not the whole book, if you refer only to that one work in
your notes. You may cite two or more specific works separately if you specifically
compare them in your text. Otherwise, cite the collection as a whole.

Heaney, Seamus. "To George Seferis in the Underworld." In *District and Circle*, 22–
23. New York: Farrar, Straus and Giroux, 2006.
Lahiri, Jhumpa. "This Blessed House." In *Interpreter of Maladies*, 136–157. Boston:
Houghton Mifflin Harcourt, 1999.

20.2.7    **Sample Bibliography, Chicago Style**
Model your Chicago-style bibliography on the following sample, drawn from
the examples in this chapter. Note that the entries appear in alphabetical order
by author or title. In your paper, you will add an extra line space between entries
(not shown here). For more advice on formatting your paper, see appendix A at
the end of this book.

**Bibliography**

Carson, Clayborne, ed. *The Papers of Martin Luther King, Jr.* Vol. 7, *To Save the
Soul of America, January 1961–August 1962*, edited by Tenisha Armstrong.
Berkeley: University of California Press, 2014.
de Blasio, Bill. "Mayor de Blasio Delivers the State of the City Address." NYC
Mayor's Office, February 13, 2018. YouTube video. https://youtu.be/yp3g
gthd8ho.
Domínguez Torres, Mónica. "Havana's Fortunes: 'Entangled Histories' in Cop-
ley's *Watson and the Shark*." *American Art* 30, no. 2 (Summer 2016): 8–13.
Fatsis, Stefan. "The Definition of a Dictionary." *Slate*, January 12, 2015. http://
www.slate.com/articles/life/culturebox/2015/01/merriam_webster_dictio
nary_what_should_an_online_dictionary_look_like.html.
Ibrahim, Abadir M. "A Not-So-Radical Approach to Human Rights in Islam."
*Journal of Religion* 96, no. 3 (July 2016): 346–377. https://doi.org/10.1086
/686568.
Kinzie, Mary. *A Poet's Guide to Poetry*. 2nd ed. Chicago: University of Chicago
Press, 2013.
Lahiri, Jhumpa. "This Blessed House." In *Interpreter of Maladies*, 136–157. Bos-
ton: Houghton Mifflin Harcourt, 1999.
Levitt, Steven D., and Stephen J. Dubner. *Freakonomics: A Rogue Economist Ex-
plores the Hidden Side of Everything*. Rev. ed. New York: HarperCollins, 2006.

Marx, Patricia. "Big Skyline." Talk of the Town. *New Yorker*, April 27, 2015. http://
www.newyorker.com/magazine/2015/04/27/big-skyline.

"Muhammad Ali." Wikipedia. Last modified September 25, 2016. https://en
.wikipedia.org/wiki/Muhammad_Ali.

*Oxford English Dictionary*. 2nd ed. 1989.

United Nations. *Basic Facts about the United Nations, 2014*. New York: UN Department of Public Information, 2014.

# 21 MLA Style

This chapter shows you how to use the MLA citation style. In this style, you use *parenthetical references* in the text to cite every instance in which you use a source. You must also create a *bibliographical entry* for each source, listing its author, title, and publication data. At the end of your paper, you collect these bibliographical entries into an alphabetical list. This list must include every source you mention in your text or in a parenthetical reference. If it includes only sources you specifically cite, it is titled "Works Cited." That list may also include all sources you consulted in your research, even if you did not cite them in your text. In that case it is titled "Works Consulted." Ask your teacher which you should use.

**How to Use This Chapter**

This chapter presents models for the most common kinds of sources, starting with articles and ending with books. You will find models of bibliographical entries in 21.2. The models are listed by category: articles; websites, blogs, and social media; personal communications and interviews; reference works; and books. Whether you are double-checking your citations or creating them from scratch, follow these steps.

1. **Find a model.**
   - Find the model that matches your kind of source. For instance, if you need to cite a scholarly journal article in an online database, find the example under "Journal."
   - If your source does not match any of the examples in this chapter,

find one that is similar. Or consult a more comprehensive guide, such as the *MLA Handbook*, 8th ed. (2016).

2.  **Match the model.**
    - Make sure your citation matches the bibliographical details in the model. Pay close attention to punctuation, capitalization, and abbreviations.
    - If your source has multiple authors, consult the information on authors' names in section 21.2.1.1.

3.  **Adjust as needed.**
    - You may make reasonable small adjustments if your source is the same kind as a model but its bibliographic information is slightly different. For example, if the person who put together a book of collected material is called a "compiler" rather than an editor, you may use the form for an edited volume and use the word "compiler" wherever the example uses "editor": Henry Jones, compiler. *The Oxford Book of . . .*
    - If your source is different from any of the models, make sure your citation answers these three questions: *Who created the source? What is it called? Who published it, where, and when?*

You will likely get many of your citations from a library or website. And you may use software that formats citations for you automatically. It's okay to let your software create a first draft of your citations, *but do not trust it to produce the correct form in every case.* Always double-check each bibliographical entry against the appropriate model. (By the time you do this, you should have already checked your data for accuracy against the sources themselves.) It's easy to miss small but important details when a citation is already formatted for you, so go slowly and be careful.

## 21.1   When and How to Cite Sources in Your Text

### 21.1.1   Parenthetical References

You must indicate in your text every place where you use the words or ideas of a source (see chapter 10). The general rule is to insert a parenthetical reference that gives readers the minimum information they need to find the cited passage. Typically that includes only the last name of the author and the page number(s) of the material in the source. The author's name tells readers how to find the details of that source in your works cited list, and the page numbers tell them where to look in the source. In some cases, however, you have to give more information to help readers identify a specific source (see 21.1.2).

You should insert the parenthetical reference immediately after the material borrowed from a source. For a quotation or paraphrase, insert the reference at the end of a sentence or clause (outside of quotation marks but inside a period or comma):

The founding fathers' commitment to religious freedom was based on their commitment to the freedom of ideas. They were adamant that the "coercion of the laws" cannot apply to "the operations of the mind" in the way that they must apply to "the acts of the body" (Jefferson 159).

If you quote or paraphrase several passages from the same work in a single paragraph, use only one parenthetical reference after the final quotation:

The founding fathers' commitment to religious freedom was based on their commitment to the freedom of ideas. They were adamant that the "coercion of the laws" cannot apply to "the operations of the mind" in the way that they must apply to "the acts of the body." The purpose of the law was, they believed, to protect us from injury. "But it does me no injury for my neighbor to say there are twenty gods, or no god" (Jefferson 159).

For a block quotation, add the parenthetical reference to the end with no period after it.

According to Jared Diamond,

> Because technology begets more technology, the importance of an invention's diffusion potentially exceeds the importance of the original invention. Technology's history exemplifies what is termed an autocatalytic process: that is, one that speeds up at a rate that increases with time, because the process catalyzes itself. (301)

For ideas or methods, insert the reference at the end of the sentence(s) in which you first introduce or explain the borrowed material. *Be sure to cite every source that influenced your thinking, even if you do not quote or paraphrase from it.* A reader might think you're guilty of plagiarism if you seem to reflect the ideas of a text that you do not cite. (See chapter 10.)

### 21.1.2  Forms of Parenthetical References

Each parenthetical reference must point to one and only one source in your works cited list. The standard form includes the author's last name and a page number. (If the work is listed by an editor or translator rather than an author, use that name but do not add "editor" or "translator.") You may, however, need more or less information. If you mention the author when you introduce a quotation or paraphrase, do not include the name again in the reference. If you list more than one work by the same author in your works cited, add a short title to identify which work you are citing. If you refer to a whole work rather than to a specific passage, do not include page numbers. There are other variants. These are the most common:

**AUTHOR NOT MENTIONED IN TEXT**
**(Name Page)**
The founding fathers' commitment to religious freedom was based on their commitment to the freedom of ideas. They were adamant that the "coercion of the laws" cannot apply to "the operations of the mind" in the way that they must apply to "the acts of the body" (Jefferson 159).

**AUTHOR MENTIONED IN TEXT**
**(Page)**
. . . their commitment to the freedom of ideas. As Thomas Jefferson put it, the "coercion of the laws" cannot apply to "the operations of the mind" in the way that they must apply to "the acts of the body" (159).

**AUTHOR WITH SAME LAST NAME AS OTHERS IN WORKS CITED**
**(Initial Name Page)**
. . . their commitment to the freedom of ideas. They were adamant that the "coercion of the laws" cannot apply to "the operations of the mind" in the way that they must apply to "the acts of the body" (T. Jefferson 159).

**MORE THAN ONE WORK BY AUTHOR**
**(Name, Short Title Page)**
. . . their commitment to the freedom of ideas. They were adamant that the "coercion of the laws" cannot apply to "the operations of the mind" in the way that they must apply to "the acts of the body" (Jefferson, *Notes* 159).

**TWO AUTHORS**
**(Name and Name Page)**
(Levitt and Dubner 47)

**THREE OR MORE AUTHORS**
**(Name et al. Page)**
(Heatherton et al. 192)

**TWO OR MORE WORKS IN ONE CITATION**
**(Name Page; Name Page)**
(Levitt and Dubner 47; Heatherton et al. 192)

21.1.3    **Footnotes**

In MLA style, you do not use notes to identify citations unless a citation is so long that it would disrupt the flow of your text. This situation typically arises when you cite many sources for a single idea. In that case, use the author + page form to refer to each source in the note:

By this time, women like Holloway were not only going to college in greater numbers and gaining crucial momentum toward attaining the right to vote but also embracing a new feminist ideal of political equality.[1] Supporters of women's rights . . .

   1. For political quality and the "New Woman," see Lepore 21. For the role of feminism in prewar American colleges, see Shalia 119–120; Zhang 212; Keller, *Women* 13; and Martinez, *Collegium* 44.

You may, of course, also use notes for substantive comments, supplemental information, and so on.

   Notes can be printed as footnotes, at the bottom of the page, or endnotes, on a separate page at the end. Because you are likely to have few notes, you should treat them as *footnotes*, which are easier for readers to find.

21.2    **Works Cited**

Because you give readers only minimal bibliographical information in your text, you must give complete information for every source in the works cited list at the end of your paper. Normally you should not include a source you did not cite in your text, but your teacher may ask you to include all sources you consulted in order to show the scope of your research.

   Start your list of sources on a new page. At the top of the first page center the heading "Works Cited." (If you include works you consulted but did not cite, use the heading "Works Consulted.") Skip two lines and list all references in alphabetical order, single-spaced, with an extra line space after each entry. Format each entry with a half-inch hanging indent. You can let your word processor put the list in alphabetical order. If you do this yourself, follow the order of the letters.

Macally, Mack, Madden, McArthur, Mecks . . .
Saint-Beuve, Schwab, Selleck, Skillen, St. Helena, Stricker . . .

   If you have to list more than one source by the same author, order those sources alphabetically by their titles. If a source does not have an author or editor, the first element in the bibliography entry will be the title, so use that to place the entry alphabetically among the authors' names.

   See the sample works cited list in MLA style at the end of this chapter.

21.2.1    **Elements Common to All Bibliographical Entries**

When you create a bibliographical entry, pay attention to the kind of source you are citing, because many elements of citations are different for different kinds of sources. But all MLA-style entries consist of three basic elements—author's name, title of the work, and publication facts (or what MLA calls the "container" for the work).

21.2.1.1    *Author's Name*

Whenever possible, begin each bibliographical entry with the name of the author(s). Spell the names exactly as they appear on the title page: use initials if that's how the name appears, but do not shorten names that are spelled out on the title page. Do not include titles such as *Sir*, *Saint*, *Sister*, *Reverend*, and *Doctor*. However, list the author's name in *inverted* order: last name–comma–first name–middle name (if any).

SINGLE AUTHOR

Gawande, Atul. *Being Mortal* . . .

Rowling, J. K. *Harry Potter and* . . .

MULTIPLE AUTHORS

List no more than two authors for any one work, in the order they appear on the title page. To allow the authors to line up in alphabetical order by last name, invert the name of the *first* author. List the name of the second author in regular order. Separate the names by commas and put *and* before the last author. A period follows the name of the last author. If a work has three or more authors, list only the first, followed by a comma and "et al." (and others).

Levitt, Steven D., and Stephen J. Dubner. *Freakonomics* . . .

Heatherton, Joyce, et al. *Meteors and Mudslides* . . .

MULTIPLE WORKS BY ONE AUTHOR

If you cite multiple works by the same author or group of authors, you will have several entries that begin the same. For all entries after the first, replace the name(s) with three hyphens (not dashes). If the work is edited or translated, add the corresponding designation after the three hyphens and a comma. *Add these hyphens only after you have sorted your final bibliography.* Note that "editor" or "translator" is ignored in alphabetizing.

NOT

Schank, Roger C. *Dynamic Memory* . . .

Schank, Roger C., editor. *Inside Multi-Media* . . .

BUT

Schank, Roger C. *Dynamic Memory* . . .

---, editor. *Inside Multi-Media* . . .

Schank, Roger C. *Reading and . . .*           ---. *Reading and . . .*
Schank, Roger C. *Tell Me a Story . . .*        ---. *Tell Me a Story . . .*

21.2.1.2    *Title*

Give the title *exactly* as it is shown in the source, including a subtitle if there is one. For articles and other short works, you will need both the article title and the title of the book, journal, website, or other work in which it appears.

Capitalize titles headline-style: capitalize the first and last words of the title and subtitle and all other words *except* articles (*a, an, the*), coordinating conjunctions (*and, but, or, nor, for*), prepositions (*of, in, at, above, under*, and so forth), and the words *to* and *as*. If a title includes a subtitle, put a colon between the main title and the subtitle. With few exceptions, titles are set off in quotation marks or italics.

Put the titles of short works that are part of longer ones in regular type, enclosed in quotation marks. These include articles, chapters in books, and other shorter works or parts of longer works. Put the titles of longer works in italics. These include books, journals, magazines, newspapers, and blogs. For additional categories, including examples, see 25.1. *Note*: MLA style puts the titles of websites in italics.

21.2.1.3    *Publication Facts*

In addition to author's name and title, a bibliographical entry usually includes facts that identify *who* published the source, *where*, and *when*. Publication facts vary from one kind of source to another, so check each model carefully.

*Note*: Except for very old works identified only by location, MLA style no longer requires including the city of publication for books.

If you cite a range of pages, include all the digits in both numbers: do not abbreviate the second (*not* 127–32).

For dates, use the day-month-year form, with no punctuation in the date: 4 May 2009. Abbreviate all months except May, June, and July: 23 Nov. 2017.

For sources consulted online, you must include a complete online address, or URL (uniform resource locator). In most cases you should copy the URL from your browser's address bar. For online sources that do not list a date of publication or posting or revision, you must also include an access date. For an example, see 21.2.3.

*Note*: MLA style does not include "http://" or "https://" in URLs. Exception: DOIs presented in the form of URLs begin with https://doi.org/ (see the section on journals at 21.2.2).

*Note*: For sources obtained through a library database or website, MLA style suggests listing the name of that resource in addition to the URL. But if you consult a database like LexisNexis Academic or one of the databases offered by EBSCOhost, you can list just the database, especially if the URL for the specific item is very long. For examples, see 21.2.2 (newspaper article) and 21.2.6.1 (book).

21.2.2   **Bibliographical Entries for Periodical Articles**

Most of the articles you will consult will be found in *periodicals*—journals, magazines, newspapers, and other works published at periodic intervals in print form, online, or both.

- **Journals** are scholarly, literary, or professional periodicals written for experts and available primarily through academic libraries. Journals often include the word *journal* in their titles (*Journal of Modern History*) but not always (*Ethics*).
- **Magazines** are not scholarly publications; they are designed for more general readers in both their content and their availability outside of academic settings. If you are unsure whether a periodical is a journal or a magazine, see whether its articles include citations; if so, treat it as a journal.
- **Newspapers and news sites** are generally daily or weekly publications whose articles are closely tied to recent events.

**THE BASIC PATTERN**

**MLA works cited entry for a journal article:** Periods after authors' names and title of article, commas between remaining elements. End with a period.

**JOURNAL**

If a journal lists both a volume and an issue number, include both. If you consult the article online, include a URL. If the article comes with a suggested form of the URL, use that. If it lists a DOI (a type of permanent identifier), add the DOI to "https://doi.org/" to create the URL. (In MLA style, other types of URLs do not begin with http:// or https://.) If you got the article from a library or commercial database, include the name of the database, in italics (and following a period), before the URL.

*Note*: If the article title includes a term in quotation marks, use single quotation marks for the term. If it includes a term in italics, retain the italics.

Domínguez Torres, Mónica. "Havana's Fortunes: 'Entangled Histories' in Copley's *Watson and the Shark*." *American Art*, vol. 30, no. 2, Summer 2016, pp. 8–13.

Ibrahim, Abadir M. "A Not-So-Radical Approach to Human Rights in Islam." *Journal of Religion*, vol. 96, no. 3, July 2016, pp. 346–377, https://doi.org/10.1086/686568.

Ivashkin, Alexander. "Who's Afraid of Socialist Realism?" *Slavonic and East European Review*, vol. 92, no. 3, 2014, pp. 430–448. *JSTOR*, www.jstor.org/stable/10.5699/slaveasteurorev2.92.3.0430.

Novak, Barbara. "Church, Humboldt, and the Politics of Display." *Getty Research Journal*, vol. 8, 2016, pp. 73–92.

## MAGAZINE

If the article is interrupted by other material, include only the first page number followed by "+.". Omit page numbers for articles consulted online.

Dempsey, David. "How to Get Published, More or Less." *Harper's Magazine*, 1 July 1955, pp. 77–80.

Fatsis, Stefan. "The Definition of a Dictionary." *Slate*, 12 Jan. 2015, www.slate.com/articles/life/culturebox/2015/01/merriam_webster_dictionary_what_should_an_online_dictionary_look_like.html.

Marx, Patricia. "Big Skyline." Talk of the Town, *New Yorker*, 27 Apr. 2015, www.newyorker.com/magazine/2015/04/27/big-skyline.

## NEWSPAPER OR NEWS SITE

Include the edition (abbreviate as "ed.") and the letter designation of the section if there is one. If the article is interrupted by other material, use only the first page number followed by "+." Omit page numbers for articles consulted online.

Bishop, Greg. "Favre Wins in Debut for Jets." *New York Times*, 7 Sept. 2008, late ed., p. D1.

"Donald Trump Is Now Hiring." Editorial. *New York Times*, 14 Nov. 2016. *LexisNexis Academic*.

Nelson, Libby. "Why Trigger Warnings Are Really So Controversial, Explained." *Vox*, 26 Sept. 2016, www.vox.com/2015/9/10/9298577/trigger-warnings-college.

Snowden, Edward. "Edward Snowden Explains How to Reclaim Your Privacy." Interview by Micah Lee, *The Intercept*, 12 Nov. 2015, theintercept.com/2015/11/12/edward-snowden-explains-how-to-reclaim-your-privacy/.

*Note*: If a news article has no author, list it by title in the works cited list.

*Note*: Interviews are listed under the name of the interviewee; the name of the interviewer follows the title of the interview. Unpublished interviews are cited as a form of personal communication (see 21.2.4).

21.2.3    **Bibliographical Entries for Websites, Blogs, and Social Media**
MLA style uses italics for the titles of named websites and blogs and the names of social media services. For descriptive titles, don't use italics. Articles and posts are in quotation marks.

WEBSITE CONTENT
To cite website content, including webpages, articles, and videos, include the following information:

- author, if any
- title of page, article, video, etc. (in quotation marks)
- website title, if any (in italics)
- owner or sponsor of the content or site (if different from website title)
- date of publication or posting or revision, if any
- URL for the page
- access date, for undated material

de Blasio, Bill. "Mayor de Blasio Delivers the State of the City Address."
    *YouTube*, uploaded by NYC Mayor's Office, 13 Feb. 2018, youtu.be/yp3ggth
    d8ho.
"History." *Columbia University*, www.columbia.edu/content/history.html. Ac-
    cessed 1 July 2016.
"Privacy Policy." *Privacy & Terms*, Google, 25 Mar. 2016, www.google.com/policies
    /privacy/.

*Note*: MLA style no longer specifies the medium of publication in works cited entries, even for videos and other multimedia.

BLOG POST
Blog posts (or entries) are cited like articles from newspapers or news sites (see 21.2.2); some blogs are hosted by news organizations, and many blogs are indistinguishable from news sites.

Jayson, Sharon. "Is Selfie Culture Making Our Kids Selfish?" *Well*, *New York Times*,
    23 June 2016, well.blogs.nytimes.com/2016/06/23/is-selfie-culture-making
    -our-kids-selfish/.
West, Lindy. "Sweden Introduces New Gender-Neutral Pronoun, Makes Being

a Man ILLEGAL." *Jezebel*, 11 Apr. 2013, jezebel.com/sweden-introduces-new
-gender-neutral-pronoun-makes-bei-472492079.

SOCIAL MEDIA CONTENT

Content shared over social media and available to the public can usually be cited
by identifying the following elements:

- The author of the post. List a screen name in addition to the name of the
  person or group on the account, if known. Otherwise, just use the screen
  name (ignore an @ in alphabetizing the name).
- In place of a title, the text of the post. Quote up to the first 160 characters
  (enough to capture the typical text message), capitalized as in the original.
- The type of post. This is usually the name of the website or service.
- The date, including month, day, and year. You can also include a time stamp
  to help differentiate a post from others on the same day.
- A URL. The URL can often be found via the date stamp for the item.

Chicago Manual of Style. "Is the world ready for singular they? We thought so
    back in 1993." *Facebook*, 17 Apr. 2015, www.facebook.com/ChicagoManual
    /posts/10152906193679151.
O'Brien, Conan (@ConanOBrien). "In honor of Earth Day, I'm recycling my
    tweets." *Twitter*, 22 Apr. 2015, 11:10 a.m., twitter.com/ConanOBrien/status
    /590940792967016448.
Souza, Pete (@petesouza). "President Obama bids farewell to President Xi of
    China at the conclusion of the Nuclear Security Summit." *Instagram*, 1 Apr.
    2016, www.instagram.com/p/BDrmfXTtNCt/.

A direct message or other private content shared with you through social media
is cited as a form of personal communication. See 21.2.4 for examples.

READERS' COMMENTS

Cite individual readers' comments in the body of your paper, in reference to the
original post (which may be cited with an appropriate in-text citation). Do not
include readers' comments in the list of works cited.

21.2.4    **Bibliographical Entries for Personal Communications
and Interviews**

Unpublished interviews, conversations, email, direct messages, texts, and other
forms of personal communications with the author are cited under the name of
the interviewee or conversation partner. If the name is withheld, use a description in place of a name.

Fenton, Emma. *Instagram* direct message to author, 25 Mar. 2018.

Home health aide. Interview by author. *Facebook Messenger*, 2 Apr. 2018.

Reid, Adam J., US Army Captain, Retired. Interview by author, 1 Nov. 2018.

For an example of a published interview, see 21.2.2 (under "Newspaper or News Site").

21.2.5   **Bibliographical Entries for Reference Works**

If the reference work is a standard one such as *Encyclopaedia Britannica* or the *Oxford English Dictionary*, do not cite the author, editor, or publication data. For print sources, list only the edition (if any) and the year. Cite the work as a whole in the list of works cited; the entries themselves are mentioned or described in the text.

*Britannica Academic*, academic.eb.com/.

*Merriam-Webster*, www.merriam-webster.com/.

*Oxford English Dictionary*, 2nd ed., 1989.

If your teacher allows, a longer article in a general reference work may be included in your works cited list, under the name of the article:

"Muhammad Ali." *Wikipedia*, last modified 25 Sept. 2016, en.wikipedia.org/wiki /Muhammad_Ali.

Specialized reference works are usually cited like books (see 21.2.6.1); an article in such a work is cited like a chapter in a book (see 21.2.6.2).

21.2.6   **Bibliographical Entries for Books**

**THE BASIC PATTERN**

**MLA works cited entry for a book:** Periods after author's name and title of book, comma between publisher's name and year of publication. End with a period.

Author's name (last name first)          Title of book (in italics)

Lepore, Jill. *The Secret History of Wonder Woman*. Vintage Books, 2015.

Publisher's name

Year of publication

21.2.6.1   *Whole Books*

**BOOK, GENERAL FORMAT**

For publishers' names, abbreviate "University" to "U" (no period) and "Press" to "P" (no period).

McCabe, Janice M. *Connecting in College: How Friendship Networks Matter for Academic and Social Success.* U of Chicago P, 2016.

Melville, Herman. *Moby-Dick; or, The Whale.* Harper & Brothers, 1851.

If the book is produced by an organization rather than a person, list the organization as the author:

United Nations. *Basic Facts about the United Nations, 2014.* UN Department of Public Information, 2014.

### ONLINE BOOK

Use the URL for the main page (if there is more than one). First list the website that hosts the book, following a period. But if you consulted the book through a library database, you don't need to list a URL, especially if the URL for the specific item is very long.

Melville, Herman. *Moby-Dick; or, The Whale.* Harper & Brothers, 1851. *Melville Electronic Archive,* mel.hofstra.edu/moby-dick-the-whale-proofs.html.

Skrentny, John David. *After Civil Rights: Racial Realism in the New American Workplace.* Princeton UP, 2014. *eBook Academic Collection,* EBSCOhost.

### E-BOOK

MLA style identifies an e-book format as an edition (abbreviated "ed.").

Austen, Jane. *Pride and Prejudice.* iBooks ed., Penguin Classics, 2007.

Miranda, Lin-Manuel, and Jeremy McCarter. *Hamilton: The Revolution.* Kindle ed., Grand Central Publishing, 2016.

### EDITED OR TRANSLATED BOOK

If a book has an editor or translator but no author, put the editor or translator in place of the author. Spell out "editor" and "translator" and the like.

Delgado-Ramos, Gian Carlo, editor. *Inequality and Climate Change: Perspectives from the South.* CODESRIA, 2015.

Silverstein, Theodore, translator. *Sir Gawain and the Green Knight.* U of Chicago P, 1974.

If a book has an author as well as an editor or a translator, identify the editor or translator after the title:

Adorno, Theodor W., and Walter Benjamin. *The Complete Correspondence, 1928–1940.* Edited by Henri Lonitz, translated by Nicholas Walker, Harvard UP, 1999.

Bonnefoy, Yves. *New and Selected Poems*. Edited by John Naughton and Anthony
   Rudolf, U Chicago P, 1995.
Menchú, Rigoberta. *Crossing Borders*. Translated and edited by Ann Wright,
   Verso, 1999.

### REVISED EDITION

If you consult a book labeled as a "revised" edition or a "second" (or subsequent)
edition, place this information between the title and the publication facts, using
abbreviations as in the following examples.

Kinzie, Mary. *A Poet's Guide to Poetry*. 2nd ed., U of Chicago P, 2013.
Levitt, Steven D., and Stephen J. Dubner. *Freakonomics: A Rogue Economist Explores
   the Hidden Side of Everything*. Rev. ed., HarperCollins, 2006.

### MULTIVOLUME WORK OR SERIES

If you cite one book from a group of books (called a *multivolume* work), list only
the specific volume you consulted. Identify the volume number ("Vol. X").

Byrne, Muriel St. Clare, editor. *The Lisle Letters*. Vol. 4, U of Chicago P, 1981.

If the one volume you cite has a different title from that of the whole group, cite
the title of the volume. You do not need to add the title of the group.

Armstrong, Tenisha, editor. *To Save the Soul of America, January 1961–August 1962*.
   U of California P, 2014.

If you consulted more than one volume in a group, list the whole group in a single
entry. State the number of volumes after the date ("X vols.").

Byrne, Muriel St. Clare, editor. *The Lisle Letters*. U of Chicago P, 1981. 6 vols.
Carson, Clayborne, editor. *The Papers of Martin Luther King, Jr.* U of California P,
   1992–. 7 vols.

In the text, you can refer a specific volume like this: (Carson 4: 123).
   If you cite a book that belongs to a named series, you can give the series title
in regular type, after the other publication data.

Hausman, Blake M. *Riding the Trail of Tears*. U of Nebraska P, 2011. Native Storiers: A Series of American Narratives.

21.2.6.2    *Parts of Books*

**CHAPTER IN AN EDITED BOOK**

Cite the specific chapter, not the whole book, if you refer only to that one chapter in your text. You may cite two specific chapters separately if you specifically compare them in your text. Otherwise, cite the edited book as a whole.

Gillespie, Kelly. "Before the Commission: Ethnography as Public Testimony."
     *If Truth Be Told: The Politics of Public Ethnography*, edited by Didier Fassin,
     Duke UP, 2017, pp. 69–95.

**INTRODUCTIONS, PREFACES, AFTERWORDS**

If you refer to a supplemental part of a book that was written by someone other than the book author, cite it separately. If the part has a title, include it in quotation marks.

McClary, Susan. "Humanizing the Humanities." Foreword. *Just Vibrations: The Purpose of Sounding Good*, by William Cheng, U of Michigan P, 2016, pp. xvii–xix.

**LETTER IN A COLLECTION**

Cite a letter from a published collection in the text, in reference to the work in which it appears.

Adams, in a letter to Charles Milnes Gaskell dated March 30, 1868 (141), . . .

Adams, Henry. *Letters of Henry Adams, 1858–1891*. Edited by Worthington
     Chauncey Ford, Houghton Mifflin, 1930.

**SHORT STORY OR POEM IN A COLLECTION**

Cite the specific work, not the whole book, if you refer only to that one work. You may cite two or more specific works separately if you specifically compare them in your text. Otherwise, cite the collection as a whole.

Heaney, Seamus. "To George Seferis in the Underworld." *District and Circle*, Farrar, Straus and Giroux, 2006, pp. 22–23.
Lahiri, Jhumpa. "This Blessed House." *Interpreter of Maladies*, Houghton Mifflin
     Harcourt, 1999, pp. 136–157.

21.2.7    **Sample Works Cited List, MLA Style**

Model your MLA-style works cited list on the following sample, drawn from the examples in this chapter. Note that the entries appear in alphabetical order by author or title. In your paper you will add an extra line space between entries (not shown here). For more advice on formatting your paper, see appendix A at the end of this book.

## Works Cited

Armstrong, Tenisha, editor. *To Save the Soul of America, January 1961–August 1962*. U of California P, 2014.

de Blasio, Bill. "Mayor de Blasio Delivers the State of the City Address." *YouTube*, uploaded by NYC Mayor's Office, 13 Feb. 2018, youtu.be/yp3ggthd8ho.

Domínguez Torres, Mónica. "Havana's Fortunes: 'Entangled Histories' in Copley's *Watson and the Shark*." *American Art*, vol. 30, no. 2, Summer 2016, pp. 8–13.

Fatsis, Stefan. "The Definition of a Dictionary." *Slate*, 12 Jan. 2015, www.slate.com/articles/life/culturebox/2015/01/merriam_webster_dictionary_what_should_an_online_dictionary_look_like.html.

Ibrahim, Abadir M. "A Not-So-Radical Approach to Human Rights in Islam." *Journal of Religion*, vol. 96, no. 3, July 2016, pp. 346–377, https://doi.org/10.1086/686568.

Kinzie, Mary. *A Poet's Guide to Poetry*. 2nd ed., U of Chicago P, 2013.

Lahiri, Jhumpa. "This Blessed House." *Interpreter of Maladies*, Houghton Mifflin Harcourt, 1999, pp. 136–157.

Levitt, Steven D., and Stephen J. Dubner. *Freakonomics: A Rogue Economist Explores the Hidden Side of Everything*. Rev. ed., HarperCollins, 2006.

Marx, Patricia. "Big Skyline." Talk of the Town, *New Yorker*, 27 Apr. 2015, www.newyorker.com/magazine/2015/04/27/big-skyline.

"Muhammad Ali." *Wikipedia*, last modified 25 Sept. 2016, https://en.wikipedia.org/wiki/Muhammad_Ali.

*Oxford English Dictionary*, 2nd ed., 1989.

United Nations. *Basic Facts about the United Nations, 2014*. UN Department of Public Information, 2014.

# 22 APA Style

This chapter shows you how to use the APA citation style. In this style you use *parenthetical references* in the text to cite every instance in which you use a source. You must also create a *bibliographical entry* for each source, listing its author, date, title, and publication data. At the end of your paper, you collect these bibliographical entries into an alphabetical list titled "Reference List." This list must include every source you mention in your text or in a parenthetical reference; conversely, every source included in your reference list must also be cited in your paper.

## How to Use This Chapter

This chapter presents models for the most common kinds of sources, starting with articles and ending with books. You will find models of bibliographical entries in 22.2. The models are listed by category: articles; websites, blogs, and social media; personal communications and interviews; reference works; and books. Whether you are double-checking your citations or creating them from scratch, follow these steps:

1. **Find a model.**
   - Find the model that matches your kind of source. For instance, if you need to cite a scholarly journal article in an online database, find the example under "Journal."
   - If your source does not match any of the examples in this chapter, find one that is similar. Or consult a more comprehensive guide,

such as the *Publication Manual of the American Psychological Association*, 6th ed. (2009).

2. **Match the model.**
   - Make sure your citation matches the bibliographical details in the model. Pay close attention to punctuation, capitalization, and abbreviations.
   - If your source has multiple authors, consult the information on authors' names in section 22.2.1.1.

3. **Adjust as needed.**
   - You may make reasonable small adjustments if your source is the same kind as a model but its bibliographic information is slightly different. For example, if the person who put together a book of collected material is called a "compiler" rather than an editor, you may use the form for an edited volume and use the word "Compiler" where the model uses "Editor": Jones, Henry. (Compiler). (1994). *The Oxford Book of* . . .
   - If your source is different from any of the models, make sure your citation answers these three questions: *Who created the source? What is it called? Who published it, where, and when?*

You will likely get many of your citations from a library or website. And you may use software that formats citations for you automatically. It's okay to let your software create a first draft of your citations, *but do not trust it to produce the correct form in every case*. Always double-check each parenthetical reference and bibliographical entry against the appropriate model. (By the time you do this, you should have already checked your data for accuracy against the sources themselves.) It's easy to miss small but important details when a citation is already formatted for you, so go slowly and be careful.

## 22.1   When and How to Cite Sources in Your Text

### 22.1.1   Parenthetical References

You must indicate in your text every place where you use the words or ideas of a source (see chapter 10). The general rule is to insert a parenthetical reference with the author's last name, the year of the publication, and the page number(s) in the source. The author's name and the date tell readers how to find the details of that source in your reference list, and the page numbers tell them where to look in the source. In some cases, however, you have to give more information to help readers identify a specific source (see 22.1.2).

In most cases you should insert the parenthetical reference immediately after the material from a source. For a quotation or paraphrase, insert the reference at the end of a sentence or clause (outside of any quotation marks and before a period or comma):

Technology feeds on itself. In many cases, the "diffusion" of an invention is more important than the invention itself (Diamond, 1997, p. 301).

If you quote or paraphrase several passages from the same work in a single paragraph, use only one parenthetical reference after the final quotation:

Technology feeds on itself. In many cases, the "diffusion" of an invention is more important than the invention itself. For example, the peel-off adhesive on Post-it notes was a valuable invention, but it also set off a whole industry of temporary adhesives. Through this "autocatalytic process," the diffusion of a technology "speeds up at a rate that increases with time, because the process catalyzes itself" (Diamond, 1997, p. 301).

If you mention the author in your text, add the year after the author and the page numbers after the quotation or paraphrase:

Technology feeds on itself. As Diamond (1997) explains, the "diffusion" of an invention can be more important than the invention itself (p. 301).

For a block quotation, add the parenthetical reference to the end with no period after it.

According to Jared Diamond (1997),

> Because technology begets more technology, the importance of an invention's diffusion potentially exceeds the importance of the original invention. Technology's history exemplifies what is termed an autocatalytic process: that is, one that speeds up at a rate that increases with time, because the process catalyzes itself. (p. 301)

For ideas or methods, insert the reference at the end of the sentence(s) in which you first introduce or explain the borrowed material. *Be sure to cite every source that influenced your thinking, even if you do not quote or paraphrase from it.* A reader might think you're guilty of plagiarism if you seem to reflect the ideas of a text that you do not cite. (See chapter 10.)

## 22.1.2    Forms of Parenthetical References

Each parenthetical reference must point to one and only one source in your reference list. The standard form for these references includes the author's last name, the year of publication, and a page number (preceded by "p." or "pp."). If the work is listed by an editor or translator rather than an author, use that name but do not add "Ed." or "Trans." You may, however, need more or less information. If two or more authors have the same last name, add initials. If you refer to a whole work rather than to a specific passage, do not include page numbers. There are other variants. These are the most common:

**AUTHOR NOT MENTIONED IN TEXT**
**(Name, Year, Page)**
Technology feeds on itself. In many cases, the "diffusion" of an invention is more important than the invention itself (Diamond, 1997, p. 301).

**AUTHOR MENTIONED IN TEXT**
**(Year) . . . (Page)**
Technology feeds on itself. As Diamond (1997) explains, the "diffusion" of an invention can be more important than the invention itself (p. 301).

**AUTHOR WITH SAME LAST NAME AS OTHERS IN REFERENCE LIST**
**(Initial + Name, Year, Page)**
Technology feeds on itself. In many cases, the "diffusion" of an invention is more important than the invention itself (J. Diamond, 1997, p. 301).

**TWO AUTHORS**
**(Name & Name, Year, Page)**
(Levitt & Dubner, 2006, p. 47)

**THREE–FIVE AUTHORS**
**First Citation: (Name, Name, . . . , & Name, Year, Page)**
(Whyte, Feng, & Cai, 2015, p. 146)

**Subsequent Citation: (Name et al., Year, Page)**
(Whyte et al., 2015, p. 147)

**SIX OR MORE AUTHORS**
**(Name et al., Year, Page)**
(Yguel et al., 2016, p. 403)

**WORK WITHOUT AN AUTHOR**
**(Short Title, Year, Page)**
("Study Finds," 2017, pp. 2–3)

**MULTIPLE CITATIONS WITH DIFFERENT AUTHORS**
**(Cite; Cite)**
(Whyte et al., 2015; Yguel et al., 2016)

MULTIPLE CITATIONS WITH THE SAME AUTHOR
(Name, Year, Year, . . . Year)
(Hardin, 2012, 2013a, 2013b, 2017)

### 22.1.3    Footnotes

In APA style you do not use notes to identify citations. You may use notes for substantive comments, supplemental information, and so on.

Notes can be printed as footnotes, at the bottom of the page, or as endnotes, on a separate page at the end. Because you are likely to have few notes, you should treat them as *footnotes*, which are easier for readers to find.

### 22.2    Reference List

Because you give readers only minimal bibliographical information in your text, you must give complete information for every source in the reference list at the end of your paper.

Start your list of sources on a new page. At the top of the first page, center the heading "Reference List." Skip two lines and list all references in alphabetical order, single-spaced, with an extra line space after each entry. Format each entry with a half-inch hanging indent. You can let your word processor put the list in alphabetical order. If you do this yourself, follow the order of the letters.

Macally, Mack, Madden, McArthur, Mecks, . . .
Saint-Beuve, Schwab, Selleck, Skillen, St. Helena, Stricker, . . .

If there is more than one entry for the same author in the same year, alphabetize them by title and add letters after the year: 2003a, 2003b, and so on.

See the sample reference list in APA style at the end of this chapter.

### 22.2.1    Elements Common to All Bibliographical Entries

When you create a bibliographical entry, you have to pay attention to the kind of source you are citing, because many elements of citations are different for different kinds of sources. But all APA-style entries consist of four basic elements—author's name, date, title of the work, and publication facts.

### 22.2.1.1    *Author's Name*

Whenever possible, begin each bibliographical entry with the name of the author(s). Spell the last name of each author exactly as it appears on the title page; use initials for all first and middle names. Do not include titles such as *Sir*, *Saint*, *Sister*, *Reverend*, and *Doctor*. The author's name is listed in *inverted* order: last name–comma–first initial–middle initial (if any).

**SINGLE AUTHOR**

Delgado-Ramos, G. C. (Ed.). 2015. *Inequality and* . . .

Gawande, A. (2014). *Being mortal* . . .

Rowling, J. K. (2007). *Harry Potter and* . . .

**MULTIPLE AUTHORS**

List as many as seven authors, in the order they appear on the title page. List *all* names in inverted order, last name first, followed by a comma followed by initial(s). Put an ampersand (&) before the name of the last author.

Levitt, S. D., & Dubner, S. J. (2006). *Freakonomics* . . .

Whyte, M. K., Feng, W., & Cai, Y. (2015). Challenging myths . . .

**MORE THAN SEVEN AUTHORS**

If there are more than seven authors, list the first six and then add three dots, followed by the name of the last author.

Yguel, B., Jactel, H., Pearse, J. S., Moen, D., Winter, M., Hortal, J., . . . Prinzing, A. (2016). The evolutionary legacy of . . .

22.2.1.2   *Date*

All bibliographical entries include a date in parentheses, immediately after the author. Most publications are identified by year: (2012). Monthly magazines or newspapers are also identified by month: (2012, May). Daily or weekly publications also include the day: (2012, November 5). Do not abbreviate months.

    If your reference list includes more than one publication in the same year for the same author, alphabetize them by titles (ignoring "A" or "The") and add a letter to each date.

Ockenfels, A., Sliwka, D., & Werner, P. (2015a). Bonus payments . . .

Ockenfels, A., Sliwka, D., & Werner, P. (2015b). Timing of kindness . . .

22.2.1.3   *Title*

Whenever possible, identify a source by its title. For articles and other short works, include both the article title and the title of the book, journal, or other work in which it occurs.

    *Note*: APA style treats titles differently in the reference list than it does in the body of the paper. In general, titles in the body of the paper are treated as you're probably used to treating them, but titles in reference lists are not. Pay attention to the differences noted here (and modeled in the examples in this chapter).

    *In your reference list*, capitalize titles of articles and books *sentence-style*: capitalize *only* the first word of the title and the subtitle and any proper nouns.

Capitalize the titles of websites, blogs, and all journals, magazines, and other periodicals *headline-style*.

*In the body of your paper*, use headline style for *all* titles: capitalize the first and last words of the title and subtitle and all other words *except* articles (*a, an, the*), coordinating conjunctions (*and, but, or, nor, for*), prepositions (*of, in, at, above, under*, and so forth), and the words *to* and *as* (see 25.1.2 for examples).

*In your reference list*, put the titles of short works that are part of longer ones in regular type, *but do not enclose them in quotation marks*. These include articles, chapters in books, and other shorter works or parts of longer works. Italicize only those words that are italicized in the original, and keep any quotation marks that are used for words in the original title. Put the titles of longer works in italics.

*In the body of your paper*, enclose the titles of shorter works in quotation marks and use italics for longer works as you normally would (see 25.1.3).

## 22.2.1.4 *Publication Facts*

In addition to the author's name and title, a bibliographical entry usually includes facts that identify *who* published the source, *where*, and *when*. Publication facts vary from one kind of source to another, so check each model carefully.

*Note*: The publication facts for books include the city of publication. For well-known cities like New York and London, you don't have to include a state or country. For all other cities, add the state or country unless it's included in the publisher's name.

For sources consulted online, you must include a complete online address, or URL (uniform resource locator). In APA style, URLs usually follow the words "Retrieved from." In most cases you should copy the URL from your browser's address bar. For online sources that do not list a date of publication or posting or revision, you must also include a date of retrieval (or access). For an example, see 22.2.3.

*Note*: If you consult a library database like LexisNexis Academic or one of the databases offered by EBSCOhost, you can list the name of the database instead of a URL, especially if the URL for the specific item is very long. For examples, see 22.2.2 (newspaper article) and 22.2.6.1 (book).

*Note*: APA style allows you to cite just the home page instead of the URL for the specific item. Examples in this chapter show full URLs.

## 22.2.2 Bibliographical Entries for Periodical Articles

Most of the articles you will consult will be found in *periodicals*—journals, magazines, newspapers, and other works published at periodic intervals in print form, online, or both.

- **Journals** are scholarly, literary, or professional periodicals written for experts and available primarily through academic libraries. Journals often include the word *journal* in their title (*Journal of Modern History*) but not always (*Ethics*).

- **Magazines** are not scholarly publications; they are designed for more general readers in both their content and their availability outside of academic settings. If you are unsure whether a periodical is a journal or a magazine, see whether its articles include citations; if so, treat it as a journal.

- **Newspapers and news sites** are generally daily or weekly publications whose articles are closely tied to recent events.

### THE BASIC PATTERN

**APA reference list entry for a journal article:** Periods between most elements, but comma before volume number and page numbers. No period after URL (end with period if no URL).

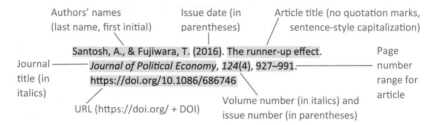

### JOURNAL

If a journal lists both a volume and an issue number, include both. If you consult the article online, include a URL, following the words "Retrieved from." If the article comes with a suggested form of the URL, use that. If it lists a DOI (a type of permanent identifier), add the DOI to "https://doi.org/" to create the URL, but do *not* include "Retrieved from."

*Note*: If the article title includes a term in quotation marks, retain the quotation marks. If it includes a term in italics, retain the italics.

Domínguez Torres, M. (2016). Havana's fortunes: "Entangled histories" in Copley's *Watson and the shark. American Art*, 30(2), 8–13.

Ibrahim, A. M. (2016). A not-so-radical approach to human rights in Islam. *Journal of Religion*, 96(3), 346–377. https://doi.org/10.1086/686568

Ivashkin, A. (2014). Who's afraid of socialist realism? *Slavonic and East European Review*, 92(3), 430–448. Retrieved from http://www.jstor.org/stable/10.5699/slaveasteurorev2.92.3.0430

Novak, B. (2016). "Church, Humboldt, and the politics of display." *Getty Research Journal*, 8, 73–92.

## MAGAZINE

Give volume or issue numbers, if any. Also include page numbers, if any. (If the article is interrupted by other material, list *all* page numbers, separated by commas.)

Dempsey, D. (1955, July 1). How to get published, more or less. *Harper's Magazine*, 211, 77–80.

Fatsis, S. (2015, January 12). The definition of a dictionary. *Slate*. Retrieved from http://www.slate.com/articles/life/culturebox/2015/01/merriam_webster _dictionary_what_should_an_online_dictionary_look_like.html

Marx, P. (2015, April 27). Big skyline. *New Yorker* (Talk of the Town). Retrieved from http://www.newyorker.com/magazine/2015/04/27/big-skyline

## NEWSPAPER OR NEWS SITE

Include all page numbers, with letters identifying sections, if available.

Bishop, G. (2008, September 7). Favre wins in debut for Jets. *New York Times*, D1, D4.

Donald Trump is now hiring [Editorial]. (2016, November 14). *New York Times*. Retrieved from LexisNexis Academic.

Nelson, L. (2016, September 26). Why trigger warnings are really so controversial, explained. *Vox*. Retrieved from http://www.vox.com/2015/9/10/9298577 /trigger-warnings-college

Snowden, E. (2015, November 12). Edward Snowden explains how to reclaim your privacy (Interview by M. Lee). *The Intercept*. Retrieved from https:// theintercept.com/2015/11/12/edward-snowden-explains-how-to-reclaim -your-privacy/

*Note*: If a news article has no author, list it by title in the reference list; if you need a parenthetical reference, refer to the first few words of the title: ("Donald Trump," 2016).

*Note*: Interviews are listed under the name of the interviewee; the name of the interviewer follows the title of the interview. Unpublished interviews are cited as a form of personal communication (see 22.2.4).

## 22.2.3    Bibliographical Entries for Websites, Blogs, and Social Media

### WEBSITE CONTENT

To cite a webpage or other website content in a reference list entry, include the following information:

- author, if any
- date of publication or posting or revision; use "n.d." for undated sources

- title of page, article, video, etc. (capitalized sentence-style, no quotation marks)
- format (in square brackets), if relevant
- website title, if any (capitalized headline-style, no italics)
- owner or sponsor of the content or site (if different from website title)
- URL for the page; for undated sources, include a date of retrieval (or access)

If there's no author, list the entry either under the title of the article or page or under the name of the website or its sponsor.

de Blasio, B. (2018, February 13). Mayor de Blasio delivers the State of the City address [Video file]. NYC Mayor's Office. Retrieved from https://youtu.be /yp3ggthd8ho

Columbia University. (n.d.). History. Retrieved July 1, 2016, from http://www .columbia.edu/content/history.html

Privacy policy. (2016, March 25). Privacy & Terms, Google. Retrieved from http:// www.google.com/policies/privacy/

### BLOG POST

Blog posts (or entries) are cited like articles from newspapers or news sites (see 22.2.2). If the blog is part of a larger publication such as a newspaper or website, give the name of the publication after the title of the blog. APA style puts the titles of blogs in regular type (capitalized headline-style).

Jayson, S. (2016, June 23). Is selfie culture making our kids selfish? [Blog post]. Well. *New York Times*. Retrieved from http://well.blogs.nytimes.com/2016/06 /23/is-selfie-culture-making-our-kids-selfish/

West, L. (2013, April 11). Sweden introduces new gender-neutral pronoun, makes being a man ILLEGAL [Blog post]. Jezebel. Retrieved from http:// jezebel.com/sweden-introduces-new-gender-neutral-pronoun-makes-bei -472492079

### SOCIAL MEDIA CONTENT

Content shared over social media and available to the public can usually be cited by identifying the following elements:

- The author of the post. List a screen name (in brackets) in addition to the name of the person or group on the account, if known. Otherwise just use the screen name (ignore an @ in alphabetizing the name).
- The date, including month, day, and year. You can also include a time stamp to help differentiate a post from others on the same day.

- In place of a title, the text of the post. Quote up to the first 160 characters (enough to capture the typical text message), capitalized as in the original.
- The type of post. Use square brackets.
- A URL. The URL can often be found via the date stamp for the item.

Chicago Manual of Style. (2015, April 17). Is the world ready for singular they? We thought so back in 1993 [Facebook]. Retrieved from https://www.facebook.com/ChicagoManual/posts/10152906193679151

O'Brien, C. [@ConanOBrien]. (2015, April 22, 11:10 a.m.). In honor of Earth Day, I'm recycling my tweets [Twitter]. Retrieved from https://twitter.com/ConanOBrien/status/590940792967016448

Souza, P. [@petesouza]. (2016, April 1). President Obama bids farewell to President Xi of China at the conclusion of the Nuclear Security Summit [Instagram photo]. Retrieved from https://www.instagram.com/p/BDrmfXTtNCt/

A direct message or other private content shared with you through social media is cited as a form of personal communication. See 22.2.4 for examples.

READERS' COMMENTS

Cite individual readers' comments in the body of your paper, in reference to the original post (which may be cited with an appropriate in-text citation). Do not include readers' comments in the reference list.

According to a comment on Jayson (2016), . . .

## 22.2.4    Bibliographical Entries for Personal Communications and Interviews

In APA style, unpublished interviews, conversations, email, direct messages, texts, and other forms of personal communications with the author are normally cited in the text only (see also 22.1.2):

(E. Fenton, personal communication, March 25, 2018)

If a reference list entry is needed for any reason (for example, if your teacher requires one), it is listed under the name of the interviewee or conversation partner. If the name is withheld, use a description in place of a name.

Fenton, E. (2018, March 25). Direct message to author [Instagram].
Home health aide. (2018, April 2). Interview by author [Facebook Messenger].
Reid, A. J. (US Army Captain, Retired). (2018, November 1). Interview by author.

For an example of a published interview, see 22.2.2 (under "Newspaper or News Site").

22.2.5   **Bibliographical Entries for Reference Works**

DICTIONARY

If the reference work is a standard one such as *Encyclopaedia Britannica* or the *Oxford English Dictionary*, do not cite the author, editor, or publication data. For print sources, list only the edition (if any) and the year. Cite the work as a whole in the reference list; the entries themselves are mentioned or described in the text.

*Britannica Academic.* Retrieved from http://academic.eb.com/
*Merriam-Webster.* Retrieved from http://www.merriam-webster.com/
*Oxford English Dictionary.* (1989). 2nd ed.

If your teacher allows, a longer article in a general reference work may be included in your reference list, under the name of the article:

Muhammad Ali. (2016, September 25). In *Wikipedia.* Retrieved from https://en
      .wikipedia.org/wiki/Muhammad_Ali

Specialized reference works are usually cited like books (see 22.2.6); an article in such a work is cited like a chapter in a book (see 22.2.6.2).

22.2.6   **Bibliographical Entries for Books**

THE BASIC PATTERN

> **APA reference list entry for a book:** Periods between elements, but colon between place of publication and publisher's name. End with a period.

Author's name   Year of publication   Title of book (in italics,
(last name, first initial)   (in parentheses)   sentence-style capitalization)

Lepore, J. (2015). *The secret history of Wonder Woman.*
New York: Vintage Books.

City of publication   Publisher's name

22.2.6.1   *Whole Books*

BOOK, GENERAL FORMAT

McCabe, J. M. (2016). *Connecting in college: How friendship networks matter for academic and social success.* Chicago: University of Chicago Press.
Melville, H. (1851). *Moby-Dick; or, The whale.* New York: Harper & Brothers.

If the book is produced by an organization rather than a person, list the organization as the author:

United Nations. (2014). *Basic facts about the United Nations, 2014.* New York: UN Department of Public Information.

**ONLINE BOOK**
Use the URL for the main page (if there is more than one). If you consulted the book through a library database, you can list that instead of a URL.

Melville, H. (1851). *Moby-Dick; or, The whale.* New York: Harper & Brothers. Retrieved from http://mel.hofstra.edu/moby-dick-the-whale-proofs.html
Skrentny, J. D. (2014). *After civil rights: Racial realism in the new American workplace.* Princeton, NJ: Princeton University Press. Retrieved from eBook Academic Collection, EBSCOhost.

**E-BOOK**
Identify the e-book format after the title, in square brackets.

Austen, J. (2007). *Pride and prejudice* [iBooks edition]. New York: Penguin Classics.
Miranda, L.-M., & McCarter, J. (2016). *Hamilton: The revolution* [Kindle edition]. New York: Grand Central Publishing.

**EDITED OR TRANSLATED BOOK**
If a book has an editor or translator but no author, treat the editor or translator as the author. *Note*: If the original has an earlier date, indicate that in parentheses at the end of the entry.

Delgado-Ramos, G. C. (Ed.). (2015). *Inequality and climate change: Perspectives from the south.* Dakar, Senegal: CODESRIA.
Silverstein, T. (Trans.). (1974). *Sir Gawain and the green knight.* Chicago: University of Chicago Press. (Original work published in late 14th century)

If a book has an author as well as an editor or a translator, identify the editor or translator in parentheses after the title and before the period.

Adorno, T. W., & Benjamin, W. (1999). *The complete correspondence, 1928–1940* (H. Lonitz, Ed., & N. Walker, Trans.). Cambridge, MA: Harvard University Press.
Bonnefoy, Y. (1995). *New and selected poems* (J. Naughton & A. Rudolf, Eds.). Chicago: University of Chicago Press.
Feydeau, G. (1970). *Four farces by Georges Feydeau* (N. R. Shapiro, Trans.). Chicago: University of Chicago Press.
Menchú, R. (1999). *Crossing borders* (A. Wright, Trans. & Ed.). New York: Verso.

## REVISED EDITION

If you consult a book labeled as a "revised" edition or a "second" (or subsequent) edition, place this information in parentheses, after the title and before the period, using abbreviations as in the following examples.

Bolt, P. J., Coletta, D. V., & Shackelford, C. G., Jr. (2005). *American defense policy* (8th ed.). Baltimore, MD: Johns Hopkins University Press.

Kinzie, M. (2013). *A poet's guide to poetry* (2nd ed.). Chicago: University of Chicago Press.

Levitt, S. D., & Dubner, S. J. (2006). *Freakonomics: A rogue economist explores the hidden side of everything* (Rev. ed.). New York: HarperCollins.

## MULTIVOLUME WORK OR SERIES

If you cite one book from a group of books (called a *multivolume* work), list only the specific volume you consulted. Identify the volume number "(Vol. X)."

Byrne, M. S. C. (Ed.). (1981). *The Lisle letters* (Vol. 4). Chicago: University of Chicago Press.

If the volume you cite has a different title from that of the whole group, use both titles, starting with the title of the group:

Armstrong, T. (Vol. Ed.). (2014). *The papers of Martin Luther King, Jr.: Vol. 7. To save the soul of America, January 1961–August 1962* (C. Carson, Series Ed.). Berkeley: University of California Press.

If you refer to more than one book in the group of books, you can cite all of them in one entry:

Byrne, M. S. C. (Ed.). (1981). *The Lisle letters* (Vols. 1–6). Chicago: University of Chicago Press.

Carson, C. (Ed.). (1992–). *The papers of Martin Luther King, Jr.* (Vols. 1–7). Berkeley: University of California Press.

In the text you can refer to a specific volume like this: (Carson, 1992–, vol. 4, p. 123).

If you cite a book that belongs to a named series, you can give the series title after the book title, in regular type.

Hausman, B. M. (2011). *Riding the Trail of Tears*. Native storiers: A series of American narratives. Lincoln: University of Nebraska Press.

22.2.6.2   *Parts of Books*

**CHAPTER IN AN EDITED BOOK**

If you refer to only one chapter, cite that chapter. You may cite two specific chapters separately if you specifically compare them in your text. Otherwise cite the edited book as a whole.

Gillespie, K. (2017). Before the commission: Ethnography as public testimony. In D. Fassin (Ed.), *If truth be told: The politics of public ethography* (pp. 69–95). Durham, NC: Duke University Press.

**INTRODUCTIONS, PREFACES, AFTERWORDS**

If you refer to a supplemental part of a book that was written by someone other than the book author, cite it separately. If the part has a title, include it.

McClary, S. (2016). Humanizing the humanities. Foreword. In W. Cheng, *Just vibrations: The purpose of sounding good* (pp. xvii–xix). Ann Arbor: University of Michigan Press.

**LETTER IN A COLLECTION**

Cite a letter from a published collection in the text, in reference to the work in which it appears.

Adams (1930), in a letter to Charles Milnes Gaskell dated March 30, 1868, . . .

Adams, H. (1930). *Letters of Henry Adams, 1858–1891* (W. C. Ford, Ed.). Boston: Houghton Mifflin.

**SHORT STORY OR POEM IN A COLLECTION**

Cite the specific work, not the whole book, if you refer only to that one work. You may cite two or more specific works separately if you specifically compare them in your text. Otherwise cite the collection as a whole.

Heaney, S. (2006). To George Seferis in the underworld. In *District and circle* (pp. 22–23). New York: Farrar, Straus and Giroux.
Lahiri, J. (1999). This blessed house. In *Interpreter of maladies* (pp. 136–157). Boston: Houghton Mifflin Harcourt.

22.2.7   **Sample Reference List, APA Style**

Model your APA-style reference list on the following sample, drawn from the examples in this chapter. Note that the entries appear in alphabetical order by author or title. In your paper you will add an extra line space between entries (not shown here). For more advice on formatting your paper, see appendix A at the end of this book.

**Reference List**

Armstrong, T. (Vol. Ed.). (2014). *The papers of Martin Luther King, Jr.: Vol. 7. To save the soul of America, January 1961–August 1962* (C. Carson, Series Ed.). Berkeley: University of California Press.

de Blasio, B. (2018, February 13). Mayor de Blasio delivers the State of the City address [Video file]. NYC Mayor's Office. Retrieved from https://youtu.be /yp3ggthd8ho

Domínguez Torres, M. (2016). Havana's fortunes: "Entangled histories" in Copley's *Watson and the shark. American Art, 30*(2), 8–13.

Fatsis, S. (2015, January 12). The definition of a dictionary. *Slate*. Retrieved from http://www.slate.com/articles/life/culturebox/2015/01/merriam_webster _dictionary_what_should_an_online_dictionary_look_like.html

Ibrahim, A. M. (2016). A not-so-radical approach to human rights in Islam. *Journal of Religion, 96*(3), 346–377. https://doi.org/10.1086/686568

Kinzie, M. (2013). *A poet's guide to poetry* (2nd ed.). Chicago: University of Chicago Press.

Lahiri, J. (1999). This blessed house. In *Interpreter of maladies* (pp. 136–157). Boston: Houghton Mifflin Harcourt.

Levitt, S. D., & Dubner, S. J. (2006). *Freakonomics: A rogue economist explores the hidden side of everything* (Rev. ed.). New York: HarperCollins.

Marx, P. (2015, April 27). Big skyline. *New Yorker* (Talk of the Town). Retrieved from http://www.newyorker.com/magazine/2015/04/27/big-skyline

Muhammad Ali. (2016, September 25). In *Wikipedia*. Retrieved from https://en .wikipedia.org/wiki/Muhammad_Ali

*Oxford English Dictionary*. (1989). 2nd ed.

United Nations. (2014). *Basic facts about the United Nations, 2014*. New York: UN Department of Public Information.

# PART III  *Style*

In part 3 we show you how to deal with issues of punctuation, matters of spelling not handled in dictionaries, and other matters of editorial style.

**Read Me First: How to Use Part 3**

We have designed this part not for reading but for reference. Use the contents at the beginning of each chapter to find the issue you need to address, and consult the appropriate section. In some cases you'll find an example that answers your question. In other cases you'll find a rule that you can follow.

# 23 Spelling: Plurals, Possessives, and Hyphenation

For most spelling questions, the rule is simple: let the dictionary or your spell-checker be your guide. But writers often face questions about spelling and related matters whose answers cannot be found in a dictionary and won't be flagged by a spell-checker. This chapter offers general guidelines and specific examples designed to answer many of those questions.

## 23.1   Spelling Basics

Model your spelling on standard American usage. When your spell-checker leaves you in doubt, consult a dictionary. Use standard spellings for anything that you write, but copy the words in quotations and titles of works exactly as they appear in the original, even if the spelling differs from standard American English.

Be aware that dictionaries can differ on how to spell a word, and many dictionaries are inaccurate or out of date. The most reliable sources for current usage and spelling are

- Merriam-Webster.com, which includes a regularly updated free version of its dictionary and a subscription-only unabridged version
- *Merriam-Webster's Collegiate Dictionary*, 11th ed. (updated regularly in print to reflect the updates at Merriam-Webster.com)

The smaller free version at Merriam-Webster.com, or the *Collegiate Dictionary* on which it is based, is good enough for most purposes. For the names of people and places, see the listings in either of those dictionaries or consult a reliable encyclopedia.

Most standard dictionaries offer more than one acceptable spelling for some words. In those cases you should use the first spelling offered. Under no circumstances use both in the same paper.

Your word processor will save you not only from misspellings but from typos as well. *But do not rely on a spellchecker alone.* Computer dictionaries are not entirely reliable, and it is easy for them to accept incorrect spellings that someone has added to a computer's custom dictionary (a serious problem for shared computers). And even if your word processor checks grammar too, it won't always alert you when you have correctly spelled the wrong word: "The teacher had and extra long nap because the students were being quite." A spellchecker is not a substitute for a good dictionary or careful proofreading.

## 23.2   Plurals

### 23.2.1   The General Rule

Most nouns form the plural by adding *s*.

| | | | | |
|---|---|---|---|---|
| dog | → | dogs | tree | → | trees |
| vehicle | → | vehicles | Emma | → | Emmas |

But there are many irregular nouns that form their plurals in different ways. When in doubt, consult a dictionary.

Do not confuse plurals with possessives. Do not use an apostrophe to make a standard plural.

| | |
|---|---|
| Plural: | dogs, vehicles, Emmas |
| Possessive: | dog's, vehicle's, Emma's |

### 23.2.2   Special Cases

**NOUNS ENDING IN CH, J, S, SH, X, OR Z**
These nouns add *es*.

| | | | | |
|---|---|---|---|---|
| beach | → | beaches | glass | → | glasses |
| dish | → | dishes | Alex | → | Alexes |

**COMMON NOUNS ENDING IN Y**
If the *y* is preceded by a vowel, add an *s*.

| Boy | → | boys | monkey | → | monkeys |
| day | → | days | decoy | → | decoys |

If the *y* is preceded by a consonant, replaced it with *ies*.

| baby | → | babies | family | → | families |
| story | → | stories | hobby | → | hobbies |

### PROPER NOUNS ENDING IN Y
These nouns add *s*.

| Harry | → | Harrys | Germany | → | Germanys |
| Sally | → | Sallys | Jay | → | Jays |

### NOUNS ENDING IN O
These nouns sometimes add *s* and sometimes *es*. If in doubt, check a dictionary.

| hero | → | heroes | potato | → | potatoes |
| memo | → | memos | auto | → | autos |

### NOUNS ENDING IN F OR FE
These nouns sometimes add *s* and sometimes replace the *f* with *ves*. If in doubt, check a dictionary.

| leaf | → | leaves | knife | → | knives |
| roof | → | roofs | proof | → | proofs |

### COMPOUND NOUNS
If the compound is made of two nouns, make the last noun plural. (It does not matter whether the words are joined, hyphenated, or just together.)

| bookkeeper | → | bookkeepers |
| actor-singer | → | actor-singers |
| district attorney | → | district attorneys |

If the compound is made of a noun followed by an adjective or prepositional phrase, make the main noun plural. (It does not matter whether the words are hyphenated or not.)

| sister-in-law | → | sisters-in-law |
| man-of-war | → | men-of-war |

attorney general    →    attorneys general
president-elect    →    presidents-elect

### LETTERS AND NUMERALS

Numerals and capital letters usually form the plural by adding an *s* without an apostrophe.

| | | | | |
|---|---|---|---|---|
| R | → | Rs | 1950 → | 1950s |
| ABC | → | ABCs | 767 → | 767s |

For lowercase letters or for instances where readers might mistake the plural combination for a word or common abbreviation, add an apostrophe before the *s*.

| | | |
|---|---|---|
| j | → | j's *not* js |
| I | → | I's *not* Is |
| A and B | → | A's and B's *not* As and Bs |

### ABBREVIATIONS

Form the plurals of most abbreviations by adding *s* alone. If the abbreviation ends in a period, add the *s* before the period. (But remember that the plural of *p*. [page] is *pp*.)

| | | | | | |
|---|---|---|---|---|---|
| URL | → | URLs | ed. | → | eds. |
| DVD | → | DVDs | vol. | → | vols. |
| PhD | → | PhDs | | | |

### TERMS IN ITALICS

For titles and other terms in italics, add *s* in regular type without an apostrophe.

| | | |
|---|---|---|
| *Chicago Tribune* | → | *Chicago Tribune*s |
| *New Yorker* | → | *New Yorker*s |

### TERMS IN QUOTATION MARKS

Do not form the plural of a term in quotation marks; rephrase the sentence to avoid the need for a plural.

| | |
|---|---|
| NOT | included many "To be continued's" |
| BUT | included many instances of "To be continued" |

23.3    **Possessives**

23.3.1    **The General Rules**

SINGULAR NOUNS

For most singular nouns, including abbreviations, add an apostrophe and *s*, even if the word ends in *s*, *x*, or *z*.

the argument's effects      Díaz's paper
Jones's paper               JFK's speech

PLURAL NOUNS ENDING IN S

For regular plural nouns, add an apostrophe without an additional *s*.

the arguments' effects      politicians' votes
the Davises' house          the Cubs' lineup

PLURAL NOUNS NOT ENDING IN S

For irregular plurals that do not end in *s*, add both an apostrophe and *s*.

the children's hour         the mice's nest
alumni's donations          the women's team

23.3.2    **Special Cases**

EXCEPTIONS FOR SINGULAR NOUNS ENDING IN S

For collective nouns that end in *s* but are treated as singular nouns, add an apostrophe without an additional *s*.

politics' true meaning      the United States' role

NOUNS FOR INANIMATE OBJECTS

In most cases you should not create possessives for inanimate objects.

NOT   the house's door
BUT   the door of the house

NOT   the shirt's color
BUT   the color of the shirt

SINGULAR COMPOUND NOUNS

Add an apostrophe and an *s* to the last word in the compound.

bookkeeper's records          district attorney's case
sister-in-law's children      attorney general's decision

### PLURAL COMPOUND NOUNS

For compounds composed of two nouns, form the possessive based on the last word in the compound.

bookkeepers' records          district attorneys' cases

Avoid possessive forms for compounds with a noun followed by an adjective or prepositional phrase; rephrase instead.

NOT    sisters-in-law's children
BUT    the children of the sisters-in-law

NOT    attorneys' general decisions
BUT    the decisions of the attorneys general

### MULTIPLE NOUNS

To indicate that two or more entities each possess something separately, make all the nouns possessive.

New York's and Chicago's teams
historians' and economists' methods

To indicate that two or more entities possess something jointly, make only the last noun possessive.

Minneapolis and St. Paul's team
historians and economists' data

### TERMS IN ITALICS

Add an apostrophe and an *s*, both in regular type. If the term ends in an *s*, add only an apostrophe.

the *Atlantic Monthly*'s editor
the *Chicago Tribune*'s readers
the *New York Times*' subscribers

### TERMS IN QUOTATION MARKS

Avoid possessive forms for terms in quotation marks; rephrase instead.

NOT    the "Ode on a Grecian Urn"'s admirers

BUT    admirers of the "Ode on a Grecian Urn"

## 23.4    Hyphenated Words

A compound word or a compound modifier may be hyphenated, left open (with a space between words), or closed (spelled as one word). To find out which form to use, check the dictionary first. If you cannot find a compound there, follow the principles outlined here to decide whether or not to hyphenate. If you cannot find the form in either place, leave the compound open.

The patterns outlined below are not hard-and-fast rules. You will have to decide many individual cases on the basis of context, personal taste, or common usage in your subject area. Although much of the suggested hyphenation is logical and will make your text more readable, some is only traditional.

### 23.4.1    Words Formed with Prefixes

#### 23.4.1.1    *The General Rule*

Words formed with prefixes are normally closed (spelled as one word), whether they are nouns (*postmodernism*), verbs (*misrepresent*), adjectives (*antebellum*), or adverbs (*prematurely*). This pattern also applies to prepositions such as *over* and *under* that can be attached to words in the same position as prefixes (*overachiever*, *underhanded*).

#### 23.4.1.2    *Special Cases That Call for Hyphens*

Use a hyphen between a prefix and the word it precedes in the following cases.

**Prefix + capitalized word**

sub-Saharan, pro-iPhone, anti-American, un-American, trans-Siberian

**Prefix + numeral**

pre-1950, mid-1980s, pro-3M

**Prefix + compound (hyphenated or open)**

non-coffee-drinking, post-high school, pro-American dream

**Stand-alone prefix in a compound phrase**

pre- and postwar, pro- and anti-iPhone, over- and underachievers

**Doubled prefix**

sub-sub-Saharan, sub-subhead, post-postmodern, mega-megatrucks

**Doubled letters at junction of prefix and root**

| | |
|---|---|
| NOT antiintellectual | BUT anti-intellectual |
| NOT megaandroid | BUT mega-android |
| NOT protooncologist | BUT proto-oncologist |
| NOT cyberrage | BUT cyber-rage |

Note: Many words with doubled letters are correct without a hyphen (check the dictionary): misspelling, posttraumatic, reexamine

**Combinations that may be confused with other words**

re-cover (cover again) vs. recover; re-creation (created again) vs. recreation

### 23.4.2 Compounds Used as Adjectives

In most cases, hyphenate a compound used as an adjective when it precedes the noun it modifies; otherwise leave it open.

| Before noun | After noun |
|---|---|
| full-length treatment | treatment is full length |
| thought-provoking commentary | commentary was thought provoking |
| over-the-counter drug | drug sold over the counter |
| emerald-green tie | tie that was emerald green |
| spelled-out numbers | numbers that are spelled out |

### 23.4.3 Compounds Used as Nouns

In most cases, compounds used as nouns are open.

master builder, middle class, cooking class

Many frequently used compounds are closed and a few are hyphenated. Check the dictionary.

bookkeeper, birthrate, smartphone, notebook, decision-making, head-hunting

There are also a number of special cases that are always hyphenated (see 23.4.4).

### 23.4.4 Compounds Normally Hyphenated

The following compounds are normally hyphenated, no matter how or where they are used. In some cases, individual compounds that are especially common are closed (check the dictionary). Any exceptions are noted.

**age terms**

a three-year-old, three-year-old children, a fifty-two-year-old woman, eight-to-ten-year-olds

Note: She is three years old

**all- (adjectives)**
all-American player, all-out effort, all-encompassing rule, the rule is all-
encompassing
*Note*: Adverbial *all-* forms are open: went all out, looked all around

**cross-**
cross-checked pages, cross-referenced term, a cross-reference, go cross-
country
*Note*: A few forms are open, and some are closed (check the dictionary): cross
section, crossbow, crossover

**e-**
e-commerce, e-book
*Note*: At least one form is now closed: email

**-elect**
president-elect, mayor-elect, chairperson-elect
*Exception*: Multiword elected offices are open: district attorney elect, county
delegate elect

**ever-**
ever-ready helper, ever-recurring problem
*Note*: everlasting

**ex-**
ex-teammate, ex-marine, ex-CEO, ex-kindergarten teacher

**familiar phrases (standardized with hyphens)**
Jack-of-all-trades, stick-in-the-mud

**fractions**
a two-thirds share, two-thirds done, four-fifths majority, seven-sixteenths
*Exception*: Use only one hyphen per fraction: one and three-quarters, three fifty-
thirds
*Note*: Combinations of fractions plus nouns follow the general rule: an eighth
note, a half mile, a half-mile run, the run was a half mile long, a one-and-
three-quarter-inch tab

**functional pairs (that could also be written with *and*)**
city-state government (i.e., city and state), a writer-director, student-teacher
internship, Arab-Israeli peace, Russian-English dictionary (avoid a slash in
such cases)

**great- (kinship)**
great-grandmother, great-grandfather, great-aunt

**-in-law**
son-in-law, mother-in-law, cousin-in-law

**-odd**
twenty-odd points, 350-odd students, a hundred-odd dollars

**on-**
on-screen, on-site
*Note:* Many *on-* words are closed: online, onboard, ongoing

**proper nouns, shortened**
Anglo-Saxon culture, Afro-American studies, the Franco-Prussian War, the
    Sino-Soviet bloc

**self-**
self-realization, self-sustaining, self-conscious
*Note:* unselfconscious

**-style**
Chicago-style pizza, headline-style capitalization, capitalized headline-style
*Note:* Adjective and adverb forms are hyphenated, but leave noun forms open:
    pizza in Chicago style, use headline style for titles

23.4.5 **Compounds Normally Open**
The following compounds are normally open (no hyphens), no matter how they
are used. In some cases, individual compounds that are especially common are
closed (check the dictionary). Any exceptions are noted.

**-book**
reference book, coupon book, comic book
*Note:* checkbook, cookbook, textbook

**chemical terms**
hydrogen peroxide, sodium chloride solution

**comparative constructions**
the least prepared students, the most talented athletes, those athletes are the
    most talented

*Note:* Add a hyphen if readers might be confused over what the term modifies:

We hired more skilled workers to fill in for the holidays (i.e., more workers who are skilled).

Our training program produces more-skilled workers (i.e., workers who are more skilled).

### -general

attorney general, postmaster general

### -ly adverbs

highly regarded teacher, widely known singer, partially chewed food

### Modified by a preceding adverb

| Without adverb | With adverb |
| --- | --- |
| thought-provoking commentary | extremely thought provoking commentary |
| ill-advised comment | highly ill advised comment |

### -percent

5 percent, a 10 percent increase, your score was 86 percent
*Note:* Use numerals.

### proper nouns

African American students, a Chinese American lawyer, the North Central Region, State Department employees, French Canadian, French Canadians

## 23.4.6    Compounds Normally Closed

The following compounds are normally closed. Any exceptions are noted.

### -ache

toothache, stomachache, heartache

### -borne, -like, or -wide

foodborne, childlike, doglike, systemwide, worldwide
*Exception 1, proper nouns:* Chicago-wide, Obama-like
*Exception 2, three or more syllables:* mosquito-borne, handkerchief-like
*Exception 3, repeated letters:* meadow-wide, bell-like

### directions

Two directions: northeast, northwest, southwest, southeast
Three directions: east-northeast, north-northwest, south-southeast
*Note:* north-south, east-west, northeast-southwest, southeast-northwest

**grand- (kinship)**

grandfather, grandmother, granddaughter, grandnephew

**step- (kinship)**

stepmother, stepfather, stepson

*Note:* step-granddaughter

# 24 Punctuation

This chapter offers general guidelines for punctuation in the text of your paper. (For punctuation in citations, see part 2.) Some rules are clear-cut, but others are not, so you often have to depend on sound judgment and a good ear.

> **How to Use This Chapter**
> This chapter is organized not by kind of punctuation but by the kind of structure you need to punctuate: sentences, clauses, series, quotations, and so

on. Find the section that corresponds to the part of your writing you want to punctuate, and then find a specific example that matches your case. If you find a grammatical term that you don't recognize or cannot define, look in the glossary (appendix B).

## 24.1 Complete Sentences

You must end every complete sentence with a *terminal punctuation* mark: a period (.), a question mark (?), or an exclamation point (!). Exclamations are rare in academic writing, and you should avoid them except in quotations.

### 24.1.1 Summary

You have three ways to end complete sentences:

1. period
2. question mark
3. exclamation point

### 24.1.2 Three Ways to Punctuate Sentences

1. Period (for declaratory statements, imperatives, and indirect questions)

   He chose to use a graph.
   Consider the advantages of this method.
   The question was whether these differences could be reconciled.

2. Question mark

   Did you consider the advantages of this method?

3. Exclamation point

   I'm really surprised that you used this method!

### 24.1.3 Sentence Fragments

Experienced writers sometimes try to achieve a stylistic or rhetorical effect by punctuating incomplete sentences as though they were complete. These are known as *sentence fragments*.

Which can be dangerous. Especially for students.

Fragments can end with any terminal punctuation.

Which can be dangerous.
For whom?
For students!

But you should avoid fragments: teachers usually disallow them because they cannot distinguish intentional fragments from grammatical mistakes.

## 24.2    Independent Clauses

A *compound sentence* is composed of two or more independent clauses that could be punctuated as complete sentences. You must separate the independent clauses within a sentence in one of eight ways. The following list groups them into the most common cases, less common cases, and cases for special effects. In all cases you could end each clause with a period or question mark and make one compound sentence into two or more complete sentences.

### 24.2.1    Summary

You have eight ways to punctuate the independent clauses in a compound sentence:

1. comma + coordinating conjunction
2. semicolon
3. semicolon + coordinating conjunction
4. coordinating conjunction (alone)
5. comma (alone)—caution!
6. colon
7. dash
8. parentheses

### 24.2.2    Eight Ways to Punctuate Compound Sentences

*Three common forms*
1. Comma + coordinating conjunction (*and, but, or, nor, for, so, yet*)
    This is the most common form. If the individual clauses are long or include internal punctuation, use a semicolon instead (see #3 below).

Students around the world want to learn English, and many young Americans are eager to teach them.

**Three or more clauses.** In this case put a comma after each clause (including the one before the conjunction) and a conjunction before the last clause.

The committee designed the questionnaire, the field-workers collected responses, and the statisticians analyzed the results.

2. Semicolon

Students around the world want to learn English; many young Americans are eager to teach them.

Watch out for words that connect sentences but are not conjunctions: *however, thus, therefore, hence, then, indeed, accordingly, besides,* and so on. Because these are not conjunctions, you cannot use them with a comma in a compound sentence. Use a semicolon instead.

Revenues from streaming music now exceed revenues for all other formats combined; however, sales of vinyl records have increased dramatically in recent years.

3. Semicolon + coordinating conjunction

This form is generally reserved for sentences with complex clauses, especially those with internal punctuation. If the clauses are short, use a comma instead (see #1 above).

Although revenues from streaming music now exceed revenues for all other formats combined, sales of vinyl records have increased dramatically in recent years; but the resurgence has come not just from older buyers, as some industry analysts had predicted, but also from those who grew up with digital formats.

**Three or more complex clauses.** In this case, put a semicolon after each clause (including the one before the conjunction) and a conjunction before the last clause.

The committee designed the questionnaire, which was short but still took more than a month to be completed; the field-workers, who were obligated to wait for the committee to finish its work, collected responses; and the statisticians analyzed the results, though not until several weeks later.

*Two less common forms:*

4. Coordinating conjunction (alone)

This form is reserved for sentences with two short, simple clauses. Do not use it if either clause has internal punctuation.

The senator arrived at noon and the president left at once.

The senator, who was late, arrived at noon, and the president left at once.

5. Comma (alone)—caution!

This form is used by many of the best writers when they want to emphasize the connection between two short independent clauses. But many teachers regard this construction as an error (called a *comma splice*). So avoid it unless you know your readers will accept it.

The senator arrived, the president left.

*Three forms for special effects:*

6.  Colon

    A colon suggests that the second clause follows closely from the first. Readers take it as shorthand for *therefore, to illustrate, for example, that is, let me expand on what I just said*, and so on. The second clause generally does not begin with a capital letter, but it can. Good writers rarely include a coordinating conjunction after a colon.

    Dance is not widely supported: no company operates at a profit, and there are few outside major cities.

    Only one question remains: What if we lose money?

    Only one choice remained: he must confront his enemy.

    A colon can also introduce a list of sentences.

    Sally was faced with few good choices: She could risk revealing what she learned. Or she could let her best friend pay the price for something she did not do. Or was there a third way?

7.  Dash

    A dash can be used to signal the same relationships as a colon or parentheses. Dashes are useful for inserting explanatory elements or to signal an abrupt break in thought. In less formal writing they are sometimes used with a coordinating conjunction or another introducer in the clause after the dash.

    Vinyl records—so recently declared obsolete—have been experiencing a renaissance.

    Writing well may be hard—but it's worth the effort.

    A perfect lawn requires constant diligence—after all, weeds are always poised to invade.

8.  Parentheses

    You can use parentheses in place of a colon or a dash, especially if the second clause is short and serves as an explanation, illustration, or afterthought. Put the period outside the last parenthesis. (*Exception*: If you place an entire sentence in parentheses, like this, the period goes inside.)

    The first moon landing captivated America (the TV ratings were the highest ever).

Writing well may be hard (but it's worth the effort).

A perfect lawn requires constant diligence (after all, weeds are always poised to invade).

## 24.3 Introductory Elements

Sentences often begin with an introductory word, phrase, or subordinate clause before the main clause begins. When they are short these introducers pose little problem for readers, as in this sentence. But when (as in this sentence) an introducer becomes long enough that readers cannot keep it all in mind at once, especially if it includes multiple elements, readers need punctuation to help them keep the grammatical units straight in their minds. We can give you a few rules to guide you in punctuating introductory elements, but in many cases you will have to rely on your judgment to decide what readers need.

### 24.3.1 Summary

Use a comma to set off the following introductory elements:

1. connecting adverb or adverb phrase (with some exceptions)
2. commenting adverb or adverb phrase
3. long introductory phrase or clause
4. introductory element that might confuse readers

### 24.3.2 Four Ways to Punctuate Introductory Elements

1. Put a comma after an initial adverb or adverb phrase that connects the current sentence to previous ones.

   Connecting adverbs include such terms as *however*, *nevertheless*, *meanwhile*, *also*, *in addition*, *therefore*, and so on. Since readers tend to hear a mental pause after these terms, they usually expect a comma.

   In the meantime, the police were distracted by a noise in the alley.

   Conversely, drivers tend to underestimate the risks of cellphone use while driving.

   *Exception*: You may omit the comma after a connecting adverb if it does not create a pause when you read aloud, especially for short terms like *now*, *thus*, *hence*, and so on.

   Perhaps we will see you there.

   Now the evidence supports no such conclusion.

2. Put a comma after an initial adverb or adverb phrase that comments on the entire sentence.

Commenting adverbs include such terms as *fortunately, surely, perhaps, of course,* and so on. Since readers usually hear a mental pause after these terms, they expect a comma.

Happily, our investigation turned up no surprises.

To be sure, some researchers offer conclusions that contradict this claim.

3. Put a comma after a long introductory phrase or clause.

Although it may be possible to meet or exceed the goals set forth at the latest summit, especially after factoring in compliance by the United States, even a return to pre-nineteenth-century emissions would provide no guarantee against rising sea levels.

Despite the many concerns about the safety of nuclear power plants and their waste disposal, it seems inevitable that the United States will increase its nuclear footprint.

This is not a hard-and-fast rule. You can often omit the comma if the introductory phrase or clause is short, as long as the sentence is clear without it.

By 2014 cellphone-only households had surpassed those with either cellphone and landline service or landline only.

4. Always put a comma after an introductory element if leaving it out might confuse readers about the structure of the sentence.

NOT   When the speaker concludes her presentation will have been seen on three continents simultaneously.

BUT   When the speaker concludes, her presentation will have been seen on three continents simultaneously.

## 24.4   Trailing Elements

Many elements that can introduce a main clause can also trail it. In most cases these trailing elements do not need punctuation. But in three cases they do.

### 24.4.1   Summary

Most trailing elements are not set off by punctuation. Here are three cases in which you can set them off.

1. Use commas to separate a trailer from a long main clause.
2. Use commas to separate one trailer from a previous one.
3. Use a comma or a dash if the trailer serves as an afterthought.

24.4.2 **Three Ways to Punctuate Trailing Elements**
In most cases you do not need to set off a trailing element with a comma.

**Introducer:** Despite the many concerns about the safety of nuclear power plants and their waste disposal, it seems inevitable that the United States will increase its nuclear footprint.

**Trailer:** It seems inevitable that the United States will increase its nuclear footprint despite the many concerns about the safety of nuclear power plants and their waste disposal.

**Introducer:** Although the IRS has few auditors and antiquated data processing, taxpayers remain fearful enough to be deterred from cheating.

**Trailer:** Taxpayers remain fearful enough to be deterred from cheating even though the IRS has few auditors and antiquated data processing.

There are, however, three situations in which you may set off a trailing element—if, that is, you think it might help your readers.

1. Use a comma to set off a trailing element if the main clause is long and complex, especially if the trailer is also long.

   Missile defense systems, which have an overwhelming number of variables that must be managed, make more sense in the abstract than in the reality,$_{main}$ $_{clause}$ because in the long run an engineering project can only be as successful as our understanding of the problem it is trying to solve.$_{trailer}$

2. Use a comma to set off one trailing element that follows another, especially if what has come before is long and complex.

   Competitors will respond$_{main\ clause}$ when a new advertising campaign reframes the terms in which customers think about a product,$_{trailer\ 1}$ because they cannot be put out of the running for "share of mind."$_{trailer\ 2}$

3. Use a comma or a dash before a trailing element that serves as an afterthought or provides information that is parenthetical to the rest of the sentence.

   I knew you would break your promise and go, because you always go.

   There are, however, several situations in which you may set off a trailing element—if, that is, you think it might help your readers.

## 24.5    Elements Internal to Clauses

### 24.5.1    Summary

*Adjective Strings*
1.  Use commas to separate adjectives when they independently modify the noun.
2.  Do not use commas when one adjective affects the meaning of the next.

*Interrupting Elements*
1.  Enclose an interrupting element in paired commas, parentheses, or dashes.

*Explanatory Elements*
1.  Set off most explanatory elements with paired commas.
2.  Use dashes to signal an abrupt break or if the element has internal punctuation.
3.  Use parentheses to make it seem like an aside or a footnote.

### 24.5.2    Adjective Strings

When two or more adjectives appear before a noun—not in a series connected by *and*, but as a string—you may need to separate them with a comma.

1.  Use commas to separate a string of adjectives when each of them independently modifies the noun.

    It was a large, well-placed, beautiful house.

    They strolled out into the warm, luminous night.

2.  Do not use a comma when one adjective affects the meaning of the next.

    She refused to be identified with a traditional political label.

    Shared social networks form the basis of modern marketing campaigns.

### 24.5.3    Interrupting Elements

Interrupting elements are words, phrases, or clauses that might have been located at the beginning or end of the current clause but that are located within the clause instead.

1.  Enclose an interrupting element in commas, parentheses, or dashes, depending on how forceful you want the interruption to seem. Always use the punctuation marks in pairs.

    The Quinn Report was, to say the least, a bombshell.

    The mandate for self-driving cars (as detailed in the report) did not specify a fuel source.

Happiness—especially when it comes through the graces of chance—is as fleeting as a hot streak at the roulette wheel.

24.5.4    **Explanatory Elements**

Explanatory elements are modifiers that add useful information but are not essential to the core meaning of the clause: technically, they are called *nonrestrictive*. In contrast, *restrictive* modifiers add essential information that specifies who or what a word refers to. They answer the question "Which one?" The following modifiers (underlined) are restrictive because they add *specifying* details:

In cases of divorce, the parent with custody receives the tax deduction for child support. [*Which parent? The one with custody.*]

Student athletes are attracted to schools that balance athletics with scholarship. [*Which schools? The ones that balance athletics with scholarship.*]

Nonrestrictive modifiers add explanatory details but do not specify who or what a word refers to. They can be removed without changing the core meaning of the clause. They answer the question "What about it?" The following modifiers (underlined) are nonrestrictive because they add *explanatory* but not specifying details:

In this case, the mother—the parent with custody—receives the tax deduction for child support. [*What about the mother? She's the parent with custody.*]

My friend told me about her new school, which balances athletics with scholarship. [*What about that school? It balances athletics with scholarship.*]

Note that for relative clauses, the restrictive form uses *that* while the nonrestrictive one uses *which*.

Restrictive modifiers (the kind that specify) are never punctuated. Nonrestrictive modifiers (the kind that explain) usually are.

1.   Set off most explanatory elements with paired commas.

These five books, which are on reserve in the library, are required reading.

These five books, all required reading, are on reserve in the library.

2.   Use dashes to signal an abrupt break or if the element has internal punctuation.

Some characters in *Tom Jones* are "flat"—if I may use a somewhat discredited term—because they are caricatures of their names.

The influence of three impressionists—Monet (1840–1926), Sisley (1839–1899), and Degas (1834–1917)—is obvious in her work.

3.  Use parentheses to make a phrase seem like an aside or a footnote.

The brain (at least the part that controls rational thinking) is a complex network of distinct units working in parallel.

Kierkegaard (a Danish philosopher) once asked, "What is anxiety?"

## 24.6    Series and Lists

### 24.6.1    Summary

*Two Coordinated Elements*
1.  Never use a comma to separate two coordinated words.
2.  Use a comma to separate coordinated phrases or clauses *only* if readers might be confused about where one ends and the next begins.

*Series of Three or More*
1.  Use a comma after each item and a conjunction before the last.
2.  Use semicolons instead of commas for long and complex items.

*Run-In Lists*
1.  Put a colon at the end of a complete introductory clause; use no punctuation after an introductory verb.
2.  Punctuate the list as a series; do not capitalize the first word.

*Vertical Lists*
1.  Put a colon or period at the end of a complete introductory clause; use no punctuation after an introductory verb.
2.  If the items are complete sentences, capitalize the first word and use terminal punctuation at the end.
3.  If the items are not complete sentences, omit terminal punctuation, even for the last item, and do not capitalize the first word.

### 24.6.2    Two Coordinated Elements
In most cases you should not put a comma between two coordinated words, phrases, or subordinate clauses. But you can add a comma if readers might otherwise be confused, which can happen when two phrases or clauses are long and complex or when the conjunction includes a confusing combination of words, such as several *and*s near one another.

1.  Never put a comma between two words connected by a coordinating conjunction.

NOT   the dogs, and cats ran
      I saw Julio, and Chandra
      we ate, but didn't drink

BUT   the dogs and cats ran
      I saw Julio and Chandra
      we ate but didn't drink

2.  Use a comma to separate two coordinated phrases or clauses if readers might be confused about where one ends and the next begins.

NOT   It is in the graveyard that Hamlet finally realizes that the inevitable end of life is the grave and decay and that pride and all plotting and counter-plotting must lead to dust.

BUT   It is in the graveyard that Hamlet finally realizes that the inevitable end of life is the grave and decay, and that pride and all plotting and counter-plotting must lead to dust.

### 24.6.3  Series of Three or More

You must punctuate any series of three or more.

1.  Put a comma after each item in a series except the last, and put a coordinating conjunction before the last item. Treat a term like *etc.*, *and so forth*, or *and the like* as an item in the list.

    a red, white, and blue shirt
    run, walk, or crawl
    including pens, pencils, paper clips, tape, and the like
    You must go home, get your homework started, and ignore your phone.

2.  If the items in a series are long, and especially if they include internal punctu-ation, put a semicolon after each item except the last, and put a coordinating conjunction before the last item.

    It was the project engineers who failed to consult the risk-management team, even though they worked in the same building; who designed the apparatus (though without user-testing and even without thinking about the needs of users); and who now have cost the company its good reputation with farmers.

### 24.6.4  Run-In Lists

1.  Put a colon at the end of a complete introductory clause.

    People expect three things of government: peace, prosperity, and respect for civil rights.

The qualifications are as follows: a doctorate in economics . . .

> **Use no punctuation after an introductory verb (or after the word *including*).**

NOT   The dieters were instructed to avoid: meat, bottled drinks, packaged foods . . .

BUT   The dieters were instructed to avoid meat, bottled drinks, packaged foods . . .

2.  **Punctuate the list as a series (see 24.6.3). Do not capitalize the first word in the list.**

## 24.6.5    Vertical Lists

1.  **Put a colon or period at the end of a complete introductory clause.**

To be as clear as possible, your sentences must do the following:

- Match characters to subjects and actions to verbs.
- Begin with old information.
- Use words that readers can picture.

> **Use no punctuation after an introductory verb.**

To be as clear as possible, your sentences must

- match characters to subjects and actions to verbs
- begin with old information
- use words that readers can picture

2.  **If the items in the list are complete sentences, capitalize the first word and use terminal punctuation at the end.**

The report offered three conclusions.

1. The securities markets will not soon recover.
2. The securities industry is largely to blame.
3. The economy will not recover until securities are better regulated.

3.  **If the items in the list are not complete sentences, omit terminal punctuation, even for the last item, and do not capitalize the first word.**

The report covers three areas:

1. the securities markets
2. the securities industry
3. the effects on the economy

## 24.7    Quotations

### 24.7.1    Summary

1.  Reproduce all quoted words exactly; indicate omitted words with an ellipsis; indicate added or changed words with square brackets.
2.  Change the first letter of a quotation so that complete sentences start with a capital and incomplete sentences begin with a lowercase letter.
3.  For the introduction to a quotation, follow complete sentences with a period or a colon; follow phrases with a comma; follow *that* with no punctuation.
4.  *Run-in*: Enclose all quoted words in pairs of quotation marks. Place the final quotation mark

    *   *outside* periods and commas
    *   *inside* colons and semicolons
    *   *outside* question marks and parentheses that are part of the quotation
    *   *inside* question marks and parentheses that are part of your sentence
    *   *inside* a parenthetical reference

5.  *Block*: Do not enclose the quotation in quotation marks; place a parenthetical reference after the final punctuation.

### 24.7.2    Punctuating Quotations

1.  Reproduce all quoted words exactly as they appeared in the original. You may omit words if you replace them with an ellipsis (three dots). You may add or change words if you put them in square brackets.

    **Original:** A notable feature of American society is religious pluralism, and we should consider how this relates to the efficacy of governance by social norms.

    **Changed version:** In his discussion of religion, Posner says of American society that "a notable feature . . . is [its] religious pluralism" (299).

2.  Change the first letter of a quotation so that complete sentences start with a capital and incomplete sentences begin with a lowercase letter. If you introduce the quotation with a clause ending in *that*, make the first letter lowercase. If you weave the quotation into your own sentence, change an initial capital to lowercase.

    **Original:** Under the influence of on-demand television, the conventions of the weekly series, including strict episode timings and the use of narrative recaps, began to erode.

    **Lowercase changed to uppercase to begin complete sentence:**

    As Javal notes, "The conventions of the weekly series, including strict episode timings and the use of narrative recaps, began to erode."

"The conventions of the weekly series," notes Javal, "including strict episode timings and the use of narrative recaps, began to erode."

**Initial capital changed to lowercase following *that*:**

Javal points out that "under the influence of on-demand television, the conventions of the weekly series, including strict episode timings and the use of narrative recaps, began to erode."

**Initial capital changed to lowercase to fit syntax of including sentence:**

Javal points out that these conventions "began to erode," but only "under the influence of on-demand television."

3. If the introduction to a quotation is a complete sentence, put a period or a colon after it. If it is a phrase or incomplete clause, put a comma. If it is a clause ending in *that*, use no punctuation.

> Posner focuses on religion for its social functions. "A notable feature . . ."
> Posner focuses on religion: "A notable feature . . ."
> Posner says, "A notable feature . . ."
> Posner says that "a notable feature . . ."

4. *Run-in*: Enclose all quoted words in pairs of quotation marks. Place the final quotation mark

   • *outside* periods and commas

   > . . . now is the time."
   > . . . now is the time," but we also . . .

   • *inside* colons and semicolons

   > . . . now is the time"; but we also . . .

   • *outside* question marks and parentheses that are part of the quotation

   > He asked, "Is now the time?"
   > . . . now is the time (or so it seems)."

   • *inside* question marks and parentheses that are part of your sentence

   > Will he say, "Now is the time"?
   > . . . yesterday (as he said, "Now is the time").

- *prior to* a parenthetical reference

    . . . now is the time" (Walker 210).

5. *Block*: Do not enclose the quotation in quotation marks. Place a parenthetical reference *after* the final punctuation.

    According to Jared Diamond,

    > Because technology begets more technology, . . . technology's history exemplifies what is termed an autocatalytic process: that is, one that speeds up at a rate that increases with time, because the process cata- lyzes itself. (301)

## 24.8   Punctuation Don'ts

1. **Titles and headings.** Do not put a period after a title or heading, even if it is a complete sentence. You may use a question mark (or, more rarely, an exclamation point).

    4.3 Headings Can Be Sentences
    4.3 Can Headings Be Sentences?

2. **Subjects-verbs-objects.** Do not put a comma between a subject and its verb or a verb and its direct object, even if they are long. If a subject or verb is so long that you feel you must have a comma, revise the sentence.

    NOT   A sentence whose subject goes on forever because it includes many complex subordinate clauses and long phrases that give readers no place to take a mental breath, may seem to some students to demand a comma to show where the subject ends and the verb begins.

    For a subject that consists of a long list, put a colon or dash after the list and add a *summative subject* such as "all these."

    The president, the vice president, the secretaries of the departments, senators, members of the House of Representatives, and Supreme Court justices—all these take an oath that pledges them to uphold the Constitution.

3. **Doubled punctuation marks.** Do not put two periods together.

    NOT   I work for Abco Inc..
          Rowling, J. K.. *Harry Potter and* . . .

    BUT   I work for Abco Inc.
          Rowling, J. K. *Harry Potter and* . . .

If a title of a work ends in a question mark or exclamation point, keep any necessary comma but do not add a period.

NOT    Albee, Edward. *Who's Afraid of Virginia Wolf?*. New York: . . .

Films such as *Airplane! This Is Spinal Tap*, and *Austin Powers* offer parodies of well-established genres.

BUT    Albee, Edward. *Who's Afraid of Virginia Wolf?* New York: . . .

Films such as *Airplane!*, *This Is Spinal Tap*, and *Austin Powers* offer parodies of well-established genres.

# 25 Titles, Names, and Numbers

## 25.1 Titles

The following conventions apply when you reproduce the title of a book, article, poem, film, or other work *in the body of your paper*. For titles in citations, see the appropriate sections of part 2.

## 25.1.1 Spelling

Reproduce a title exactly as it appears in the original. Preserve the original spelling (including hyphenation) even if it departs from the dictionary or standard usage.

## 25.1.2 Capitalization

In your text, capitalize titles headline-style. In this style you should capitalize the first letter of all words except the following:

- articles (*a, an, the*)
- coordinating conjunctions (*and, but, or, nor, for*)
- prepositions (*of, in, at, above, under*, and so forth)
- the words *to* and *as*
- parts of proper nouns that are in lowercase (Ludwig van Beethoven, Charles de Gaulle)

- the second word of a hyphenated compound that starts with a prefix (Anti-intellectual, Re-establishment)

Always capitalize the first and last words of the title and subtitle, even if they are on the list of words that are not capitalized.

*The Economic Effects of the Civil War in the Mid-Atlantic States*
*To Have and to Hold: A Twenty-First-Century View of Marriage*
*All That Is True: The Life of Vincent van Gogh, 1853–1890*
*Four Readings of the Gospel according to Matthew*
*Self-Government and the Re-establishment of a New World Order*

*Note*: The principles of capitalization have nothing to do with word length. Capitalize all short words that are not on the do-not-capitalize list; use lowercase for all words that are on the list, no matter how long they might be.
*Exception*: APA headline style capitalizes all words of four letters or more, including prepositions. You may follow this rule if you use APA style to cite your sources (see chapter 22).
For titles of works published in the eighteenth century or earlier, retain the original capitalization (and spelling), except that words spelled out in all capital letters should be given with an initial capital only.

*A Treatise of morall philosophy Contaynyge the sayings of the wyse*

## 25.1.3    Italics and Quotation Marks
Set off most titles either in italics or by enclosing them in quotation marks.

### Italics
Most long, separately published works are printed in italics. Italicized works include

- books

    *Culture and Anarchy*        *The Great Gatsby*

- plays and very long poems, especially those of book length

    *A Winter's Tale*        Dante's *Inferno*

- journals, magazines, newspapers, and other periodicals; an initial *the* is treated as part of the surrounding text (and is dropped in source citations)

*Signs*
*Time*
the *Washington Post*

- long musical compositions such as operas and albums

  *The Marriage of Figaro*      Michael Jackson's *Thriller*

- paintings, sculptures, photographs, and other works of art

  *Mona Lisa*
  Michelangelo's *David*
  *North Dome* by Ansel Adams

- movies, television shows, and radio programs

  *Citizen Kane*
  *Sesame Street*
  *All Things Considered*

## Quotation Marks

Titles of most short works are enclosed in quotation marks, especially those that are part of a larger work. Works set within quotation marks include

- chapters or other titled parts of books

  "The Later Years"

- short stories, short poems, and essays

  "The Dead"
  "The Housekeeper"
  "Of Books"

- articles or other features in journals, magazines, newspapers, and other periodicals

  "The Function of Fashion in Eighteenth-Century America"
  "Who Should Lead the Supreme Court?"
  "Election Comes Down to the Wire"

- individual episodes of television series

"The Opposite"

- short musical compositions

"The Star-Spangled Banner"

**Exceptions**
For a few special types of titles, you should capitalize them but print them in regular type.

- book series

Studies in Legal History

- scriptures and other sacred works

| | |
|---|---|
| the Bible | the Koran |
| the King James Bible | Genesis |
| the Upanishads | Exodus |

- websites

Facebook
Google
JSTOR

*Note*: MLA style puts the titles of websites in italics. You may follow this rule if you use MLA style to cite your sources (see chapter 21).

Do not treat terms for the parts of books as titles; do not capitalize or set them off.

your bibliography
the preface to *Style*
see chapter 4

## 25.2    Proper Names

### 25.2.1    People, Places, and Organizations
Capitalize the first letter of each main element in the names of specific people, places, and organizations. Names that contain particles (such as *de* and *van*) or compound last names are capitalized unpredictably. When in doubt, consult the

biographical listings from Merriam-Webster or an up-to-date encyclopedia or other reliable authority. Do not capitalize prepositions (*of*) and conjunctions (*and*) that are parts of names. If *the* precedes a name, it is not capitalized.

Eleanor Roosevelt
W. E. B. DuBois
Ludwig van Beethoven
Victoria Sackville-West
Chiang Kai-shek
Sierra Leone
Central America
New York City
the Atlantic Ocean
the Republic of Lithuania
the United States Congress
the State Department
the European Union
the University of North Carolina
the Honda Motor Company
Skidmore, Owings & Merrill
the National Conference for Community and Justice
the Roman Catholic Church
the Allied Expeditionary Force

A professional title that immediately precedes a personal name is treated as part of the name and should be capitalized. If you use the title alone or after the personal name, it becomes a generic term and should be lowercased. This also applies to other generic terms that are in place of organization names.

| | |
|---|---|
| President Harry Truman announced | the president announced |
| Professors Liu and Prakash wrote | the professors wrote |
| next to the Indian Ocean | next to the ocean |

Names of ethnic and national groups are also capitalized. Terms denoting socioeconomic level, however, are not.

| | |
|---|---|
| Arab Americans | the middle class |
| Latinos | white-collar workers |

Capitalize adjectives derived from names, unless they have become part of everyday language.

| | |
|---|---|
| Machiavellian scheme | french fries |
| Roman and Arabic art | roman and arabic numerals |

## 25.2.2   Historical Events and Periods

The names of many historical periods and events are traditionally capitalized; more generic terms usually are not, except for any names they include.

| | |
|---|---|
| the Bronze Age | ancient Rome |
| the Depression | the nineteenth century |
| the Industrial Revolution | the Shang dynasty |
| Prohibition | the colonial period |
| the Seven Years' War | the gold rush |

## 25.2.3   Other Types of Names

Other types of names also follow specific patterns for capitalization, and some require italics.

### Acts, Treaties, and Government Programs

Capitalize the formal or accepted titles of acts, treaties, government programs, and similar documents or entities, but lowercase informal or generic titles.

| | |
|---|---|
| the United States (or US) Constitution | the due process clause |
| the Treaty of Versailles | the treaty |
| the Kyoto Protocol | the protocol |
| Head Start | social programs |

### Brand Names

Capitalize the brand names of products, but do not use the symbol ® or ™ after the names. Unless you are discussing a specific product, use a generic term instead of a brand name.

| | |
|---|---|
| Coca-Cola | cola |
| Xerox | photocopy |

### Devices and Applications

Capitalize proper names of devices and applications, networks, browsers, systems, and languages. Generic terms that are not trademarked can usually be lowercased.

Apple iOS 10; iPhone
the Kindle app for Android

the internet
the World Wide Web Consortium (W3C); the web; website; webpage

**Ships, Aircraft, and Other Vessels**
Capitalize and italicize the names of ships, aircraft, and the like. If the names are preceded by such abbreviations as USS (United States ship) or HMS (Her [or His] Majesty's ship), do not italicize these abbreviations or use the word *ship* in addition to the name.

| | |
|---|---|
| USS *Constitution* | *Spirit of St. Louis* |
| HMS *Saranac* | the space shuttle *Endeavor* |

## 25.3  Numbers

### 25.3.1  Words or Numerals?

#### 25.3.1.1  *The General Rule*
**Either:** Spell out numbers from one through one hundred. If the number has two words, use a hyphen (fifty-five). Also spell out round numbers followed by *hundred, thousand, hundred thousand, million,* and so on. For all other numbers, use arabic numerals. Follow this pattern for numbers that are part of physical quantities (distances, lengths, temperatures, and so on), and do not use abbreviations for the units in such quantities.

After seven years of war came sixty-four years of peace.

The population of the three states was approximately twelve million.

He cataloged more than 527 works of art.

Within fifteen minutes the temperature dropped twenty degrees.

**Or:** If your topic relies heavily on numerical data, follow a different rule: spell out only single-digit numbers (one through nine) and use numerals for all others (10 and up).

Use the same principles for ordinal numbers (*first, second,* etc.) that you use for standard ones. Add "st," "nd," "rd," or "th" as appropriate.

On the 122nd and 123rd days of his trip, he received his eighteenth and nineteenth letters from home.

25.3.1.2    *Special Cases*

**Numbers at the Beginning of a Sentence**

Never begin a sentence with a numeral. Either spell out the number or, especially when there are other numerals of a similar type in the sentence, recast the sentence.

Two hundred fifty soldiers in the unit escaped injury while 175 sustained minor injuries.

Of the soldiers in the unit, 250 escaped injury and 175 sustained minor injuries.

*Note*: When spelling out numbers over one hundred, omit the word *and* within the term (*two hundred fifty*, not *two hundred and fifty*).

**Series of Numbers**

Ignore the general rule when you have a series of numbers in the same sentence that are both above *and* below the threshold, especially when those numbers are being compared. In these examples, all are expressed in numerals.

Of the group surveyed, 78 students had studied French and 142 had studied Spanish for three years or more.

We analyzed 62 cases; of these, 59 had occurred in adults and 3 in children.

25.3.2    **Inclusive Numbers**

To express a range of numbers, such as pages or years, give the first and last (or *inclusive*) numbers of the sequence. If the numbers are spelled out, express the range with the words *from* and *to*; if they are expressed in numerals, use either these words or a connecting hyphen with no space on either side. In citations, always use hyphens (see chapters 20–22).

from 45 to 50        NOT from 45–50
45–50                NOT forty-five–fifty

For inclusive numbers of one hundred or greater, use full numbers on both sides of the hyphen (245–280, or 1929–1994).

25.3.3    **Percentages and Decimal Fractions**

Use numerals to express percentages and decimal fractions, except at the beginning of a sentence. Spell out the word *percent*, except when you use many percentage figures and in the sciences, where the symbol % is usually preferred (with no space between number and symbol). Notice that the noun *percentage* should not be used with a number.

Scores for students who skipped summer school improved only 9 percent.

The percentage of students who failed was about 2.4 times the usual rate.

Within this system, the subject scored 3.8, or 95%.

**When you use fractional and whole numbers for the same type of item in the same sentence or paragraph, give both as numerals.**

The average number of children born to college graduates dropped from 2.4 to 2.

**Put a zero in front of a decimal fraction of less than 1.00 if the quantity expressed is capable of exceeding 1.00; otherwise, omit the initial zero (as for batting averages, probabilities, and the like).**

a mean of 0.73          a batting average of .372

a loss of 0.08          $p < .05$

**For fractions standing alone, follow the general rule for spelling out the parts (see 25.3.1.1). If you spell out the parts, include a hyphen between them. A unit composed of a whole number and a fraction can be expressed in numerals; if you use a symbol for the fractional part, there is no intervening space between the number and the fraction.**

Trade and commodity services accounted for nine-tenths of all international receipts and payments.

One year during the Dust Bowl era, the town received only 15/16 of an inch of rain.

The main carving implement used in this society measured 2½ feet.

25.3.4 **Money**

If you refer only occasionally to US currency, follow the general rule (see 25.3.1.1) and spell out the words *dollars* and *cents*. Otherwise use numerals along with the symbol $ (or, if needed, ¢). Omit the decimal point and following zeros for whole-dollar amounts, unless you refer to fractional amounts as well.

Rarely do they spend more than five dollars a week on recreation.

The report showed $135 collected in fines.

Prices ranged from $0.95 up to $10.00.

After peaking at $200.00, shares of the stock plummeted to $36.75.

**Express large round numbers in a combination of numerals and words.**

The deficit that year was $420 billion.

### 25.3.5   Time

For references to times of day in increments of an hour, half hour, or quarter hour, spell out the times. If necessary, specify *in the morning* or *in the evening*. You may use *o'clock*, although it is now rare in research writing.

The participants planned to meet every Thursday around ten thirty in the morning.

When emphasizing exact times, use numerals and, if necessary, "a.m." or "p.m." (lowercase, regular type, no intervening space). Always include zeros after the colon for even hours.

Although scheduled to end at 11:00 a.m., the council meeting ran until 1:37 p.m.

In either situation, use the words *noon* and *midnight* (rather than numerals) to express these specific times of day.

### 25.3.6   Addresses and Thoroughfares

Follow the general rule (see 25.3.1.1) for the names of local numbered streets. State, federal, and interstate highways are always designated with numerals, as are street or building addresses and telephone and fax numbers. Note that the elements of a full address are separated by commas, except before a zip code.

The National Park Service maintains as a museum the house where Lincoln died (516 10th Street NW, Washington, DC 20004; 202-426-6924).

Ludwig Mies van der Rohe designed the apartments at 860–880 North Lake Shore Drive.

Interstate 95 serves as a critical transportation line from Boston to Miami.

### 25.3.7   Dates

#### 25.3.7.1   *Month, Day, and Year*

Spell out the names of months when they occur in your text, whether alone or in dates. Express days and years in numerals, and avoid using them at the beginning of a sentence, where they would have to be spelled out (see 25.3.1.2). Do not abbreviate references to the year ("the great flood of '05").

Every September, we recall the events of 2001.

NOT    Two thousand one was a memorable year.

For full references to dates, give the month, the day (followed by a comma), and the year, in accordance with US practices. If you omit the day, omit the comma. Also omit the comma for dates given with seasons instead of months; do not capitalize the names of seasons. (*Note*: Names of seasons are capitalized in source citations.)

President John F. Kennedy was assassinated on November 22, 1963.

By March 1865 the war was nearly over.

The research was conducted over several weeks in spring 2017.

25.3.7.2  *Decades, Centuries, and Eras*
In general, refer to decades using numerals, including the century (1920s, *not* 20s). If the century is clear, you can spell out the name of the decade (*the twenties*). The first two decades of any century do not lend themselves to either style and should be described fully for clarity.

The 1920s brought unheralded financial prosperity.

During the fifties, the Cold War dominated the headlines.

Many of these discoveries were announced during the first and second decades of the twenty-first century.

Refer to centuries using either numerals or lowercase spelled-out names. If the century is spelled out and used as an adjective preceding a noun that it modifies, as in the second example, use a hyphen; otherwise, do not.

The Ottoman Empire reached its apex in the 1600s.

She teaches nineteenth-century novels but would rather teach poetry from the twentieth century.

# Appendix A: Formatting Your Paper

The following guidelines for formatting your class paper, including the sample title page and text, are provided for general reference only. Any directions provided by your teacher take precedence over the guidelines presented here. For more advice and examples, consult Turabian.org.

### A.1.1 Title

Every paper must have a title and other identifying information (name, class, date). For papers of five pages or more, put this information on a title page. For papers of four pages or less, put it at the top of your first page. Find out what your teacher prefers.

- **Title page.** On a separate page, position the title about one-third from the top. Add your identifying information about one-third from the bottom.
- **Title on first page of text.** Position the title at the top of the first page of your paper. Skip two lines and add your identifying information. Skip two more lines and begin the main text of your paper.

Format the title and identifying information in the same font as the main text, centered, but use bold for the title. If you have a subtitle, put the main title on the first line, followed by a colon, with the subtitle on the next line. Capitalize your title headline-style (see 25.1.3). For identifying information, enter on separate lines your name, your course (and, if required, the name of your teacher), and the date you turn in the paper. See figure A.1.

### A.1.2 Text

Apply the following formatting for the text of your paper:

- Choose a standard font. Use the equivalent of at least 12-point Times New Roman or 10-point Arial (some fonts take up more space and appear larger than others).
- Double-space all text (except for block quotations, which should be single-spaced, with a blank line before and after the quotation).
- Set margins of at least 1 inch on all sides and no more than 1.5 inches.
- Align all text flush left (with a "ragged" right margin).
- Indent the first line of each new paragraph by half an inch.

See figure A.2.

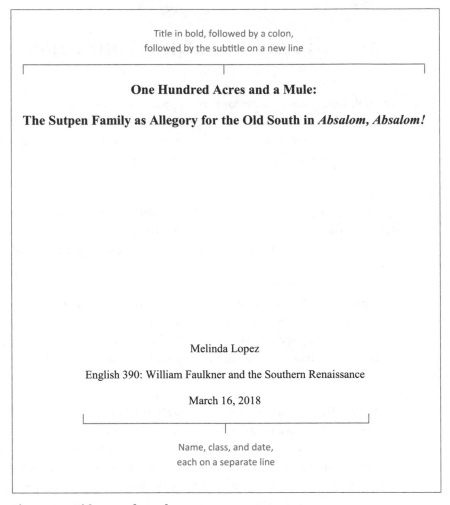

Title in bold, followed by a colon,
followed by the subtitle on a new line

**One Hundred Acres and a Mule:**

**The Sutpen Family as Allegory for the Old South in *Absalom, Absalom!***

Melinda Lopez

English 390: William Faulkner and the Southern Renaissance

March 16, 2018

Name, class, and date,
each on a separate line

**Figure A.1. Title page for a class paper**

### A.1.3   Header

Create a header for all pages except the first. If you include a title page, that counts as page 1, but your header skips that page and begins on the first page of text. If your title is on the first page of text, the header skips that page and begins on the next one. In either case, the header starts on page 2.

On the right-hand side of the header (flush right), add the page number. Use the same font and size that you are using for the text. Some teachers will want you to include your name before the page number; find out what your teacher prefers.

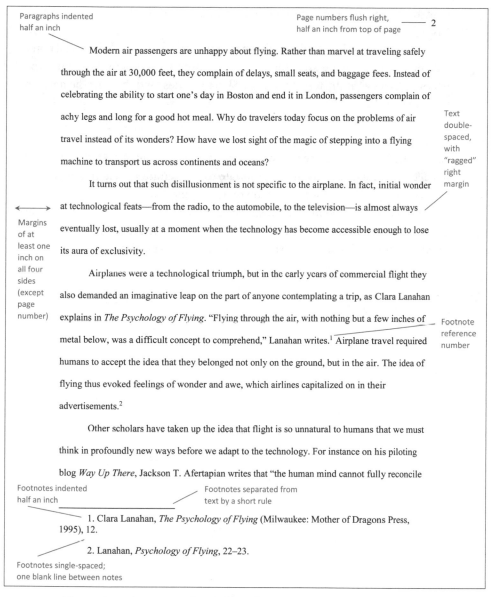

Paragraphs indented
half an inch

Page numbers flush right,
half an inch from top of page        2

Modern air passengers are unhappy about flying. Rather than marvel at traveling safely

through the air at 30,000 feet, they complain of delays, small seats, and baggage fees. Instead of

celebrating the ability to start one's day in Boston and end it in London, passengers complain of

achy legs and long for a good hot meal. Why do travelers today focus on the problems of air

travel instead of its wonders? How have we lost sight of the magic of stepping into a flying

machine to transport us across continents and oceans?

Text double-spaced, with "ragged" right margin

It turns out that such disillusionment is not specific to the airplane. In fact, initial wonder

at technological feats—from the radio, to the automobile, to the television—is almost always

eventually lost, usually at a moment when the technology has become accessible enough to lose

its aura of exclusivity.

Margins of at least one inch on all four sides (except page number)

Airplanes were a technological triumph, but in the early years of commercial flight they

also demanded an imaginative leap on the part of anyone contemplating a trip, as Clara Lanahan

explains in *The Psychology of Flying*. "Flying through the air, with nothing but a few inches of

metal below, was a difficult concept to comprehend," Lanahan writes.[1] Airplane travel required

Footnote reference number

humans to accept the idea that they belonged not only on the ground, but in the air. The idea of

flying thus evoked feelings of wonder and awe, which airlines capitalized on in their

advertisements.[2]

Other scholars have taken up the idea that flight is so unnatural to humans that we must

think in profoundly new ways before we adapt to the technology. For instance on his piloting

blog *Way Up There*, Jackson T. Afertapian writes that "the human mind cannot fully reconcile

Footnotes indented
half an inch

Footnotes separated from
text by a short rule

1. Clara Lanahan, *The Psychology of Flying* (Milwaukee: Mother of Dragons Press, 1995), 12.

2. Lanahan, *Psychology of Flying*, 22–23.

Footnotes single-spaced;
one blank line between notes

**Figure A.2. First page of text for a class paper, including footnotes**

## A.1.4    Footnotes

Use your word processor to insert footnotes. Let your word processor put a short rule between the body text and the first footnote on each page. For the text of each note, use single spacing. The text can be the same size as the main text or one or two points smaller. Insert a blank line after each note. Indent the first line of each note half an inch. Number each note with a superscript in both the text and at the beginning of the corresponding note. In the note, however, it is okay to instead use a regular number followed by a period: 1. Jill Lepore, *The Secret History* . . .

If your teacher directs you to use endnotes instead of footnotes, list all notes starting on a new page after the text but before the bibliography; center the heading "Notes" at the top of the page. Skip two lines, and then list the notes in numerical order.

## A.1.5    Bibliography

List all your sources on a separate page at the end of the paper. At the top of the page, center the title of the list appropriate to your citation style (Bibliography, Works Cited, or Reference List). Skip two lines and list bibliographical entries in the same font as the main text, single-spaced, with an extra line space after each entry. Format each entry with a half-inch hanging indent. Consult part 2 for detailed information on how to create bibliographical entries.

# Appendix B: Glossary

In this section we gather terms used in this book to denote, first, elements of argument and research and, second, elements of grammar and style. These are not technical definitions, however. They simply help you understand the discussions here.

## Terms for Argument and Research

**acknowledgment and response.** That part of argument that raises objections or other questions that you anticipate readers may have.

**argument.** The answer to a question addressed to a particular audience. Its core consists of a claim, reasons, and evidence.

**chart.** A graphic that presents quantitative evidence in bars, circles, points, or other shapes.

**citation.** A documentary record of a source of evidence.

**citation style.** A recognized convention for citations. Three common citation styles are Chicago (also known as Turabian), MLA (Modern Language Association), and APA (American Psychological Association).

**claim.** The assertion that the rest of an argument supports. It must be something that a reader will not accept without support. A *practical claim* concerns what we do; a *conceptual claim* concerns what we think.

**counterclaim/counterpoint.** An opposing claim to an argument. In most cases, a well-structured argument entertains relevant counterclaims fairly.

**data.** The objects and raw observations from which you draw evidence.

**evidence.** That part of an argument that reports on the objects or observations that you expect readers to accept as hard facts and that support your reasons.

**figure.** Any graphic except a table.

**graph.** A graphic that presents quantitative evidence as continuous lines.

**graphic.** A visual image offered as evidence. Graphics include charts and graphs, tables, diagrams, photographs, and so on.

**hypothesis.** A provisional claim. An assertion that you think might be a good answer to your research question but that you cannot yet support with reliable evidence.

**main claim.** The sentence asserting the claim that a whole argument supports and that serves as the point around which an entire paper is organized.

**point.** The most important sentence in a document, section, or paragraph. It states the idea that everything else supports and develops.

**reason.** A part of an argument that directly supports your claim. Reasons are based on evidence, but they are your judgments—subclaims—that you must support before you can expect readers to accept them.

**research question.** The specific question to which your claim, supported by reasons and evidence, is an answer.

**source.** Any material on which a researcher draws for evidence.

**table.** A grid with columns and rows that present data in numbers or words organized by categories.

**theme.** A concept that is important to the point of a paper or section and that is repeated through the body. It helps readers to organize their memory of the whole.

**thesis statement.** Another widely used term for *main claim*.

**topic.** The subject matter around which you pose your research question.

**warrant.** The part of an argument that states the principle of reasoning that connects a reason to its claim. Warrants are most explicitly stated in this form: *whenever this condition applies, we can conclude this.*

## Terms for Grammar and Style

**action.** Traditionally we say that action is expressed by a verb: *move, hate, think, discover.* But actions also appear in nominalizations: *movement, hatred, thought, discovery.* Actions are also implied in some adjectives: *advisable, explanatory,* etc.

**active voice.** A verb is *active* when its subject is the agent of its action and the direct object is the receiver of that action: *the dog chased the cat.*

**adjectival clause.** Adjectival clauses modify nouns. Also called *relative clauses,* they usually begin with a relative pronoun: *which, that, whom, whose, who.* There are two kinds: restrictive and nonrestrictive.

> **restrictive.** A restrictive clause modifies a noun whose referent you *cannot* identify without the added information in the clause. *I drove the car that was dirty.* Unless there is only one possible car in question, the noun phrase, *the car,* does not identify which car I drove, but with the added clause it does: the dirty one. We call that clause *restrictive* because it "restricts" or uniquely identifies what the noun phrase names.
>
> **nonrestrictive.** A nonrestrictive clause modifies a noun whose referent you *can* identify without the added information in the clause. *I drove my car, which was dirty.* The noun phrase, *my car,* identifies which car I drove; its lack of cleanliness is just added information. We call the clause "which was dirty" *nonrestrictive* because it does not "restrict" or uniquely identify what the noun phrase names.

**adjective.** A word you can put *very* in front of: *very old*, *very interesting*. There are exceptions—e.g., *major, additional*. Since this is also a test for adverbs, distinguish adjectives from adverbs by putting them between *the* and a noun: *the **occupational** hazard, the **major** reason*, etc.

**adjective phrase.** An adjective and what attaches to it: *so **full** that it burst*.

**adverb.** Adverbs can modify all parts of speech except nouns: ***especially** old, walk **quickly**, **very quickly***.

**adverbial clause.** A subordinate clause that modifies a verb or adjective, indicating time, cause, condition, etc. It usually begins with a subordinating conjunction such as *because, when, if, since, while, unless*.

**adverb phrase.** An adverb and what attaches to it: *as **soon** as I could*.

**agent.** Traditionally, a person who performs an action (its "doer"). But for our purposes, an agent is the *seeming* source of any action: ***She** criticized the program in this report. **This report** criticizes the program*.

**appositive.** A noun phrase that is left after *which* and *be* are deleted: *My dog, **a Dalmatian**, ran away*.

**article.** They are easier to list than to explain: *a, an, the, this, these, that, those*.

**character.** The person you talk about in your sentences. Also, the thing or idea that you tell a story about by making it the subject of several sentences in a passage.

**clause.** A clause has at least one subject + verb, where the verb agrees with the subject in number and can be made past or present. These are clauses:

she left              if she left
that they leave       why he is leaving

These next are not, because the verbs cannot be made past tense nor do they agree in number with the putative subject:

for them to **go**      her **having gone**

**comma splice.** You create a comma splice when you join two independent clauses with only a comma.

**complement.** Whatever completes a verb:

I am **home**.          You seem **tired**.      She helped **me**.

**conjunction.** Usually defined as a word that links words, phrases, or clauses. They are easier to illustrate than define (the first two are also categorized as subordinating conjunctions).

adverbial: *because, although, when, since*
relative: *who, whom, whose, which, that*

coordinating: *and, but, yet, for, so, or, nor*
correlative: *both X and Y, not only X but Y, (n)either X (n)or Y, X as well as Y*

**dependent clause.** Any clause that cannot stand alone as a sentence. It usually begins with a subordinating conjunction such as *because, if, when, which, that*.

**direct object.** The noun that follows a transitive verb and can be made the subject of a passive verb:

I found **the money**.    **The money** was found by me.

**fragment.** A phrase or dependent clause that begins with a capital letter and ends with a period, question mark, or exclamation mark:

Because I left.    Though I am here!    Which is why I did that.

**goal.** That toward which the action of a verb is directed. In most cases, goals are direct objects:

I see **you**.    I broke **the dish**.    I built **a house**.

**independent clause.** A clause that can stand alone as a sentence.

**infinitive.** A verb that cannot be made past or present. It often is preceded by the word *to: he decided to **stay***. But sometimes not: *we helped him **repair** the door.*

**main clause.** A main clause is a part of a larger sentence that could stand alone as a sentence of its own.

**nonrestrictive clause.** *See* adjectival clause.

**noun.** A word that fits this frame: *The [_____] is good*. Some are concrete: *dog, rock, car*; others abstract: *ambition, space, speed*. The nouns that most concern us are abstractions derived from verbs or adjectives: *act/action, wide/width*.

**noun clause.** A noun clause functions like a noun, as the subject or object of a verb: *That you are here **proves** that you love me.*

**object.** There are three kinds.

1.  **direct object:** the noun following a transitive verb

I read **the book**.    We *followed* **the car**.

2.  **prepositional object:** the noun following a preposition

*in* **the house**    *across* **the street**
*by* **the walk**    *with* **fervor**

3. **indirect object:** the noun or pronoun between a verb and its direct object

*I gave **him** a tip.*

**passive voice.** A verb is *passive* when its subject is the receiver of its action and the verb is preceded by a form of *be*; if the agent is named, it is in a *by* phrase: *the cat was chased by the dog.*

**personal pronoun.** Easier to list than define: *I, me, my, mine; we, us, our, ours; you, your, yours; he, him, his; she, her, hers; they, them, their, theirs.*

**phrase.** A group of words constituting a unit but not including both a subject and a finite verb: *the dog, too old, was leaving, in the house, ready to work.*

**possessive.** *My, your, his, her, its, their,* or a noun ending with *-'s* or *-s'*: the **dog's** tail.

**predicate.** Whatever follows the whole subject, beginning with the verb phrase, including the complement and what attaches to it:

He **left yesterday to buy a hat**.<sub>predicate</sub>

**preposition.** Easier to list: *in, on, up, over, of, at, by,* etc.

**prepositional phrase.** The preposition plus its object: *in + the house.*

**relative clause.** *See* adjectival clause.

**relative pronoun.** *Who, whom, which, whose, that* when used in a relative clause.

**restrictive clause.** *See* adjectival clause.

**run-on sentence.** A sentence consisting of two or more clauses not separated by either a coordinating conjunction or any mark of punctuation. *This example illustrates a run-on sentence it just keeps going.*

**subject.** The subject is what the verb agrees with in number:

**Two men** *are* at the door.       **One man** is at the door.

**subordinate clause.** A clause that usually begins with a subordinating conjunction such as *if, when, unless,* or *which, that, who.* There are three kinds of subordinate clauses: noun, adverbial, and adjectival.

**subordinating conjunction.** *because, if, when, since, unless, which, who, that, whose,* etc.

**transitive verb.** A verb with a direct object. The direct object prototypically "receives" an action. The prototypical direct object can be made the subject of a passive verb:

We **read** the book.       The book **was read** by us.

**verb.** The word that must agree with the subject in number and that can be inflected for past or present.

The book **is** ready.       The books **were** returned.

**whole subject.** You can identify a whole subject once you identify its verb: Put a *who* or a *what* in front of the verb and turn the sentence into a question. The fullest answer to the question is the whole subject.

# Appendix C: Resources for Research and Writing

There is a large literature on finding and presenting information. What we have listed here are those works that provide beginners with a useful overview (primarily specialized dictionaries and encyclopedias) and those that help beginners find sources. We have also included citation and writing guides for specialized research papers. If there is no date listed for an item, the publication appears annually. URLs are provided here for sources available online (in addition to or in place of traditional print formats). Other sources may also be available online or in an e-book format; consult your library. This list is divided as follows:

For most of those areas, six kinds of resources are listed:

1. specialized dictionaries that offer short essays defining concepts in a field
2. general and specialized encyclopedias that offer more extensive overviews of a topic
3. guides to finding resources in different fields and using their methodologies
4. bibliographies, abstracts, and indexes that list past and current publications in different fields
5. writing manuals for different fields
6. style manuals that describe required features of citations in different fields

## Internet Databases (Bibliographies and Indexes)

### General

*Academic OneFile*. Farmington Hills, MI: Gale Cengage Learning, 2006–. http://www.gale.com/.

*Academic Search Premier*. Ipswich, MA: Ebsco Information Services, 1975–. https://www.ebsco.com/.

*ArticleFirst*. Dublin, OH: OCLC, 1990–. http://www.oclc.org/.

*AP Images*. New York: Associated Press, 2013–. http:// http://www.apimages.com.

*Biography Reference Center*. Ipswich, MA: Ebsco Information Services. https://www.ebsco.com/.

*Booklist Online*. Chicago: American Library Association, 2006–. http://www.booklistonline.com/.

*CQ Researcher*. Washington, DC: CQ Press, 1991–. http://library.cqpress.com/cqresearcher/.

*EBSCOhost*. Ipswich, MA: EBSCO Publishing. https://www.ebsco.com/products/ebscohost-platform.

*ERIC*. Educational Resources Information Center. Washington, DC: US Department of Education, Institute of Education Sciences, 2004–. http://www.eric.ed.gov/.

*Essay and General Literature Index (H. W. Wilson)*. Ipswich, MA: EBSCO Publishing, 2000s–. https://www.ebsco.com/.

*General OneFile*. Farmington Hills, MI: Gale Cengage Learning, 2006–. http://www.gale.cengage.com/.

*ISI Web of Science* (formerly *Web of Knowledge*). New York: Thomson Reuters, 1990s–. http://wokinfo.com/.

*Issues & Controversies Online*. New York: Infobase. http://www.infobase.com/databases.

*LexisNexis Academic*. Dayton, OH: LexisNexis, 1984–. http://www.lexisnexis.com/.

*Library Literature and Information Science Full Text (H. W. Wilson)*. Ipswich, MA: EBSCO Publishing, 1999–. https://www.ebsco.com/.

*Library of Congress Online Catalog*. Washington, DC: Library of Congress. http://catalog.loc.gov/.

*Omnifile Full Text Select (H. W. Wilson)*. Ipswich, MA: EBSCO Publishing, 1990–. https://www.ebsco.com/.

*Opposing Viewpoints in Context*. Farmington Hills, MI: Gale Group. https://www.gale.com/c/opposing-viewpoints-in-context.

*Periodicals Index Online*. ProQuest Information and Learning, 1990–. http://www.proquest.com.

*Points of View Reference Center*. Ipswich, MA: EBSCO Publishing, 2009–. https://www.ebsco.com/.

*Pop Culture Collection*. Farmington Hills, MI: Gale Group. https://www.gale.com/c/pop-culture-collection.

*ProQuest Research Library*. Ann Arbor, MI: ProQuest Information and Learning, 1998–. http://www.proquest.com/products-services/ProQuest-Research-Library.html.

*SIRS Issues Researcher*. Ann Arbor, MI: ProQuest Information and Learning. http://www.proquest.com/.

*Teen Health and Wellness Database*. New York: Rosen Publishing, 2007–. https://teenhealthandwellness.com/.

*WorldCat*. Dublin, OH: Online Computer Library Center, 2001. http://www.oclc.org/worldcat/.

## Humanities

*American History Online*. New York: Infobase. http://www.infobase.com/.

*Humanities Full Text (H. W. Wilson)*. Ipswich, MA: EBSCO Publishing, 2011–. https://www.ebsco.com/.

*Humanities International Index* (formerly *American Humanities Index*). Ipswich, MA: EBSCO Publishing, 2005–. https://www.ebsco.com/products/research -databases/humanities-international-index.

*Literary Reference Center.* Ipswich, MA: EBSCO Publishing, 2006–. https://www .ebsco.com/products/research-databases/literary-reference-center.

*Modern World History Online.* New York: Infobase. http://www.infobase.com /product/libraries/modern-world-history-online/.

*Poetry & Short Story Reference Center.* Ipswich, MA: EBSCO Publishing. https:// www.ebsco.com/products/research-databases/poetry-short-story-refer ence-center.

*Religion & Philosophy Collection.* Ipswich, MA: Ebsco Information Services, 2002–. https://www.ebsco.com/products/research-databases/religion -philosophy-collection.

*Soundzabound.* Atlanta: Soundzabound, 2010–. http://www.soundzabound .com/.

*U.S. History in Context.* Farmington Hills, MI: Gale Group, 2007–. https://www .gale.com/c/us-history-in-context.

*World History Collection.* Farmington Hills, MI: Gale Group. https://www.gale .com/c/world-history-collection.

## Social Sciences

*Anthropological Literature.* Cambridge, MA: Tozzer Library, Harvard University, 1984–. https://library.harvard.edu/services-tools/anthropological-literature.

*Anthropology Plus.* Ipswich, MA: EBSCO Publishing. https://www.ebsco.com.

*AnthroSource.* American Anthropological Association. Arlington, VA. https:// anthrosource.onlinelibrary.wiley.com.

*APA PsycNET.* Washington, DC: American Psychological Association, 1990s–. http://www.apa.org/pubs/databases/psycnet/.

*ASSIA: Applied Social Sciences Index and Abstracts.* Ann Arbor, MI: ProQuest Information and Learning. https://www.proquest.com/.

*CultureGrams.* Ann Arbor, MI: ProQuest Information and Learning. http://www .proquest.com/products-services/culturegrams.html.

*PAIS International with Archive.* Public Affairs Information Service. Ann Arbor, MI: ProQuest. http://www.proquest.com/.

*Political Science.* Research Guide. Ann Arbor: University of Michigan. http:// guides.lib.umich.edu/polisci/.

*Psychology Collection.* Farmington Hills, MI: Gale Group. https://www.gale.com /c/psychology-collection.

*Social Sciences Abstracts (H. W. Wilson).* Ipswich, MA: EBSCO Publishing, 1990s–. https://www.ebsco.com/.

*Social Sciences Citation Index*. Philadelphia: Institute for Scientific Information, 1990s–. http://wokinfo.com/.

*Sociological Abstracts*. Ann Arbor, MI: ProQuest, 1990s–. http://www.proquest .com/products-services/socioabs-set-c.html.

*War and Terrorism Collection*. Farmington Hills, MI: Gale Group. https://www .gale.com/c/war-and-terrorism-collection.

## Natural and Health Sciences

*Applied Science and Technology Index (H. W. Wilson)*. Ipswich, MA: EBSCO Publishing, 1997–. https://www.ebsco.com/.

*The Human Body: How It Works Online*. New York: Infobase. http://www.infobase .com/product/schools/the-human-body-how-it-works-online.

*National Agricultural Library Catalog*. Washington, DC: National Agricultural Library, 1970–. https://www.nal.usda.gov.

*PubMed.gov*. US National Library of Medicine, National Institutes of Health. http://www.ncbi.nlm.nih.gov/pubmed.

*Science Online*. New York: Infobase, 2004–. http://www.infobase.com/product /academia/science-online/.

*Science Reference Center*. Ipswich, MA: Ebsco Information Services. https://www .ebsco.com/products/research-databases/science-reference-center.

*Web of Science*. Philadelphia: Institute for Scientific Information, 1990s–. http:// wokinfo.com/.

## Print and Electronic Resources

## General

1. *American National Biography*. New York: Oxford University Press, 2000–. http://www.anb.org/.

1. Matthew, H. C. G., and Brian Howard Harrison, eds. *Oxford Dictionary of National Biography, in Association with the British Academy: From the Earliest Times to the Year 2000*. New York: Oxford University Press, 2004. Also at http://www.oxforddnb.com/.

1. *World Biographical Information System*. Berlin: De Gruyter. https://wbis .degruyter.com.

2. Lagassé, Paul, ed. *The Columbia Encyclopedia*. 6th ed. New York: Columbia University Press, 2008.

2. *New Encyclopaedia Britannica*. 16th ed. 32 vols. Chicago: Encyclopaedia Britannica, 2010. Also at http://www.britannica.com/.

3. Hacker, Diana, and Barbara Fister. *Research and Documentation in the Digital Age, with 2016 MLA Update*. 6th ed. Boston: Bedford / St. Martin's, 2016.

3. Lipson, Charles. *Doing Honest Work in College: How to Prepare Citations, Avoid*

*Plagiarism, and Achieve Real Academic Success*. 3rd ed. Chicago: University of Chicago Press, 2018.

3. Mann, Thomas. *Oxford Guide to Library Research*. 4th ed. New York: Oxford University Press, 2015.

4. *Alternative Press Index*. Chicago: Alternative Press Centre; Ipswich, MA: EBSCO Publishing, 1969–. https://www.ebsco.com/products/research-databases/alternative-press-index.

4. *Book Review Digest Plus*. New York: H. W. Wilson; Ipswich, MA: EBSCO Publishing, 2002–. https://www.ebsco.com/.

4. *Book Review Digest Retrospective: 1903–1982 (H. W. Wilson)*. Bronx, NY: H. W. Wilson Co.; Ipswich, MA: EBSCO Publishing, 2011–. https://www.ebsco.com/.

4. *Book Review Index*. Detroit: Gale Research, 1965–. Also at https://www.gale.com.

4. *Books in Print*. New Providence, NJ: R. R. Bowker, 2011. Also at http://www.booksinprint.com/.

4. *Kirkus Reviews*. New York: Kirkus Media, 1933–. Also at http://www.kirkusreviews.com/.

4. *National Newspaper Index*. Farmington Hills, MI: Gale Cengage, 1977.

4. *New York Times Index*. New York: New York Times, 1913–. Also at https://archive.nytimes.com/www.nytimes.com/ref/membercenter/nytarchive.html.

4. *Periodicals Index Online*. Ann Arbor, MI: ProQuest Information and Learning, 1990–. http://proquest.com/pio.

4. *Readers' Guide to Periodical Literature (H. W. Wilson)*. Ipswich, MA: EBSCO Publishing, 2003–. https://www.ebsco.com/.

4. *Subject Guide to Books in Print*. New York: R. R. Bowker, 1957–. Also at http://www.booksinprint.com/.

5. Miller, Jane E. *The Chicago Guide to Writing about Numbers*. 2nd ed. Chicago: University of Chicago Press, 2015.

5. Strunk, William, and E. B. White. *The Elements of Style*. 50th anniversary ed. New York: Pearson Longman, 2009.

5. Williams, Joseph M., and Joseph Bizup. *Style: Lessons in Clarity and Grace*. 12th ed. Boston: Pearson Longman, 2017.

6. *The Chicago Manual of Style*. 17th ed. Chicago: University of Chicago Press, 2017. Also at http://www.chicagomanualofstyle.org/.

## Visual Representation of Data (Tables, Figures, Posters, Etc.)

2. Evergreen, Stephanie. *Effective Data Visualization: The Right Chart for the Right Data*. Thousand Oaks, CA: Sage, 2016.

5. Alley, Michael. *The Craft of Scientific Presentations: Critical Steps to Succeed and Critical Errors to Avoid*. 2nd ed. New York: Springer, 2013.

5. Larkin, Greg. "Storyboarding: A Concrete Way to Generate Effective Visuals." *Journal of Technical Writing and Communication* 26, no. 3 (1996): 273–89.

5. Nicol, Adelheid A. M., and Penny M. Pexman. *Displaying Your Findings: A Practical Guide for Creating Figures, Posters, and Presentations.* 6th ed. Washington, DC: American Psychological Association, 2010.

5. Robbins, Naomi B. *Creating More Effective Graphs.* New York: John Wiley and Sons, 2005. Paperback reprint. Houston: Chart House, 2013.

## Humanities

### General

1. Hornblower, Simon, and Antony Spawforth, eds. *The Oxford Classical Dictionary.* 4th ed. Oxford: Oxford University Press, 2012. Also at http://www.oxfordreference.com/.

4. *Arts and Humanities Citation Index.* Philadelphia: Institute for Scientific Information, 1976–. Compact disc ed. 1994. Also at http://mjl.clarivate.com.

### Art

1. Chilvers, Ian, ed. *The Oxford Dictionary of Art and Artists.* 5th ed. Oxford: Oxford University Press, 2015. https://doi.org/10.1093/acref/9780191782763.001.0001.

1. *Oxford Art Online.* Oxford: Oxford University Press, 2007–. http://www.oxfordartonline.com/.

1. Sorensen, Lee. *Dictionary of Art Historians.* Durham, NC: Duke University Press. http://www.dictionaryofarthistorians.org/.

2. Myers, Bernard S., ed. *Encyclopedia of World Art.* 17 vols. New York: McGraw-Hill, 1959–87.

4. *International Bibliography of Art.* Los Angeles: J. Paul Getty Trust; Ann Arbor, MI: ProQuest, 2008–. http://www.proquest.com.

5. Barnet, Sylvan. *A Short Guide to Writing about Art.* 11th ed. Upper Saddle River, NJ: Prentice Hall, 2015.

### History

1. Cook, Chris. *A Dictionary of Historical Terms.* 3rd ed. Houndmills, UK: Macmillan, 1998.

3. Benjamin, Jules R. *A Student's Guide to History.* 13th ed. Boston: Bedford / St. Martin's, 2016.

3. Brundage, Anthony. *Going to the Sources: A Guide to Historical Research and Writing.* 6th ed. Chichester, UK: Wiley-Blackwell, 2017.

3. Kyvig, David E., and Myron A. Marty. *Nearby History: Exploring the Past around You.* 3rd ed. Walnut Creek, CA: AltaMira Press, 2010.

4. *America: History and Life*. Ipswich, MA: EBSCO Publishing, 1990s-. https://www.ebsco.com/.
4. Blazek, Ron, and Anna H. Perrault. *United States History: A Multicultural, Interdisciplinary Guide to Information Sources*. 2nd ed. Westport, CT: Libraries Unlimited, 2003.
4. *Historical Abstracts*. Ipswich, MA: EBSCO Publishing, 1990s-. https://www.ebsco.com/.
5. Barzun, Jacques, and Henry F. Graff. *The Modern Researcher*. 6th ed. Belmont, CA: Thomson/Wadsworth, 2004.
5. Marius, Richard, and Melvin E. Page. *A Short Guide to Writing about History*. 9th ed. New York: Pearson Longman, 2015.

## Literary Studies

1. Abrams, M. H., and Geoffrey Galt Harpham. *A Glossary of Literary Terms*. 11th ed. Boston: Wadsworth Cengage Learning, 2015.
1. Baldick, Chris, ed. *The Oxford Dictionary of Literary Terms*. 4th ed. Oxford: Oxford University Press, 2015.
1. Greene. Roland, and Stephen Cushman, eds. *Princeton Handbook of Poetic Terms*. Princeton, NJ: Princeton, 2016.
2. Birch, Dinah, ed. *The Oxford Companion to English Literature*. 7th ed. New York: Oxford University Press, 2009. Also at http://www.oxfordreference.com/.
2. Hart, James D., and Phillip W. Leininger, eds. *The Oxford Companion to American Literature*. 7th ed. New York: Oxford University Press, 2009. Also at http://www.oxfordreference.com/.
2. Lentricchia, Frank, and Thomas McLaughlin, eds. *Critical Terms for Literary Study*. 2nd ed. Chicago: University of Chicago Press, 1995.
2. Parini, Jay, ed. *The Oxford Encyclopedia of American Literature*. 4 vols. New York: Oxford University Press, 2004. Also at http://www.oxfordreference.com/.
4. *MLA International Bibliography*. New York: Modern Language Association of America. https://www.mla.org/Publications/MLA-International-Bibliography.
5. Barnet, Sylvan, and William E. Cain. *A Short Guide to Writing about Literature*. 12th ed. New York: Longman/Pearson, 2011.
6. Griffith, Kelley. *Writing Essays about Literature: A Guide and Style Sheet*. 9th ed. Boston: Wadsworth Cengage Learning, 2014.
6. *MLA Handbook for Writers of Research Papers*. 8th ed. New York: Modern Language Association of America, 2016.

## Music

1. *Oxford Music Online*. New York: Oxford University Press, 2001-. Includes *Grove Music Online*. http://www.oxfordmusiconline.com/.

1. Randel, Don Michael, ed. *The Harvard Dictionary of Music*. 4th ed. Cambridge, MA: Belknap Press of Harvard University Press, 2003.

1. Sadie, Stanley, and John Tyrrell, eds. *The New Grove Dictionary of Music and Musicians*. 2nd ed. 29 vols. New York: Grove, 2001. Also at http://www .oxfordmusiconline.com/ (as part of *Grove Music Online*).

4. *Music Index*. Ipswich, MA: EBSCO Publishing, 2000s–. https://www .ebsco.com/.

5. Herbert, Trevor. *Music in Words: A Guide to Researching and Writing about Music*. 2nd ed. London: ABRSM, 2012.

5. Wingell, Richard. *Writing about Music: An Introductory Guide*. 4th ed. Upper Saddle River, NJ: Pearson Prentice Hall, 2009.

6. Bellman, Jonathan. *A Short Guide to Writing about Music*. 2nd ed. New York: Pearson Longman, 2006.

6. Holoman, D. Kern. *Writing about Music: A Style Sheet*. 3rd ed. Berkeley: University of California Press, 2014.

*Philosophy*

1. Blackburn, Simon. *The Oxford Dictionary of Philosophy*. 3rd ed. Oxford: Oxford University Press, 2016. Also at http://www.oxfordreference.com/.

2. Borchert, Donald, ed. *The Encyclopedia of Philosophy*. 8 vols. 2nd ed. Detroit: Macmillan Reference USA, 2006.

2. Craig, Edward, ed. *Routledge Encyclopedia of Philosophy*. 10 vols. New York: Routledge, 1998. Also at http://www.rep.routledge.com.

2. Zalta, Edward N. *Stanford Encyclopedia of Philosophy*. Stanford, CA: Stanford University, 1997–. http://plato.stanford.edu/.

4. *The Philosopher's Index*. Bowling Green, OH: Philosopher's Information Center, 1968–. Also at http://philindex.org/.

6. Martinich, A. P. *Philosophical Writing: An Introduction*. 4th ed. Malden, MA: Wiley-Blackwell, 2015.

## Social Sciences

*General*

1. Calhoun, Craig, ed. *Dictionary of the Social Sciences*. New York: Oxford University Press, 2002. Also at http://www.oxfordreference.com/.

1. *Statistical Abstract of the United States*. Washington, DC: US Census Bureau, 1878–2011. Also at https://www.census.gov/library/publications/time-series /statistical_abstracts.html.

2. Darity, William, ed. *International Encyclopedia of the Social Sciences*. 2nd ed. 9 vols. Detroit: Macmillan, 2008.

4. *Ethnic NewsWatch*. Ann Arbor, MI: ProQuest. http://www.proquest.com /products-services/ethnic_newswatch.html.

4. *Social Sciences Index.* New York: H. W. Wilson, 1974–. Also at https://www
.ebsco.com/ (as *Social Sciences Abstracts*).

5. Becker, Howard S. *Writing for Social Scientists: How to Start and Finish Your
Thesis, Book, or Article.* 2nd ed. Chicago: University of Chicago Press, 2007.

5. Bell, Judith, and Stephen Waters. *Doing Your Research Project: A Guide for First-
Time Researchers in Education, Health, and Social Science.* 6th ed. rev. Maiden-
head, UK: McGraw-Hill Open University Press, 2014.

5. Northey, Margot, Lorne Tepperman, and Patrizia Albanese. *Making Sense:
A Student's Guide to Research and Writing; Social Sciences.* 6th ed. Don Mills,
ON: Oxford University Press, 2015.

## African American and Africana Studies

2. *African American Biographical Database.* Ann Arbor, MI: ProQuest. http://www
.proquest.com/products-services/af_am_biographical.html.

2. Appiah, Kwame Anthony, and Henry Louis Gates Jr., eds. *The Encyclopedia
of Africa.* New York: Oxford University Press, 2010. Also at http://www
.oxfordreference.com/view/10.1093/acref/9780195337709.001.0001/acref
-9780195337709.

2. Europa Publications, ed. *Africa South of the Sahara.* London: Routledge, 2018.

2. Finkelman, Paul, ed. *Encyclopedia of African American History, 1896 to the Present.* New York: Oxford University Press, 2009.

2. Palmer, Colin, ed. *Encyclopedia of African-American Culture and History: The
Black Experience in the Americas.* 6 vols. Detroit: Thompson Gale, 2006.

3. Higginbotham, Evelyn Brooks, Leon F. Litwack, and Darlene Clark Hine, eds.
*The Harvard Guide to African-American History.* Cambridge, MA: Harvard
University Press, 2001.

4. Danky, James Philip, and Maureen E. Hady. *African-American Newspapers
and Periodicals: A National Bibliography.* Cambridge, MA: Harvard University Press, 1998.

## Anthropology

1. Barfield, Thomas, ed. *The Dictionary of Anthropology.* 13th pr. Malden, MA:
Blackwell, 2009.

2. Barnard, Alan, and Jonathan Spencer, eds. *Routledge Encyclopedia of Social and
Cultural Anthropology.* 2nd ed. London: Routledge, 2012.

2. Ingold, Tim, ed. *Companion Encyclopedia of Anthropology: Humanity, Culture,
and Social Life.* London: Routledge, 2007.

2. Levinson, David, ed. *Encyclopedia of World Cultures.* 10 vols. Boston: G. K.
Hall, 1991–96.

3. Glenn, James R. *Guide to the National Anthropological Archives, Smithsonian
Institution.* Rev. and enl. ed. Washington, DC: National Anthropological Ar-

chives, 1996. Revised and amended, as *Guide to the Collections of the National Anthropological Archives*, at http://anthropology.si.edu/naa/guide/_toc.htm.

4. *Annual Review of Anthropology*. Palo Alto, CA: Annual Reviews, 1972–. Also at http://www.annualreviews.org/journal/anthro.

4. *The Urban Portal*. Chicago: University of Chicago Urban Network. http://urban.uchicago.edu/.

## Business

1. Friedman, Jack P. *Dictionary of Business Terms*. 4th ed. Hauppauge, NY: Barron's Educational Series, 2012.

2. Folsom, W. Davis, and Stacia N. VanDyne, eds. *Encyclopedia of American Business*. Rev. ed. 2 vols. New York: Facts on File, 2011. Also at http://www.infobasepublishing.com/.

2. McDonough, John, and Karen Egolf, eds. *The Advertising Age Encyclopedia of Advertising*. 3 vols. New York: Fitzroy Dearborn, 2003.

2. Warner, Malcolm, and John P. Kotter, eds. *International Encyclopedia of Business and Management*. 2nd ed. 8 vols. London: Thomson Learning, 2002.

3. Bryman, Alan, and Emma Bell. *Business Research Methods*. 4th ed. New York: Oxford University Press, 2015.

3. Moss, Rita W., and David G. Ernsthausen. *Strauss's Handbook of Business Information: A Guide for Librarians, Students, and Researchers*. 3rd ed. Westport, CT: Libraries Unlimited, 2012.

3. Sekaran, Uma, and Roger Bougie. *Research Methods for Business: A Skill Building Approach*. 7th ed. New York: John Wiley and Sons, 2016.

3. Woy, James B., ed. *Encyclopedia of Business Information Sources*. 33rd ed. 2 vols. Detroit: Gale Cengage Learning, 2016.

4. *Business Periodicals Index*. New York: H. W. Wilson, 1958–. Also at https://www.ebsco.com/ (as *Business Periodicals Index Retrospective*).

## Communication, Journalism, and Media Studies

1. Miller, Toby, ed. *Television: Critical Concepts in Media and Cultural Studies*. London: Routledge, 2003.

1. Newton, Harry. *Newton's Telecom Dictionary*. 30th ed. New York: Telecom Publishing, 2016.

1. Watson, James, and Anne Hill. *A Dictionary of Communication and Media Studies*. 9th ed. New York: Bloomsbury Academic, 2015.

2. Littlejohn, Stephen W., and Karen Foss, eds. *Encyclopedia of Communication Theory*. Los Angeles: Sage, 2009.

2. Vaughn, Stephen L. *Encyclopedia of American Journalism*. New York: Routledge, 2008.

3. Stokes, Jane. *How to Do Media and Cultural Studies*. 2nd ed. London: Sage, 2012.

3. Storey, John. *Cultural Studies and the Study of Popular Culture*. 3rd ed. Edinburgh: Edinburgh University Press, 2010.

4. Cates, Jo A. *Journalism: A Guide to the Reference Literature*. 3rd ed. Westport,
CT: Libraries Unlimited, 2004.

4. *Communication Abstracts*. Los Angeles: Dept. of Journalism, University of
California, Los Angeles, 1960–. Also at https://www.ebsco.com/ (as *Communication Source*).

4. *FIAF International Index to Film Periodicals*. Ann Arbor, MI: ProQuest. http://
www.proquest.com/products-services/fiaf.html.

6. Christian, Darrell, Sally Jacobsen, and David Minthorn, eds. *Associated Press
Stylebook and Briefing on Media Law*. Updated annually. New York: Associated Press. Also at http://www.apstylebook.com/.


## Economics

1. Pearce, David W., ed. *MIT Dictionary of Modern Economics*. 4th ed. Cambridge,
MA: MIT Press, 1992.

2. Durlauf, Steven N., and Lawrence E. Blume, eds. *The New Palgrave Dictionary
of Economics*. 8 vols. 2nd ed. New York: Palgrave Macmillan, 2008. Also at
http://www.dictionaryofeconomics.com/dictionary.

2. Mokyr, Joel, ed. *The Oxford Encyclopedia of Economic History*. 5 vols. Oxford:
Oxford University Press, 2003. Also at http://www.oxfordreference.com/.

4. *Journal of Economic Literature*. Nashville: American Economic Association,
1969–. Also at https://www.aeaweb.org/journals/jel.

5. McCloskey, Deirdre N. *Economical Writing*. 3rd ed. Chicago: University of Chicago Press, 2019.


## Education

1. Collins, John Williams, and Nancy P. O'Brien, eds. *The Greenwood Dictionary
of Education*. 2nd ed. Santa Barbara, CA: Greenwood, 2011.

2. Guthrie, James W., ed. *Encyclopedia of Education*. 2nd ed. 8 vols. New York:
Macmillan Reference USA, 2002.

2. Peterson, Penelope, Eva Baker, and Barry McGaw, eds. *The International Encyclopedia of Education*. 3rd ed. 8 vols. Oxford: Elsevier, 2010.

2. Unger, Harlow G. *Encyclopedia of American Education*. 3rd ed. 3 vols. New York:
Facts on File, 2007. Also at http://www.infobasepublishing.com/.

3. Tuckman, Bruce W., and Brian E. Harper. *Conducting Educational Research*.
6th ed. Lanham, MD: Rowman and Littlefield, 2012.

4. *Education Index*. New York: H. W. Wilson, 1929–. Also at https://www.ebsco
.com/ (as *Education Index Retrospective* and *Education Abstracts*).

4. *ERIC Database*. Lanham, MD: Educational Resources Information Center,
2004–. http://www.eric.ed.gov/.

### Geography

1. Witherick, M. E., Simon Ross, and John Small. *A Modern Dictionary of Geography*. 4th ed. London: Arnold, 2001.
1. *The World Factbook*. Washington, DC: Central Intelligence Agency, 1990s–. https://www.cia.gov/library/publications/the-world-factbook/.
2. McCoy, John, ed. *Geo-Data: The World Geographical Encyclopedia*. 3rd ed. Detroit: Thomson/Gale, 2003. Also at http://www.gale.com/.
3. *Historical GIS Clearinghouse and Forum*. Washington, DC: Association of American Geographers. http://www.aag.org/.
3. Walford, Nigel. *Geographical Data: Characteristics and Sources*. New York: John Wiley and Sons, 2002.
4. *Geographical Abstracts*. Norwich, UK: Geo Abstracts, 1966–.
5. Northey, Margot, David B. Knight, and Dianne Draper. *Making Sense: A Student's Guide to Research and Writing; Geography and Environmental Sciences*. 6th ed. Don Mills, ON: Oxford University Press, 2015.

### Latino and Latin American Studies

2. Oboler, Suzanne, and Dena J. González, eds. *The Oxford Encyclopedia of Latinos and Latinas in the United States*. 4 vols. New York: Oxford University Press, 2006.
4. *Chicano Database*. Ipswich, MA: EBSCO Publishing. https://www.ebsco.com/products/research-databases/chicano-database.
4. *Hispanic American Periodicals Index (HAPI)*. Los Angeles: UCLA Latin American Center Publications, 1977–. Also at http://hapi.ucla.edu.
4. *HLAS Online: Handbook of Latin American Studies*. Washington, DC: Library of Congress. http://lcweb2.loc.gov/hlas/.
4. *LANIC: Latin American Network Information Center*. Austin: University of Texas. http://lanic.utexas.edu.

### Law

1. Law, Jonathan, and Elizabeth A. Martin, eds. *A Dictionary of Law*. 8th ed. Oxford: Oxford University Press, 2015.
2. *Gale Encyclopedia of American Law*. 3rd ed. 14 vols. Detroit: Gale Cengage Learning, 2011. Also at http://www.gale.cengage.com/.
2. Hall, Kermit, and David Scott Clark, eds. *The Oxford Companion to American Law*. New York: Oxford University Press, 2002. Also at http://www.oxfordreference.com/.
4. *Index to Legal Periodicals and Books*. New York: H. W. Wilson, 1924–. Also at https://www.ebsco.com/.
5. Bast, Carol M., and Margie Hawkins. *Foundations of Legal Research and Writing*. 5th ed. Clifton Park, NY: Delmar Cengage Learning, 2012.

6. Yelin, Andrea, and Hope Viner Samborn. *The Legal Research and Writing Handbook: A Basic Approach for Paralegals*. 8th ed. Waltham, MA: Wolters Kluwer, 2018.

## Native American Studies

2. Deloria, Philip J., and Neal Salisbury, eds. *A Companion to American Indian History*. Hoboken, NJ: Wiley-Blackwell, 2004.

2. Hoxie, Frederick E., ed. *Encyclopedia of North American Indians: Native American History, Culture, and Life from Paleo-Indians to the Present*. Boston: Houghton Mifflin, 1996.

4. *America: History and Life with Full Text*. Ipswich, MA: EBSCO Publishing. https://www.ebsco.com/products/research-databases/america-history-and -life-with-full-text.

4. *Bibliography of Native North Americans*. Ipswich, MA: EBSCO Publishing. https://www.ebsco.com/products/research-databases/bibliography-of -native-north-americans.

## Political Science

1. Robertson, David. *A Dictionary of Modern Politics*. 4th ed. London: Routledge, 2007.

2. *The Almanac of American Politics*. Washington, DC: National Journal, 1972–. Also at http://nationaljournal.com/almanac.

2. Hawkesworth, Mary E., and Maurice Kogan, eds. *Encyclopedia of Government and Politics*. 2nd ed. 2 vols. London: Routledge, 2004.

2. Miller, David, ed. *The Blackwell Encyclopaedia of Political Thought*. Oxford: Blackwell, 2004.

3. Johnson, Janet Buttolph, and H. T. Reynolds. *Political Science Research Methods*. 8th ed. Los Angeles: Congressional Quarterly Press, 2015.

4. *PAIS International Journals Indexed*. New York: Public Affairs Information Service, 1972–. Also at http://www.proquest.com/.

4. *Worldwide Political Science Abstracts*. Bethesda, MD: Cambridge Scientific Abstracts, 1976–. Also at http://www.proquest.com/.

5. LaVaque-Manty, Mika, and Danielle LaVaque-Manty. *Writing in Political Science: A Brief Guide*. New York: Oxford University Press, 2016.

5. Schmidt, Diane E. *Writing in Political Science: A Practical Guide*. 4th ed. Boston: Longman, 2010.

6. American Political Science Association. *APSA Style Manual for Political Science*. Rev. ed. Washington, DC: American Political Science Association, 2006. http://www.apsanet.org/files/APSAStyleManual2006.pdf.

## Psychology

1. Colman, Andrew M. *A Dictionary of Psychology*. 4th ed. Oxford: Oxford University Press, 2015. Also at http://www.oxfordreference.com/.

1. Hayes, Nicky, and Peter Stratton. *A Student's Dictionary of Psychology*. 4th ed. London: Arnold, 2003.
2. Craighead, W. Edward, Charles B. Nemeroff, and Raymond J. Corsini, eds. *The Corsini Encyclopedia of Psychology and Behavioral Science*. 4th ed. 4 vols. New York: John Wiley and Sons, 2010.
2. Kazdin, Alan E., ed. *Encyclopedia of Psychology*. 8 vols. Washington, DC: American Psychological Association; Oxford: Oxford University Press, 2000.
3. Breakwell, Glynis M., Sean Hammond, Chris Fife-Schaw, and Jonathan A. Smith. *Research Methods in Psychology*. 4th ed. London: Sage, 2012.
3. Shaughnessy, John J., Eugene B. Zechmeister, and Jeanne S. Zechmeister. *Research Methods in Psychology*. 10th ed. Boston: McGraw-Hill, 2014.
4. *Annual Review of Psychology*. Palo Alto, CA: Annual Reviews, 1950–. Also at http://arjournals.annualreviews.org/journal/psych.
4. *PubMed*. Bethesda, MD: US National Library of Medicine. http://www.ncbi.nlm.nih.gov/pubmed/.
5. Sternberg, Robert J., and Karin Sternberg. *The Psychologist's Companion: A Guide to Writing Scientific Papers for Students and Researchers*. 6th ed. Cambridge: Cambridge University Press, 2016.
6. *Publication Manual of the American Psychological Association*. 6th ed. Washington, DC: American Psychological Association, 2009.

## Religion

1. Bowker, John, ed. *The Concise Oxford Dictionary of World Religions*. New ed. Oxford: Oxford University Press, 2007. Also at http://www.oxfordreference.com/.
2. Cesari, Jocelyne. *Encyclopedia of Islam in the United States*. London: Greenwood Press, 2007.
2. Freedman, David Noel, ed. *The Anchor Yale Bible Dictionary*. 6 vols. New Haven, CT: Yale University Press, 2008.
2. Jones, Lindsay, ed. *Encyclopedia of Religion*. 2nd ed. 15 vols. Detroit: Macmillan Reference USA, 2005.
2. Martin, Richard C., ed. *Encyclopedia of Islam and the Muslim World*. 2 vols. New York: Macmillan Reference USA, 2003.
2. Skolnik, Fred, and Michael Berenbaum, eds. *Encyclopaedia Judaica*. 2nd ed. 22 vols. Detroit: Macmillan Reference USA, 2007.
2. Swatos, William H., ed. *Encyclopedia of Religion and Society*. Lanham, MD: Rowman and Littlefield, 1998.
4. *Index of Articles on Jewish Studies (RAMBI)*. Jerusalem: Jewish National and University Library, 2002–. http://jnul.huji.ac.il/rambi/.

4. *Index to Book Reviews in Religion.* Chicago: American Theological Library Association, 1990–. Also at https://ebsco.com/ (as *ATLA Religion Database*).

4. *Islamic Book Review Index.* Berlin: Adiyok, 1982–.

6. *CNS Stylebook on Religion: Reference Guide and Usage Manual.* 4th ed. Washington, DC: Catholic News Service, 2012.

## Sociology

1. Abercrombie, Nicholas, Stephen Hill, and Bryan S. Turner. *The Penguin Dictionary of Sociology.* 5th ed. London: Penguin, 2006.

1. Scott, John, and Marshall Gordon, eds. *A Dictionary of Sociology.* 4th ed. rev. Oxford: Oxford University Press, 2009. Also at http://www.oxfordreference.com/.

2. Levinson, David L., Peter W. Cookson, and Alan R. Sadovnik, eds. *Education and Sociology: An Encyclopedia.* New York: Routledge, 2014.

2. Ritzer, George, ed. *Encyclopedia of Social Theory.* 2 vols. Thousand Oaks, CA: Sage, 2005.

4. *Annual Review of Sociology.* Palo Alto, CA: Annual Reviews, 1975–. Also at http://www.annualreviews.org/journal/soc.

4. *Social Science Research.* San Diego, CA: Academic Press, 1972–. Also at http://www.sciencedirect.com/science/journal/0049089X/.

4. *Sociological Abstracts.* Bethesda, MD: Sociological Abstracts, 1952–. Also at http://www.proquest.com/.

5. Smith-Lovin, Lynn, and Cary Moskovitz. *Writing in Sociology: A Brief Guide.* New York: Oxford University Press, 2016.

5. Sociology Writing Group. *A Guide to Writing Sociology Papers.* 7th ed. New York: Worth, 2013.

## Women's and Gender Studies

1. Bataille, Gretchen M., and Laurie Lisa, eds. *Native American Women: A Biographical Dictionary.* 2nd ed. New York: Routledge, 2001.

1. Hendry, Maggy, and Jennifer S. Uglow, eds. *The Palgrave Macmillan Dictionary of Women's Biography.* 4th ed. New York: Palgrave Macmillan, 2005.

1. Salem, Dorothy C., ed. *African American Women: A Biographical Dictionary.* New York: Garland, 1993.

2. Hine, Darlene Clark, ed. *Black Women in America.* 2nd ed. 3 vols. New York: Oxford University Press, 2005.

2. Kramarae, Cheris, and Dale Spender, eds. *Routledge International Encyclopedia of Women: Global Women's Issues and Knowledge.* 4 vols. New York: Routledge, 2000.

2. Tierney, Helen, ed. *Women's Studies Encyclopedia.* Rev. ed. 3 vols. Westport, CT: Greenwood Press, 2007.

2. Willard, Frances E., and Mary A. Livermore, eds. *Great American Women of the 19th Century: A Biographical Encyclopedia*. Amherst, NY: Humanity Books, 2005.

4. *LGBT Life*. Ann Arbor, MI: ProQuest. https://www.ebsco.com/products /research-databases/lgbt-life.

4. *ViVa: A Bibliography of Women's History in Historical and Women's Studies Journals*. Amsterdam: International Institute of Social History, 1995–. http:// www.iisg.nl/womhist/vivahome.php.

## Natural Sciences

*General*

1. *McGraw-Hill Dictionary of Scientific and Technical Terms*. 7th ed. New York: McGraw-Hill, 2017. Also at http://www.accessscience.com/.

1. Porter, Roy, and Marilyn Bailey Ogilvie, eds. *The Biographical Dictionary of Scientists*. 3rd ed. 2 vols. New York: Oxford University Press, 2000.

2. *McGraw-Hill Encyclopedia of Science and Technology*. 11th ed. 20 vols. New York: McGraw-Hill, 2012. Also at http://www.accessscience.com/.

2. *Nature Encyclopedia: An A–Z Guide to Life on Earth*. New York: Oxford University Press, 2001.

4. *Applied Science and Technology Index*. New York: H. W. Wilson, 1913–. Also at https://www.ebsco.com/.

4. *General Science Index*. New York: H. W. Wilson, 1978–. Also at https://www .ebsco.com/ (as *General Science Full Text*).

5. Montgomery, Scott L. *The Chicago Guide to Communicating Science*. 2nd ed. Chicago: University of Chicago Press, 2017.

5. Valiela, Ivan. *Doing Science: Design, Analysis, and Communication of Scientific Research*. 2nd ed. Oxford: Oxford University Press, 2009.

*Biology*

1. Lawrence, Eleanor, ed. *Henderson's Dictionary of Biology*. 16th ed. New York: Benjamin Cummings, 2016.

1. Martin, Elizabeth, and Robert S. Hine, eds. *A Dictionary of Biology*. 7th ed. Oxford: Oxford University Press, 2015. Also at http://www.oxfordreference .com/.

2. Dulbecco, Renato, ed. *Encyclopedia of Human Biology*. 3rd ed. 10 vols. San Diego, CA: Academic Press, 2008.

2. Eldredge, Niles, ed. *Life on Earth: An Encyclopedia of Biodiversity, Ecology, and Evolution*. 2 vols. Santa Barbara, CA: ABC-Clio, 2002.

4. *Biological Abstracts*. Philadelphia: BioSciences Information Service of Biological Abstracts, 1926–. Also at https://www.ebsco.com/products/research -databases/biological-abstracts/.

4. *Biological and Agricultural Index*. New York: H. W. Wilson, 1964–. Also at https://www.ebsco.com/.

5. McMillan, Victoria E. *Writing Papers in the Biological Sciences*. 6th ed. Boston: Bedford / St. Martin's, 2016.

5. Roldan, Leslie Ann and Mary-Lou Pardue. *Writing in Biology: A Brief Guide*. New York: Oxford University Press, 2016.

## Chemistry

1. Hawley, Gessner Goodrich, and Richard J. Lewis Sr. *Hawley's Condensed Chemical Dictionary*. 16th ed. New York: Wiley, 2016.

2. Meyers, Robert A., ed. *Encyclopedia of Physical Science and Technology*. 3rd ed. 18 vols. San Diego, CA: Academic, 2002. Also at http://www.sciencedirect .com/science/referenceworks/9780122274107/.

4. *ACS Publications*. Columbus, OH: American Chemical Society. http://pubs .acs.org/.

4. *Chemical Abstracts*. Columbus, OH: American Chemical Society, 1907–. Also at http://www.cas.org/.

4. *ScienceDirect*. New York: Elsevier Science, 1999–. http://www.sciencedirect .com/.

5. Davis, Holly B., Julian F. Tyson, and Jan A. Pechenik. *A Short Guide to Writing about Chemistry*. Boston: Longman, 2010.

6. Dodd, Janet S., ed. *The ACS Style Guide: Effective Communication of Scientific Information*. 3rd ed. Washington, DC: American Chemical Society, 2006.

## Computer Sciences

1. LaPlante, Phillip A. *Dictionary of Computer Science, Engineering, and Technology*. Boca Raton, FL: CRC Press, 2001.

1. *Random House Concise Dictionary of Science and Computers*. New York: Random House Reference, 2004.

2. Henderson, Harry. *Encyclopedia of Computer Science and Technology*. Rev. ed. New York: Facts on File, 2009. Also at http://www.infobasepublishing.com/.

4. *ACM Digital Library*. New York: Association for Computing Machinery. https://www.acm.org/publications/digital-library.

## Geology and Earth and Environmental Sciences

1. *McGraw-Hill Dictionary of Geology and Mineralogy*. 2nd ed. New York: McGraw-Hill, 2003.

1. Smith, Jacqueline, ed. *The Facts on File Dictionary of Earth Science*. Rev. ed. New York: Facts on File, 2006. Also at http://www.infobasepublishing.com/.

2. Bishop, Arthur C., Alan R. Woolley, and William R. Hamilton. *Cambridge Guide to Minerals, Rocks, and Fossils*. Rev. ed. Cambridge: Cambridge University Press, 2001.

2. Dasch, E. Julius, ed. *Macmillan Encyclopedia of Earth Sciences*. 2 vols. New York: Macmillan Reference USA, 1996.

2. Hancock, Paul L., and Brian J. Skinner, eds. *The Oxford Companion to the Earth*. Oxford: Oxford University Press, 2000. Also at http://www.oxfordreference.com/.

2. Selley, Richard C., et al., eds. *Encyclopedia of Geology*. 5 vols. Amsterdam: Elsevier Academic, 2005.

4. *Bibliography and Index of Geology*. Alexandria, VA: American Geological Institute, 1966–2005. Also at http://www.proquest.com/ (as *GeoRef*).

4. *Environmental Sciences and Pollution Management*. Bethesda, MD: Cambridge Scientific Abstracts. Also at http://www.proquest.com/.

4. *Geobase*. New York: Elsevier Science. Also at http://www.elsevier.com/online -tools/engineering-village/geobase/.

4. *GreenFILE*. Ipswich, MA: EBSCO Publishing. https://www.ebsco.com/products /research-databases/greenfile.

4. *GREENR (Global Reference on the Environment, Energy, and Natural Resources)*. Farmington Hills, MI: Gale Cengage. https://www.gale.com/c/greenr.

## Mathematics

1. Borowski, E. J., and J. M. Borwein, eds. *Collins Dictionary: Mathematics*. 2nd ed. Glasgow: HarperCollins, 2002.

1. Nelson, David, ed. *The Penguin Dictionary of Mathematics*. 4th ed. London: Penguin, 2008.

1. Nicholson, James. *The Concise Oxford Dictionary of Mathematics*. 5th ed. Oxford: Oxford University Press, 2014.

2. Weisstein, Eric W. *CRC Concise Encyclopedia of Mathematics*. 3rd ed. Boca Raton, FL: Chapman and Hall / CRC, 2009.

4. *MathSci*. Providence, RI: American Mathematical Society. Also at http://www .ams.org/mathscinet/.

## Physics

1. Daintith, John, ed. *A Dictionary of Physics*. 7th ed. Oxford: Oxford University Press, 2015. Also at http://www.oxfordreference.com/.

2. *McGraw-Hill Concise Encyclopedia of Physics*. New York: McGraw-Hill, 2005.

4. American Institute of Physics. Journals. College Park, MD: AIP. http://aip .scitation.

4. *IEEE Xplore*. New York: Institute of Electrical and Electronics Engineers. http://ieeexplore.ieee.org/Xplore/.

4. *Physics Abstracts*. London: Institution of Electrical Engineers, 1967–.

6. American Institute of Physics. *AIP Style Manual*. 4th ed. New York: American Institute of Physics, 1990.

# Authors

Kate L. Turabian (1893–1987) was the graduate school dissertation secretary at the University of Chicago for nearly three decades. She is the original author of this work and *A Manual for Writers of Research Papers, Theses, and Dissertations*, also published by the University of Chicago Press and currently in its ninth edition (2018).

Gregory G. Colomb (1951–2011) was professor of English at the University of Virginia and the author of *Designs on Truth: The Poetics of the Augustan Mock-Epic*.

Joseph M. Williams (1933–2008) was professor emeritus of English and linguistics at the University of Chicago. He is the author of *Style: Lessons in Clarity and Grace*. Colomb and Williams jointly wrote *The Craft of Argument*.

Joseph Bizup is associate professor of English and associate dean for undergraduate academic programs and policies in the College of Arts & Sciences at Boston University. He is the author of *Manufacturing Culture*, coeditor of recent editions of the *Norton Reader*, and editor of recent editions of Williams's *Style*.

William T. FitzGerald is associate professor of English and director of the Writing Program and the Teaching Matters and Assessment Center at Rutgers University–Camden. He is the author of *Spiritual Modalities*.

Together with Wayne C. Booth (1921–2005), Colomb and Williams authored *The Craft of Research*, which Bizup and FitzGerald revised for its fourth edition (University of Chicago Press, 2016). And first Booth, Colomb, and Williams, and now Bizup and FitzGerald, have revised Turabian's *Manual for Writers*.

The University of Chicago Press Editorial Staff produces *The Chicago Manual of Style*, currently in its seventeenth edition (2017).

# Index